Maynooth College is two hundred years old. Age is honourable and achievement is to be honoured, and both age and achievement will be widely celebrated on the bicentenary. The occasion will see the celebration of Maynooth's original purpose, still continued, the training of priests for Ireland. It will also mark the development of that purpose over two centuries, eventually to include third-level education of men and women in philosophy and theology, in the sciences, and in the arts.

To honour in an appropriate way these two hundred years of teaching, members of the college staff are publishing a series of books in a number of academic disciplines. Edited by members of the College Faculty, these books will range from texts based on standard theology courses to interdisciplinary studies with a theological or religious involvement.

The venture is undertaken with pride in the long Maynooth academic tradition and in modest continuance of it.

Editorial Board:

Patrick Hannon
Ronan Drury
Gerard Watson

Saturday, 20th May, 2000 A.D.

ONLY LIFE GIVES LIFE

Dear Francesca,

A little souvenir of your visit to Maynooth for the symposium on 'Fides et Ratio'.

Tom Morris.

For
Alma, John, Edward and Mary

Thomas J. Norris

Only Life Gives Life
Revelation, Theology and Christian Living according to Cardinal Newman

the columba press

First published in 1996 by

the columba press

55A Spruce Avenue, Stillorgan Industrial Park,
Blackrock, Co Dublin

Cover by Bill Bolger
Origination by The Columba Press
Printed in Ireland by Colour Books, Dublin

ISBN 1 85607 141 3

Acknowledgements

The author is sincerely grateful to the editors of The *Irish Theological Quarterly*, Maynooth, for the permission to publish chapter 3, originally published as 'On the Personal Appropriation of the Meaning of Revelation', *ITQ*, 1 (1979), 40-50; for chapter 5, originally published, in large part, as 'Tradition: Variations on the Theme' in *ITQ*, 1 & 2 (1981), 60-79; for chapter 6, originally published as 'Cardinal Newman and the Liberals', 1 (1987), 1-16; for chapter 8, originally published as 'Did Newman Preach a Gospel of Gloom?', in *ITQ*, 2-3-4 (1983/84), 198-211.

Contents

List of Abbreviations

References to Newman's works are usually to the uniform edition of 1869-81 (36 vols), which was published by Longmans, Green, and Co of London until the stock was destroyed in the Second World War. References to volumes which are not in the uniform edition are identified by the addition of distinguishing details.

Apo.	*Apologia pro Vita Sua.*
Ari.	*The Arians of the Fourth Century*
Artz	Johannes Artz, *Newman-Lexikon,* (Mainz, 1975)
Ath I, II	*Select Treatises of St Athanasius*, 2 vols.
AW	*John Henry Newman: Autobiographical Writings,* ed. Henry Tristram, (London and New York, 1956)
Call.	*Callista: A Tale of the Third Century*
Campaign	*My Campaign in Ireland,* part I, ed. W. Neville, (privately printed, 1896)
CS	*Catholic Sermons of Cardinal Newman,* ed. at the Birmingham Oratory (London, 1957)
Cons.	*On Consulting the Faithful in Matters of Doctrine,* ed. John Coulson, (London, 1961)
DA	*Discussions and Arguments on Various Subjects*
Dev.	*An Essay on the Development of Christian Doctrine*
Diff. I, II	*Certain Difficulties felt by Anglicans in Catholic Teaching,* 2 vols.
Ess. I, II	*Essays Critical and Historical,* 2 vols.
GA	*An Essay in Aid of a Grammar of Assent*
HS I, II, III	*Historical Sketches,* 3 vols.
Idea	*The Idea of a University*
Jfc	*Lectures on the Doctrine of Justification*
Ker	Ian Ker, *John Henry Newman A Biography,* (Oxford and New York, 1990)

LD	*The Letters and Diaries of John Henry Newman,* ed. Charles Stephen Dessain et al., vols i-vi (Oxford, 1978-84), xi-xxii (London, 1961-72), xxiii-xxxi (Oxford, 1973-7)
LG	*Loss and Gain: The Story of a Convert*
Life	C.S. Dessain, *John Henry Newman,* (London, 1966)
MD	*Meditations and Devotions of the late Cardinal Newman,* (London, 1893)
Mir.	*Two Essays on Biblical and on Ecclesiastical Miracles*
Mix.	*Discourses addressed to Mixed Congregations*
Moz. I, II	*Letters and Correspondence of John Henry Newman during his Life in the English Church,* ed. Anne Mozley, 2 vols. (London, 1891)
NO	*Newman the Oratorian: His Unpublished Oratory Papers,* ed. Placid Murray, OSB (Dublin, 1969)
OS	*Sermons preached on Various Occasions*
PS I-VIII	*Parochial and Plain Sermons,* 8 vols.
Prepos.	*Present Position of Catholics in England*
Red.	J. Coulson and A.M. Allchin, eds., *The Rediscovery of Newman,* (London, 1967)
SD	*Sermons bearing on Subjects of the Day*
SE	*Stray Essays on Controversial Points ,* (privately printed, 1890)
SN	*Sermon Notes of John Henry Cardinal Newman, 1849-1878,* ed. Fathers of the Birmingham Oratory, (London, 1913)
TT	*Tracts Theological and Ecclesiastical*
US	*Fifteen Sermons preached before the University of Oxford*
VM, I, II	*The Via Media,* 2 vols.
VV	*Verses on Various Occasions*
Ward I, II	Wilfrid Ward, *The Life of John Henry Cardinal Newman,* 2 vols. (London, 1912)
Weidner	*The Via Media of the Anglican Church,* Edited with Introduction and Notes by H.D. Weidner, (Oxford, 1990)

Prelude

John Henry Newman continues to fascinate. And to intrigue. At the Second Vatican Council so many of his concerns appeared on the agenda – the church and the world, the role of the lay faithful, the dignity of conscience, Christianity as a call and way to holiness for all, the renewal of theology, the issue of secular humanism, education. The very year after the conclusion of the Second Vatican Council scholars from all the churches gathered in his beloved Oxford for the First Oxford Newman Symposium. The Oxford Symposium brought Newman home. It was the rediscovery of Newman as a theologian of originality, a thinker of profound insight, and an ecumenist of genius before his time.[1] The centenary of his death six years ago saw a rash of conferences around the world, two outstanding biographies,[2] and a shelf of new studies. When the new *Catechism* appeared in 1992 it quoted Newman four times,[3] the only one so honoured since the Middle Ages who was not already a saint or doctor of the church. He seems to have grown on the church and on humanity by the tranquil influence of his genius after a temporary demise in the early part of the century.[4]

The reasons for this fascination are many. His journey all the way from an early attraction to simple unbelief into the Catholic faith was, in the words of Pope Paul VI, 'the most toilsome, but also the greatest, the most meaningful, the most conclusive, that human thought ever travelled during the last century, indeed one might say during the modern era'.[5] When half-way through that life, on the 9th of October 1845, he left the Anglican fold for the Catholic, one of his closest friends saw in the step 'perhaps the greatest event which has happened since the communion of churches has been interrupted'.[6] Having become a Catholic he continued to think, to write and to work for unity. 'Never was a mind so unceasingly in motion. But the motion was always growth, and never revolution'.[7] His analysis of the difficulties for faith being thrown up by the great cultural currents of the Enlightenment, also fascinates.[8]

9

This book explores what is perhaps both the key to his life and the central reason why he fascinates. As a teenager he discovered the living God. In a vivid encounter God manifested himself to the sensitive youngster as the undying reality and as the purpose of life. He went on to live by that vision of 'two only supreme and luminously self-evident beings, myself and my creator'.[9]

Part One of this book outlines his thinking on divine revelation, its content and action in the historical life of the church. The first chapter presents his thinking on revelation as the initial and essential idea of Christianity. But since it was 'the fathers who made (him) a Catholic',[10] the second chapter highlights his involvement with the Fathers who were always his special 'paradise of delight':[11] they provided the first, indeed the normative exposition of divine revelation. The third chapter addresses a concern that was an abiding one for Newman, the process by which believers appropriate the contents of revelation. This concern is the principal key to the great trilogy of *An Essay on the Development of Christian Doctrine*, the *Apologia pro Vita Sua* and the *Grammar of Assent*. This first part may be considered the roots of Newman's life, from which the shoots of his vibrant theology sprang up and grew into the fruits of a Christian life lived out in the imitation and following of Christ.

Part Two deals with these shoots. There is a chapter on his discovery of tradition as the life of revelation pervading the church and invading the world with the reality of the risen Christ. A further chapter shows how Newman's insight in this regard emerged in the Second Vatican Council's *Constitution on Divine Revelation*, albeit in incognito fashion. The third chapter in this part shows that, since 'theology is the fundamental and regulating principle of the whole church system',[12] it is incumbent upon it to demonstrate the need for dogma, and the truth that 'religion, as a mere sentiment, is ... a dream and a mockery'.[13]

From these shoots come, in the third part, the fruits of praxis manifest in the rich reality of Christian life. Like the fathers, Newman loved to stress the truth that to be a Christian is the most awful and the most wonderful thing a person can be in this world. Fidelity to conscience, 'the aboriginal vicar of Christ',[14] is the way to the truth that frees. The good news of revelation issues in the gospel of the joy of Christian living. But since Christ came and sent his spirit 'to gather together the scattered children of God' (Jn 12:52), it is necessary to overcome 'the division of churches (which) is the corruption of hearts'.[15] Here we outline Newman's method of ecumenism, highlighting the tension, sometimes dramatic, between the ardent convert and the committed ecumenist. The concluding chapter tries to gather together his principal insights and to suggest, however sketchily, their applicability to our own age.

That is the structure of the book now in your hands. The Anglican Newman provides perhaps a justification of that structure. It is to be found in one of those marvellous meditations on faith and reason that are now known as the *Oxford University Sermons*. In the final meditation on 'developments in religious doctrines' he begins with the witness of the Blessed Virgin at the incarnation and subsequently, in order to show the proper sequence of revelation, theology and Christian living. In her he notices that revelation and faith lead immediately into 'pondering' and so to theology as an ongoing activity, and this leads, in the second instance, to concrete action. 'And accordingly, at the marriage feast in Cana, her faith anticipated his first miracle, and she said to the servants, "Whatsoever he saith unto you, do it".'[16] This Marian paradigm provides the very shape and structure of the book before you: part one deals with revelation and faith, part two with the pondering that is theology, and part three with the vision and action that lie at the heart of Christian life. 'He had taken the focus of theology away from a code of ideas existing, however perfectly, in a passive state vouched for by authority, and located it in the orthopraxis of the loving and reverent believer thinking and doing.'[17]

It is not to be assumed that all the elements relevant to each of these component parts are treated. It is hoped, however, that an adequate sample of themes is present in each part and that the resultant architecture of the work enjoys clear definition. In any case, the book is constructed in such a way that one may read any one part on its own, and even any chapter for itself. Still, the sweep of the book is to be seen in the unfolding structure of the parts, in the vision of the whole, just as the completed course of a life is the true key to its many stages.

Part One: Roots

'Newman had a remarkable mission, the revival of so much of the
Revealed Religion of Christianity.'
(C. S. Dessain, John Henry Newman, *London 1966, 44).*

CHAPTER 1

The Initial and Essential Idea of Christianity: Revelation

Champion of Revealed Truth

The unique focus of practically all of John Henry Newman's enormous literary output was a pastoral focus: 'to make us realise what it means to be called children of God and to make us become such in fact in Christ'.[1] This was a definite but difficult enterprise. The course of thought running from the eighteenth into the nineteenth century and growing throughout his lifetime increasingly preoccupied John Henry Newman. From about 1833, the year which saw the beginning of the Oxford Movement, he noticed around him a rising tide of opposition to the faith of his church and country. He observed a subtle marginalisation of faith in English society, 'an age of evidences' when 'love was cold'.[2] The meeting of the challenge posed by this marginalisation is the real context of his life and the clue to the dramatic direction which his life was to take.

The great Londoner, who was to become the inspiration of the Oxford Movement, provided an exposition of the faith and developed a style of theology that were pastorally influential, culturally appropriate and, as time has told, theologically seminal. He had a 'clear and profound realisation of what is fundamental and permanent in Christianity – Christianity as a reality of life, divine and human, which by its very nature calls for constant development and renewal'.[3] Still, his fear was that 'this age will substitute its human cistern for the wells of truth; it will be afraid of the deep well, the abyss of God's judgements and God's mercies'.[4] In fact, in the course of his providentially long life he saw the fortunes of the Enlightenment flourish, and the cause of revealed religion wane, in his beloved England. In 1876 he wrote to Robert Charles Jenkins:

> I do not look at the divisions of Christendom so very anxiously as you do, for the Catholic (i.e. the Catholic Roman) Church presents a continuous history of fearful falls and as strange and successful recoveries. We have a series of catastrophes each unlike the others, and that diversity is the

14

> pledge that the present ordeal, though different from any of the preceding, will be overcome, in God's good time, also … Of course one's forecasting may be wrong – but we may be entering on quite a new course, for which the civil ignoring of Christianity may be the necessary first step.[5]

In the face of those difficulties, cultural, historical and theological, Newman followed a clear strategy: he expounded revelation, divine revelation, with the absolute conviction that this was the best way both to meet the difficulties of the day, and to nourish God's people. 'Christianity', he writes in 1865, 'is eminently an objective religion. For the most part it tells us of persons and facts in simple words, and leaves that announcement to produce its effect on such hearts as are prepared to receive it'.[6] Because it is from God and not from man, revealed and not man-made, Christian revelation 'brings us into a new world – a world of overpowering interest, of the sublimest views and the tenderest and purest feelings'.[7]

The renewal and development of the church, as well as the advancement of its ministry of salvation on the plane of the world, has, indeed may have, only one source – the historical revelation that God has made of himself beginning with Israel and culminating in the missions of Christ and the Holy Spirit. Christopher Dawson has remarked that Newman was the first to perceive this supreme need of the church in the modern world.[8] Divine revelation, by which the living God out of the greatness of the love with which he loved us (Eph 2:4) communicates his eternal life and love to the human family (see 1 Jn 1:1-4), must be the supreme concern of the church. Revelation is 'the inherent and indefeatible principle of her supernatural life'.[9]

John Henry Newman set out to unfold divine revelation in such a way 'that people by hearing it, would believe, by believing it, would hope and by hoping would love'.[10] Of himself he could confidently say, 'From the age of fifteen, dogma has been the fundamental principle of my religion: I know no other religion, I cannot enter into the idea of any other sort of religion; religion, as a mere sentiment, is to me a dream and a mockery. As well can there be filial love without the fact of a father, as devotion without the fact of a Supreme Being'.[11] Newman 'had a remarkable mission, the revival of so much of the revealed religion of Christianity',[12] as Charles Stephen Dessain wrote in his well-known biography. It is little wonder, then, that he dwells extensively on the subject and provides a fascinating treatment of it. It may be convenient to list the key themes comprising that treatment. First, we will consider his thought on what is in revelation. Then we will focus on Christ as the fullness of all revelation. After that we will see how the Holy Spirit acts as the agent and instrument by which revelation is received. In the fourth place we will highlight the mysterious character of revelation. Then we may expound his teaching on the perception and 'realisation' of revelation. Finally, we will show the originality and vitality of Newman's thinking on divine revelation.

I. WHAT IS IN CHRISTIAN REVELATION?

The whole of Christianity is senseless without the God who made us communicating himself to us as the form of our real life with God. Steeped as he was in the scriptures of the Old and New Testaments, as well as in the fathers of the church, particularly the Greek fathers, Newman appropriated through prayer, study and the following of Christ, as the core of Christianity, God communicating himself in the twofold mission of his Son into our human flesh, and of the Holy Spirit as the animator and soul of that first communication. The meaning, the content and the purpose of Christianity consist in the divine self-communication, indeed the trinitarian self-communication to human flesh. In that way God comes in the flesh, the Son becoming the Son of Man, so that we are saved not *from* the flesh, but *in* the flesh.

Not Only a Mystery

For Newman the 'doctrine of the Blessed Trinity is not proposed in scripture as a mystery'![13] Rather it is the very shape of God's approach to us, being the form and the outline of his loving communication and saving presence. This divine self-communication appears as the venturing forth of the triune love that is God into the human family in fulfilment of the revelation already made to Israel. Its purpose is to engage us and involve us to the point where we now have access to the Father through the Son in the Holy Spirit (Eph 2:18). 'What a source of light, freedom and comfort it is to know we cannot love them too much or humble ourselves before them too reverently, for both the Son and the Spirit are inseparably God. Such is the *practical* effect of the doctrine; but what a mystery also is herein involved!'[14] The doctrine, then, may not be seen *only* as mystery, though the world opened up by the doctrine is mysterious, as we will soon see.

Here Newman is doing no more than reiterating St Paul's formulation of the core of the faith as when, to take one example, Paul writes, 'When the appointed time came, God sent his Son, born of a woman ... God has sent the Spirit of his Son into our hearts: the Spirit that cries "Abba, Father"' (Gal 4:4,6). Revelation, therefore, provides not only the object of faith and its content, but also our access to God and the very substance of our communication with God. It opens up an extraordinary and otherwise inaccessible milieu in which the real life of Christians is lived. So he writes, 'We are assured of some real though mystical fellowship with the Father, Son, and Holy Spirit, in order to this: so that both by a real presence in the soul, and by the fruits of grace, God is one with every believer, as in a consecrated temple'.[15]

This vision of the faith and the possibilities for faith-life which it opens up make Christianity unique among all religions. Besides, it lays the foundations for an attractive and competitive Christian statement. And since the mystery of the Holy Trinity is the core of Christianity, the rediscovery of the Trinity is indispensable to a competitive Christianity.

A Competitive Christianity

Newman was acutely aware that Christianity needed to be 'developed to meet the age'.[16] His own gradual relentless discovery of the full circle of revealed truth had taught him 'what Christians had to rediscover if they wanted to have once again a Christianity with a view of the world and the life of man within it that could prove "competitive", that is, able to face the unbelief of an age which, for Newman, was to be the near future'.[17] And so his purpose was to find once more and to repropose the saving truths of revelation, convinced it was only the God of Christian revelation who could cope with 'the greatness and littleness' of the human being. In fact, he was always convinced that a principal reason for the persistence of the faith was its relevance to needs and wants ineradicable from the human heart. The God revealed in his Son made flesh and communicated to us in the Holy Spirit is the ultimate and abiding ground for our hope. If God is so much on our side – 'He did not spare his only Son, but gave him up for us all' (Rom 8:32) – who can be against us? Life is hope-filled: it not only *can* be such, but *must* be such as a result of revelation.

The Dilemma of Humankind

To appreciate what a gift revelation is, what a superlative blessing on men and women, it is necessary to look, at least a little, on the human condition, on what might be called the dilemma of humankind. For God's self-revelation is not spoken into a vacuum but into the teeming flux of life and the vicissitudes of history. This dilemma is highlighted in the inbuilt and apparently insuperable paradox of human life as great yet small, promising so much yet delivering so little, aspiring after immortality yet dominated by mortality, struggling between hope and despair, good and evil. Now this dilemma is illuminated, resolved and overcome in the mystery of Christ. By 'mystery' Newman did not mean the later idea of that which is beyond human understanding, but rather the Pauline and Patristic sense of the term. 'Christ among you' is 'the hope of glory', wrote St Paul to the Colossians (1:27). Men and women are mysteries since they are made in the image of the revealed mystery, but they are mysteries that are illuminated in what St Paul loves to call 'the mystery of Christ'. If human existence is perplexing, why should anyone hesitate at the fact of mysteries in religion? 'It seems, then, that difficulties in religion are especially given to prove the reality of our faith. What shall separate the insincere from the sincere follower of Christ? When the many own Christ with their lips, what shall try and discipline his true servant, and detect the self-deceiver? Difficulties in religion mainly contribute to this end ... (Faith) receives with reverence and love whatever God gives, when convinced it is his gift'.[18]

II. CHRIST THE FULLNESS OF REVELATION

To rediscover the trinitarian mystery, then, is to find the unifying, indeed the energising core of divine revelation. But this core comes into view only in and through the mystery of the incarnate Son and in the economy of his passion, death and resurrection. Christology is thus the second pillar of revelation. Newman underlines the point. 'The invisible God was then revealed in the form and history of man, revealed in those respects in which sinners most require to know him, and nature spoke least distinctly, as a holy yet merciful Governor of his creatures'.[19] As God from God, Jesus Christ is the full and perfect revealer of the Father: 'the only Son nearest the Father's heart, he can make him known' (Jn 1:18). Now there is a significance in the fact that he is the Son of God. '... it is surely not so marvellous and mysterious that the Son of God should be God, as that there should be a Son of God at all ... He must be God because he is the Son'.[20]

Newman sees an appropriateness in the fact that it was the Son of the Father, and not one of the other divine Persons, who became flesh. 'As the Son was God, so on the other hand was the Son suitably made man; it belonged to him to have the Father's perfections, it became him to assume a servant's form'.[21] Here Newman differs from St Augustine for whom any one of the three divine persons could have become flesh. 'We shall see fitness, ... now that the sacred truth is revealed, in the *Son* of God taking flesh'.[22] This enables us all the better to understand both what our Saviour says of himself in the gospels and what he does for us through his Paschal Mystery. In particular, the fittingness of the Son becoming incarnate is seen in the great truth of our salvation, already alluded to, namely, that the eternal Son makes us sons and daughters of the Father in himself and with himself. For revelation teaches us that the effect of the incarnation and of the Paschal Mystery is precisely to make us children of the Father through participation in the only-begotten Son.

Making the Invisible Visible

The form of his existence here below, then, achieves a perfect trans-lation to earth of his life in the blessed Trinity, his eternal homeland, if one may dare so to speak. Jesus is the visibility of the invisible God, in the sense in which the first Preface for Christmas formu-lates the point, 'In him (Jesus) we see our God made visible and so are caught up in love of the God we cannot see'.[23] Not only does he make the invisible Father visible to us, he also makes the ultimately inaccessible and mysterious near in a wonderful way. In a memo-rable homily preached in July 1837, 'The Invisible World', he explained:

> Almighty God the Being of beings, is ... among 'the things which are not seen'. Once, and only once, for thirty-three years, has he condescended to become one of the beings which are seen, when he, the second person of the ever-blessed Trinity, was, by an unspeakable mercy, born of the Virgin Mary into this sensible world. And then he was seen, heard, handled; he ate, he drank, he slept, he conversed, he went about.[24]

In that way 'the design of Christ's incarnation is a manifestation of the unseen Creator'.[25]

The apostles for their part saw him, and spoke with him, and touched him. They were with him on the holy mountain, and ate with him in the Upper Room, and saw him risen (Acts 1:21-2). We, for our part, have not seen him and heard him as the apostles did. But we believe in their witness, accept their testimony, and venture all on their authority and truthfulness. However, as the invisible

Creator was manifested and made visible to the apostles in his enfleshed Son, so too the day is coming when he will be made visible to us also. 'Men think', Newman writes, 'that they are lords of the world and may do as they will. They think this earth their property and its movements in their power; whereas it has other lords besides them and is the scene of a higher conflict than any are capable of conceiving. It contains Christ's little ones whom they despise.'[26]

To Look and to Obey
Since the Father has made himself known in Christ, the whole task of the Christian is to look upon that sacred form and then to obey him, just as he always obeys the will of the Father. Here is the true image and picture of God: the Christian is bound to look on it. He may not look at any other. Revelation is no mere piece of information, however sacred, offered to human curiosity. It is rather the communication of a life that is to be lived. We are bound to look and to obey. 'The whole duty and work of a Christian is made up of two parts, faith and obedience; "looking unto Jesus", the divine object as well as the author of our faith, and acting according to his will.'[27] This implies, indeed requires, meditating on him – his person, his words, his deeds, his example, his virtues, in a word as he is portrayed in the gospels. In a famous sermon on the Passion, Newman wrote:

> Now I bid you consider that that face, so ruthlessly smitten, was the face of God himself; the brows bloody with the thorns, the sacred body exposed to view and lacerated with the scourge, the hands nailed to the cross, and, afterwards, the side pierced with the spear; it was the blood, and the sacred flesh, and the hands, and the temples, and the side, and the feet of God himself, which the frenzied multitude then gazed upon. This is so fearful a thought, that when the mind masters it, surely it will be difficult to think of anything else.[28]

The Obedience of Faith
Commentators, both contemporary with Newman and in this century, have remarked on the emphasis he places on obedience to the revealed word. The famous historian of the Oxford Movement and his friend, Dean Church, writes, 'Evangelical theology had dwelt upon the work of Christ, and laid comparatively little stress on his example, on the picture left of personality and life.' But now there

was a change. 'The great Name stood no longer for an abstract symbol of doctrine, but for a Living Master, who could teach as well as save ... It was a change in the look and use of scripture, which some can still look back to as an epoch in their religious history.'[29] In our own day, Hans Urs von Balthasar writes of the power and authority of the word which Newman breathed into all his pastoral work and preaching, and which lends a unique and unmistakable quality to every page he wrote.[30] 'Those stumble who disobey his word' (1 Peter 2:8), would be Newman's guiding principle.

The Right Way to see Life

To the sincere Christian, the one who looks upon him whom he has pierced (Jn 19:37), the crucified Christ becomes the power and the wisdom of God (I Cor 1:24). There are many ways of looking at life. Newman stresses, however, that there is but one ultimately complete and right way. And that is the way God looks at it. We must try to look at it that way.[31] What is the vantage point, the true perspective on which to judge the world? In the sermon, 'The Cross of Christ the Measure of the World', Newman presents the crucifixion of the Son of God as the key to the Christian interpretation of life.

> It is the death of the eternal Word of God, made flesh, which is our lesson how to think and how to speak of this world. It has put its due value upon everything which we see, upon all fortunes, all advantages, all ranks, all dignities, all pleasures ... Go to the political world ... to the world of intellect and science ... look at misery, look at poverty and destitution, look at oppression and captivity; go where food is scanty and lodging unhealthy ... Would you know how to rate all these? Gaze upon the cross.[32]

Thus the crucified Christ is the most learned book ever written, and the Christian who reads regularly in this book enjoys the best hermeneutic of humankind and history.

III. THE ROLE OF THE HOLY SPIRIT

The unseen Creator of the whole universe, the invisible almighty God, makes himself visible to the believer *in* and *through* the flesh of his Son become man. But there was something else needed as well, a need to which we have already alluded. The revelation was incomplete, since the Holy Spirit had not yet been sent and the reason, as given by St John, was that 'Jesus had not yet been glorified' (Jn 7:39). Almost like the refrain in a psalm, the New Testament

points out the simple incomprehension of the first witnesses of the
incarnate Christ, and this even *after* his resurrection and ascension.
In truth, the gospel according to St Mark is almost a protracted presentation of the human incomprehension of the manner of revelation adopted by the Son of God. The Holy Spirit supplied for this
difficulty, as Jesus foretold: 'when the spirit of truth comes he will
lead you to the complete truth' (Jn 16:13).

In the *Lectures on Justification*, one of his greatest theological
works, Newman spells out this insight.

> Christ's work of mercy has two chief parts; what he did for
> all men, what he does for each; what he did once for all, what
> he does for one by one continually; what he did externally to
> us, what he does within us; what he did on earth, what he
> does in heaven; what he did in his own person, what he does
> by his Spirit ... There was but one atonement; there are ten
> thousand justifications ... He atoned, I repeat, in his own per-
> son; he justifies through his Spirit.[33]

The Holy Spirit leads Christians into the truth of the Father which is
in the Son enfleshed, crucified and glorified in the resurrection.

Being Drawn into the Drama

To use a metaphor from the theatre, it is the task of the Holy Spirit
to interpret the action of the Son to us the spectators who are then
drawn into the action. With the Holy Spirit revelation becomes a
divine and human drama. Now drama is, in the memorable
description of W.B. Yeats, 'character disclosed in an action which
engrosses the present and dominates memory'. The Holy Spirit is
the key to our perception of the drama of the incarnate Son revealing the heart of the Father and drawing us into communion with
him and with one another. He grants us the perception of what is
revealed to lead us to the knowledge of the Father of our Lord Jesus
Christ (Eph 1:17-8). He enlightens the eyes of our minds to see what
hope his call holds for us, and as Theodor Adorno, the German
Marxist philosopher, saw, 'Hope is the only form in which love
appears'. The Holy Spirit engenders a deep remembering in the
church among believers, and turns the events of the redemption
into a living *anamnesis*. The past becomes a present, and this present
inspires the future.

The Sweetness of Living Waters

With frequency Newman returns to the mission of the Spirit in the application of Christ's mercy, grace and truth to Christians. He explains this application in terms of the teaching of the Greek fathers. 'The Holy Spirit himself, perchance in his mysterious nature, is the eternal love whereby the Father and the Son have dwelt in each other, as ancient writers have believed; and what he is in heaven, that he is abundantly on earth. He lives in the Christian's heart as the never failing fount of charity, which is the very sweetness of the living waters'.[34]

The Grace of the Gospel

Here, then, is Newman's teaching on the inhabitation of the Holy Spirit in the heart of the Christian as in a temple. The Holy Spirit is 'that divine influence, which has the fullness of Christ's grace to purify us, has also the power of Christ's blood to justify'.[35] Here we find the distinguishing grace and gift of the gospel of revelation, by which the Christian 'in St Peter's forcible language, becomes "partaker of the divine nature", and has "power" or authority, as St John says, "to become the son of God". Or, to use the words of St Paul, "he is a new creation; old things are passed away, behold all things are become new". His rank is new; his parentage and service new.'[36]

The Spirit Makes Christ Present

It is a mistake, therefore, to see in the indwelling of the Holy Spirit a replacement or substitution for the risen Lord, 'the hope of glory'. Far from replacing the Redeemer, the Sanctifier has come 'to make him present'. In that way the indwelling Spirit engenders 'the indwelling of Christ risen and glorified'.[37] 'God the Son,' he writes, 'has graciously vouchsafed to reveal the Father to his creatures from without; God the Holy Ghost by inward communications.'[38] And our reaction? 'We can but silently adore the Infinite Love which encompasses us on every side.'

Revelation, then, begins with the Father, who, in the fullness of time, as the New Testament loves to repeat, sends his only-begotten Son in our flesh, to redeem it. This revelation, though glorious and unsurpassable, is still 'external' so to speak. Christ, crucified and risen, is the revealer of the Father, the burning bush between heaven and humankind. But this external revelation becomes internal through the Holy Spirit: he finishes Christ's revelation with regard to us. In that way the Holy Spirit makes the divine Persons present to us, and we to them! We truly become the sons and daughters of the Father, the brothers and sisters of Christ, and the temples of their Holy Spirit. 'Let us never lose sight of this great and simple view, which the whole of scripture sets before us. What was actually done by Christ in the flesh eighteen hundred years ago, is in type and resemblance really wrought in us one by one even to the end of time.'[39]

The Holy Spirit therefore places the Redeemer within us, vivifying him for us. He raises us to the thought of Christ, and then Christ in the same Spirit shows us the Father. In that way the Spirit glorifies Christ, just as Christ glorifies the Father. Newman aimed to forward fully and candidly the great Christian privileges. In the process he raised the minds and wills of people to a new awareness. This was the key to his influence in Oxford during the early part of his life. 'I held a large bold system of religion, very unlike the Protestantism of the day.'[40]

Obedience, not Emotion, the Test
He was always worried, however, by an emotionalism such as was sometimes evident among Evangelicals, and still more worried at the horror of any unreality in religion. He was relentless in reminding us of the price to be paid before Christ's redeeming love can take proper possession of us.

> I must say plainly this, that, fanciful though it may appear at first sight to say so, the comforts of life are the main cause of our want of love of God ... Till we, in a certain sense, detach ourselves from our bodies, our minds will not be in a state to receive divine impressions, and to exert heavenly aspirations. A smooth and easy life, an uninterrupted enjoyment of the goods of providence, full meals, soft raiment, well furnished homes, the pleasures of sense, the feeling of security, the consciousness of wealth – these and the like, if we are not careful, choke up all the avenues of the soul, through which the life and breath of heaven might come to us.[41]

To be a Christian is to live by detailed obedience to the Word of God and the prompting of the Holy Spirit.

IV. CHRISTIAN REVELATION: MYSTERIOUS BUT PRACTICAL

For Newman revelation opens up vistas unseen and beyond our wildest expectations, since revelation grants the knowledge of a love that surpasses all knowing (Eph 3:18). It leads into a world of overpowering interest, a world of the sublimest views, as we have seen. What kind of knowledge does it provide? In other words, what is the *nature* of Christian knowledge? This seems to be a key question that both deserves radical attention and promises to repay serious consideration.

It is true that the Holy Spirit comes to finish in us what Jesus had already finished in himself. This was 'the second part' of the Saviour's work, in which the Holy Spirit becomes the agent of reception of revelation, as we have just seen. This is the real key to the kind of knowledge afforded in and by revelation. That knowledge, however, is of an eminently practical nature in as much as revelation 'is given, not that we may know more, but that we may do better'. The Holy Spirit places Christ in us and makes us realise his presence in such a way that we are able to live better lives. In particular, he obviates the danger of preferring knowledge to holiness, a danger that is real, 'since men are apt to prize knowledge above holiness'. The Holy Spirit, in fact, 'is not a light accorded to the reason, the gifts of the intellect; in as much as the gospel has its mysteries, its difficulties and secret things, which the Holy Spirit does not remove'. The kind of knowledge given in revelation, then, is not given at all to satisfy our curiosity but rather to initiate, sustain and advance our Christian living. It is, in a word, *practical* knowledge, being 'practical and useful knowledge about our souls'.[42]

But it is also *mysterious* knowledge. Newman likes to highlight this characteristic of revelation. 'It is indeed a remarkable circumstance, that the very revelation that brings us practical and useful knowledge about our souls, in the very act of doing so, may (as it would seem), in consequence of doing so, brings us mysteries.' This is the very law of revelation, both as event and as content, 'We gain spiritual light at the price of intellectual perplexity and the more we gain of spiritual light the greater the intellectual perplexity.'[43]

Religious Light is Intellectual Darkness
That 'religious light is intellectual darkness' is something that must be understood in order to avoid 'very grievous mistakes respecting the nature of Christian knowledge' and so of revelation.[44] The first of these mistakes sees in Christianity a merely 'rational religion', and so a religion without mysteries. According to these 'philosophical Christians',[45] revelation removes mystery, since it draws back the veil covering 'the hidden things of God'. But for Newman it is precisely this drawing back that blinds the intellect. This is the remarkable principle of revelation. He formulates it by putting these words on the lips of Our Lord:

Scripture does not aim at making mysteries, but they are as shadows brought out by the Sun of Truth. When you knew nothing of revealed light, you knew nothing of revealed darkness. Religious truth requires that you be told *something*, your own imperfect nature prevents you knowing *all*; and to know *something* and *not all* – partial knowledge – must of course perplex; doctrines imperfectly revealed must be mysteries.[46]

It is 'the weakness of the human intellect', coupled with the 'various, complex, progressive' occurrence of revelation, that are responsible for the mysterious character of divine revelation.

Mysteries in Nature and Scripture

Newman sets out to drive home the point. He does so particularly in the sermon called 'The Christian Mysteries' where he enlarges upon his thesis that 'religious light is intellectual darkness'. In rapid succession he surveys the mysteries present in nature, in the Old Testament and in the New Testament. As for the mysteries of nature, they rise precisely where everything seems full of light and radiant with beauty until the fact of pain sternly insinuates itself. While Christianity fulfils the revelation made to the children of Abraham, it does not remove the difficulties thrown up by Judaism. In fact, it introduces fresh and still more perplexing mysteries. 'How stupendous a mystery is the incarnation and suffering of the Son of God.'[47] Newman, in truth, is deeply penetrated by the height and depth of these new mysteries, which only serve to make the one revelation highly mysterious. That is why he returns frequently in the course of his preaching to the theme. To take but a few examples, he highlights for his hearers in St Mary's in the 1830s 'the mysteriousness of our present being', the mystery of 'the humiliation of the eternal Son', which is as great as the mystery of the Holy Trinity. And he warns against irreverent speculation on the mysteries in religion.[48]

Revelation, then, is bright darkness. Or dark brightness. It masters us through its unfathomable depths, through what Newman calls in one place its 'Catholic fullness'.[49] Any revelation involves 'almost in its very idea as being something new, a collision with the human intellect, and demands accordingly … a sacrifice of private judgement'. This, in fact, is the ultimate reason why the only attitude appropriate to revelation is that of a faith that is 'unassuming, modest, thankful, obedient'. Those who lack these dispositions allow their difficulties to grow into objections, and their objections into scepticism when their insincerity as believers is finally unmasked.[50] And this is the reason too for Newman's lifelong antagonism towards every form of religious rationalism, towards what he called religious liberalism and which we will consider in Chapter VI.

The Mistake of Oversystematisation

If the Christian mysteries are 'the shadows brought out by the Sun of Truth', it would be a damaging error to eliminate this mysterious quality. There is, however, a second 'grievous mistake' that can be made, namely, the attempt to oversystematise the content of revelation. This mistake has in common with religious rationalism the denial, at least by implication, of the principle that divinely revealed truth is intellectual darkness. Oversystematisation is guilty of a presumption. That presumption of the capacity to systematise is an error about the nature of revelation. 'It is ever hunting for a fabulous primitive simplicity.'[51] In Tract 73, 'On the Introduction of Rationalistic Principles into Religion', written in 1835 at the height of the Oxford Movement, Newman states the matter with precision:

> No revelation can be complete or systematic from the weakness of the human intellect; so far as it is not such, it is mysterious ... Revelation is religious doctrine viewed on its illuminated side; a Mystery is the selfsame doctrine viewed on the side unilluminated. Thus religious truth is neither light nor darkness, but both together; it is like the dim view of a country seen in the twilight, with forms half extracted from the darkness, with broken lines, and isolated masses. Revelation is not a revealed system, but consists of detached and incomplete truths belonging to a vast system unrevealed, of doctrines and injunctions mysteriously linked together.[52]

This passage harmoniously combines theoretic penetration with imaginative analogy. As for theoretic insight, it stands out in his balancing revelation between an illuminated doctrinal side and an unilluminated or mysterious side, as well as in the insinuation that the differentiation of doctrine and mystery is to be found in 'the weakness of the human intellect' when confronted by the informing, but blinding, light of revelation. As for imaginative analogy, Newman uses the vivid simile of a tourist catching a first glance of a strange country whose massive shapes and dim forms suggest a picture but do not complete it. Who can combine in one vision such enormous facts of revelation as the Trinity, the humiliation of the eternal Son and the resurrection of the body? Relate them indeed one may, use the one to throw light on the other one ought. But this effort only serves to impress on the imagination the vastness of the new world which revelation opens.

Revelation both Personal and Propositional

Religious light then is intellectual darkness. Darkness for the intellect, but brightness for the human spirit. Newman wants to avoid any suggestion that thinking about the mysteries of the faith is improper or impossible. On the contrary, he insists that God wants to reveal himself, and not only truths about himself. And God actually does this in the twofold mission of his Son and Holy Spirit. In his review of Sir John Seeley's, *Ecce Homo*, written in 1866 and reductive of the mysterious side of revelation, Newman brings out the personal, and therefore, informative side of revelation. 'What Catholics,' he writes, 'what church doctors, as well as apostles, have ever lived on, is not any number of theological canons or decrees, but ... the Christ himself, as he is represented in concrete existence in the gospels.'[53] It is Christ who is the summation of revelation. He is the Father's ultimate witness *of* himself and ultimate witness *to* us. He is able to cross, as it were, the infinite abyss distancing the Creator from creatures, and creatures from the Creator. The 'faith of Catholics seemed like the profession of a formula' for critics such as Seeley, but the reality is that Catholics are all inhabited by one image, one picture, and that is the idea of Christ. Revelation, in a word, is eminently personal even while it is dogmatic and so also propositional.

Here we are face-to-face with the issue of whether revelation is more personal than propositional for Newman.[54] Let it be said at once that it is both, or rather that it is so eminently personal as to be propositional, and so propositional as to be personal. To appreciate the enriching tension between the personal and propositional faces of revelation, it is best perhaps to follow, though briefly, Newman's discovery of the true face of Christianity in the writings of the early church.

We know that when he was researching for the writing of *The Arians of the Fourth Century*, which appeared in 1833 and which studied in depth the Christianity of the fourth century, Newman discovered the great school of Alexandria. This centre of Christian life, action and thought flourished in a particular way from the third to the fifth centuries. There Newman encountered its great theologians and philosophers, Clement and Origen, Dionysius and

Athanasius. Their teaching came like music to his inner ear. In what did it consist? It consisted in the principle of the economy. The teaching of Clement and Origen is 'based on the mystical or sacramental principle, and spoke of the various economies or dispensations of the Eternal'. The church's 'mysteries are but the expressions in human language of truths to which the human mind is unequal'.[55]

Dogmas: Undesirable but Necessary!

The result of this enterprise was the conviction that dogmas were undesirable yet still necessary! He explained his views only gradually. As for the early centuries he held the position that 'freedom from symbols and articles is abstractedly the highest state of Christian communion, and the peculiar privilege of the primitive church'. The reason for this higher state is to be found in the fact that 'when confessions do not exist, the mysteries of divine truth, instead of being exposed to the gaze of the profane and uninstructed, are kept hidden in the bosom of the church, far more faithfully than is otherwise possible'.[56] This is an ideal order. The order of history, however, where the fortunes of revelation are committed to human hearts and consciences, soon required the clear formulation of dogma and authoritative teaching.

Their value is largely negative, at least for the younger Newman, since they are 'intended to forbid speculations, which are sure to spring up in the human mind, and to anticipate its attempts at systematic views by showing the ultimate abyss at which all rightly conducted inquiries arrive, not to tell us anything definite and real, which we did not know before, or which is beyond the faith of the most unlearned'.[57] That was in 1837. When he comes six years later to sketch his first tentative outline of a theory of doctrinal development, his attitude is more positive. Doctrines are a witness to the vitality of revelation, its inexhaustible riches, and assist in the realisation of these riches. They represent a folding out of the one great idea that is Christ, and must always be made to fold in to their mysterious source. 'One thing alone has to be impressed on us by scripture,' he writes in the fifteenth of the *Oxford University Sermons*, 'the Catholic idea, and in it they (doctrines) are all included. To object, then, to the number of propositions upon which an anathema is placed, is altogether to mistake their use; for their multiplication is not intended to enforce many things, but to express one.'[58]

Revelation then is both personal and propositional in unique harmony. That harmony is best understood against the background

of Christian revelation as revealed mystery which 'far from being
compassed by those very propositions, would not be exhausted nor
fathomed by a thousand'.[59]

V. 'REALISING THE INVISIBLE'[60]

What amazed Newman about the faith was its gift-quality. A gift,
however, is not fully such until the person to whom it is offered
actually accepts it and recognises it for what it is. Reception thus
enters into the very essence of the revelatory process, as also realisation, which is the rising of that reception to the level of awareness.
Concern for that level of consciousness in the recipients of revelation is a hallmark of Newman's theology of revelation and faith. As
we will see in our third chapter on the appropriation of revelation,
that concern preoccupies Newman continually and calls forth some
of his most stimulating thinking, as, to take but one instance, in the
Grammar of Assent. Here, however, our immediate task is to unfold
Newman's teaching on realisation as the raising of consciousness
by the reception of a revelation.

He scales heights in expressing it. He had the experience of
God's inbreaking love, whose principal characteristic was its maxi-
malism, its extremism. 'God so loved the world that he gave his
only Son' (Jn 3:16), and gave him even unto death, yes death on the
Roman *patibulum*, as ransom for sinners. Now while this gift was an
enormous and mysterious response to the question that the human
being is, still it could not be reduced to this. Indeed, any attempt to
present Christianity exclusively as an answer to the questions in the
human heart would inevitably reduce and deform the revelation. It
might be of help to look at the rudimentary shape of religion in the
ancient world.

The Drama of the Ancient World

The drama of the ancient world consisted in the search for the
divine origin of all reality. Newman picks up the theme in the second of the *Oxford University Sermons*, 'The influence of natural and
revealed religion respectively,' which was delivered in 1830.[61]
People went out in search of the Ultimate Principle of all reality.
And the achievements of many cultures in the ancient world witnessed to the depth of this search, the greatness of its achievements,
as well as the wisdom it yielded, so that it is true to claim that 'no
people (to speak in general terms) has been denied a revelation
from God, though but a portion of the world has enjoyed an
authenticated revelation'. With Christian revelation God goes in

search of lost and sinful humankind. The difference between these two searches is, in the final analysis, the difference between natural and revealed religion. 'The philosopher aspires towards a divine principle; the Christian, towards a divine agent.'[62] Of course, the insights of natural religion were true as far as they went. But that was not far enough. The inner being of God was utterly beyond the wisdom and insight of all natural religion, until, by an unspeakable mercy, in the final times, God spoke to us through his Son and in the Son's whole life as this was then illumined by the light of the Holy Spirit. Natural religion might discover an Unmoved Mover or the Ultimate Good, but this divinity had no face.

A Face at the Centre

Not so with revelation, 'for it is the God who said, "Let light shine out of darkness", who has shone in our hearts to give the light of the knowledge of the glory of God in the face of Christ' (2 Cor 4:6). At the very epicentre of revelation, then, is a 'face', the face of the co-eternal Son of the Father made flesh in order to be offered up for us and to be raised for our justification (Rom 4:25). Thus his great sermon, 'The Incarnate Son a Sufferer and Sacrifice'.[63] Newman drives home the point, 'Here, then, revelation meets us with simple and distinct facts and actions, not with painful inductions from existing phenomena, not with generalised laws or metaphysical conjectures, but with Jesus and the resurrection ... facts such as this are not simply evidence of the truth of the revelation, but the media of its impressiveness.' As a result, 'the life of Christ brings together and concentrates truths concerning the chief good and the laws of our being, which wander idle and forlorn over the surface of the moral world ... It collects the scattered rays of light.'[64] Newman's idea is splendidly put by Vladimir Soloviev, the man who has been called 'the Russian Newman'. Soloviev writes, 'Before Christianity ... divinity was something that was sought for (the ideal), and it worked on man in an "ideal" way, simply as the object of seeking. But in Christ what was sought was given to us, the ideal becomes fact ... the Word became flesh, and it is this new spiritualised and divinised flesh that remains the divine substance of the church.'[65] Now this communication of the divine is so bright that it dazzles and blinds our sight somewhat, whereas 'the so-called philosophical Christians' wish to 'be rid altogether of the shackles of a revelation'.[66]

From Notional to Real

We are now able to appreciate what Newman means by 'realising the invisible'. The Creator has intervened in his creation in an extra-

ordinary manner. That intervention created a drama of redemption
and made 'a history supernatural and almost scenic: it tells us what
its Author is, by telling us what he has done'.[67] God has chosen
with sublime freedom the way of incarnation and resurrection of
his eternal Son and the sending of the Holy Spirit, as his precise
form in the world. He has 'determined', if that is not an irreverent
thing to say, and circumscribed his revelation and has placed his
own tokens and signs upon it.

This incoming revelation finds its own form. It establishes its
own shape. In a word, the eternal God makes himself both concrete
and real. He 'realises' himself for us in the form and history of a
man, and so in a shape and condition most appropriate to the
human condition. Now this 'revelation-realisation' on the divine
side calls forth a 'faith-realisation' on our side. The intensity of this
realisation varies from person to person, a fact that is at once obvious, but is not often noticed. For Newman this fact was of central
importance and engaged his attention at frequent intervals. He
devotes many of his sermons to the subject, as well as some of his
best theological pages. As an example of the former, it is enough to
think of sermons like 'Unreal Words' and again 'The Difficulty of
Realising Sacred Privileges'.[68] As an example of the latter, one
could mention the *Grammar of Assent* where he elaborates the
famous distinction between the 'real' and the 'notional', and then
applies the distinction on the levels of both our perception of
revealed truths and our assent to them.

He wanted people to realise the 'Unseen World' made visible in
Christ, and in the whole economy of the church and her sacraments.
Thus he writes:

> It is not an easy thing to learn that new language which
> Christ has brought us. He has interpreted all things for us in
> a new way; he has brought us a religion which sheds a new
> light on all that happens. Try to learn this language. Do not
> get it by rote, or speak it as a thing of course. Try to under-
> stand what you say. Time is short, eternity is long; God is
> great, man is weak; he stands between heaven and hell;
> Christ is his saviour, Christ has suffered from him. The Holy
> Ghost sanctifies him, repentance purifies him, faith justifies,
> works save ... That a thing is true is no reason that it be said
> but 'that it should be made our own inwardly.'[69]

This theme of realisation will return for more formal treatment in
our third chapter on the appropriation of revelation.

VI. THE ORIGINALITY OF THIS THEOLOGY OF REVELATION

The originality of Newman's idea of revelation deserves noticing. His thinking seems to have anticipated many emphases in Vatican II and since. Unlike Vatican I, Vatican II did not begin by proving the existence of God or by showing the harmony of faith and reason. Rather, it set out 'to say and show today that God alone, more exactly the God of Jesus Christ, is the full and completely certain answer to the question that the human person is'.[70] This seems to be the key to its great constitutions on *Divine Revelation*, *The Church*, and *The Church in the Modern World*. Christ is the hope of humankind, because his revelation both fits with the human paradox and opens up vistas beyond it closed to human reason.[71] Here we have the carrying out into practice of that kind of 'proof' of Christianity which Newman will later draw out in the *Grammar of Assent*.

We should focus in a brief but particular way on the council's *Dogmatic Constitution on Divine Revelation*. According to this constitution, the core of revelation consists in the dramatic saving intervention of the divine Persons by which created and fallen persons have access to God. 'Through this revelation the invisible God (see Col 1:15; I Tim 1:17) out of the abundance of his love speaks to men as friends (see Ex 33:11; Jn 15:14-5) and lives among them (see Bar 3:38), so that he may invite and take them into fellowship with himself ... By this revelation then, the deepest truth about God and the salvation of man is made clear to us in Christ, who is the mediator and at the same time the fullness of all revelation.'[72] Here we have Newman's repeated assertion that 'Christianity is the presence of Persons'.[73]

The mediator of this wondrous revelation is Christ, while he is also its fullness. The *Dogmatic Constitution on Divine Revelation* presented its fascinating statement on revelation against an horizon which is clearly Christocentric. As the only Son who is nearest the Father's heart, Christ is able to reveal the Father. Thus God becomes his own exegete, as it were.[74]

Does Newman see revelation in these Christ-centred and trinitarian terms? The point of this opening chapter is to make this claim. Revelation puts before us, Newman insists, the 'marvellous and mysterious' fact that God has a Son, and that this Son assumed a servant's form. The incarnation of the Son, however, did not alter his essential relationship to his Father. Rather it brought that eternal relationship of Father and Son down to earth for us. 'He was the Son of God before his incarnation, and, by a second mystery, after it. From eternity he had been the Only-begotten in the bosom of the Father; and when he came on earth this essential relationship to the Father remained unaltered.'[75]

Here Newman anticipates by more than a century some of the better revelation theology of today. To take but one instance, Hans Urs von Balthasar describes revelation as the Trinitarian ecstatic love for humankind manifesting and communicating itself in history, so that the human family can live and move and have a new being in the divine milieu thus opened up to us.

> The object with which we are concerned is man's participation in God, which from God's perspective is actualised as 'revelation' (culminating in Christ's Godmanhood) and which from man's perspective is actualised as 'faith' (culminating in participation in Christ's Godmanhood). This double and reciprocal ekstasis – God's 'venturing forth' to man and man's to God – constitutes the very content of dogmatics.[76]

Interestingly, both thinkers achieve a fresh currency for the patristic idea of wondrous exchange, God becoming man so that men and women might become God.

Christ, then, does not come only to teach us the truths about God and about ourselves. Nor does he arrive like a divine Socrates to address 'the more universal and eternal questions, (such as) the secrets of the human heart and conscience, the confrontation between life and death, the triumph over spiritual sorrow, the laws of the history of mankind that were born in the depths of time immemorial and that will cease to exist only when the sun ceases to shine'.[77]

Of course, all these questions he answers with authority. As revealer, however, he is much more. 'He is the Word that speaks and the Word spoken about. He not only expounds, but is the truth.'[78] Henri de Lubac makes the point with customary incisiveness, 'Christianity is the only (religion) whose revelation is incarnate in a person who does not only pass on a doctrine but presents himself as the truth ... Mohammed, Buddha or Zoroaster ... preached a doctrine which is in some way external to the person ... Jesus is the master who proposes himself as the object of our faith.'[79] In Jesus, the eternal Son made flesh, the messenger and the message coalesce and converge. One and the same person mediates and is the ultimate self-manifestation of God or, in the language now current, the ultimate self-communication of God.[80] Thus Jesus Christ is both the absolute mediator of Trinitarian life, truth and communion to human flesh and human history, as well as this same life, truth and communion in person. Or in Newman's own words, 'To know Christ is to discern the Father of all, as manifested through his only-begotten Son incarnate,' and again, 'The love which he inspires lasts for it is the love of the unchangeable, it satisfies for he is inexhaustible. The nearer we draw to him, the more triumphantly does he enter into us, the more intimately have we possession of him. It is an espousal for eternity.'[81]

CHAPTER 2

'The Fathers Made Me a Catholic'

In his epoch-making volume, *Catholicism*, written in 1937, Henri de Lubac describes John Henry Newman as the 'heir to their (the fathers') way of thought'.[1] Sheridan Gilley of Durham claims in his centenary biography, *Newman and His Age*, that while 'the study of the fathers has always been a distinctive feature of Anglican theology, no Anglican had ever studied them with the intensity and passion of Newman'.[2] Gilley's judgement merely re-echoes the clear comments of Newman himself. Early in 1830 he wrote to a friend, 'I am hungry for Irenaeus and Cyprian – I long for the Long Vacation.'[3] Twenty years later and now a Catholic he commented that 'the vision of the fathers was always, to my imagination, I may say, a paradise of delight to the contemplation of which I directed my thoughts from time to time.'[4] Not only their writings, but also their very persons rise up before Newman as guides, models and prophets inspiring him along his own itinerary from the fringes of scepticism to the very fullness of truth in the Catholic church.

The 'much-enduring Athanasius' and the 'majestic Leo' were images continually before his eyes, 'whose musical words were ever in his ears and on his tongue'.[5] In 1865 in his *Letter to Pusey* on the Immaculate Conception he paid his greatest tribute to the fathers when he said, 'The fathers made me a Catholic'.[6] Erich Przywara is perhaps that person who first rescued Newman from an impending theological oblivion by translating into German in seven great tomes his principle works, in that way making them available to the world of German scholarship. His judgement of Newman was to call him 'Augustinus Redivivus'.[7] This chapter will suggest that the great German scholar, himself the master and teacher of no less a patristic giant than Hans Urs von Balthasar, was not indulging in praise for its own sake, but actually proffering his own personal estimation of the English cardinal.

The Purpose of this Chapter

The primary purpose, however, of this chapter is to study Newman's discovery of the fathers, his fondness for their theological style, and the reasons for this predilection. In their very persons he saw the face of early Christianity and recognised the first major expositors of revelation. Since it was they who first appropriated in scientific fashion the revelation given in Christ and witnessed to by scripture and the church's living tradition, they possess a perennial fruitfulness and enjoy a providential place of honour in the elaboration and transmission of revelation. Revelation indeed 'brings us into a new world – a world of overpowering interest, of the sublimest views, and the tenderest and purest feelings'.[8] But if we are going to seek and find a reliable map of that world, and sure guides to its riches, then we have to turn to the first great expositors of revelation. In this chapter then we will give an account of Newman's discovery of the fathers, his early difficulty in reading and appreciating them, an illustration of their presence and power in his theology of grace and justification, and, finally, how they opened up the issue of catholicity and the way to the church embodying this same catholicity.

I. JOHN HENRY NEWMAN'S DISCOVERY OF THE FATHERS

Newman's love for the fathers begins almost at the same time as his well known conversion at the age of fifteen while at school in Ealing. The school principal, Walter Mayers gave the adolescent boy John Milner's *Church History*. Here he read long extracts from St Augustine and St Ambrose which simply delighted him. 'I have never lost, I never have suffered a suspension of the impression, deep and most pleasurable, which his sketches of St Ambrose and St Augustine left on my mind.'[9] Fascinated and intrigued by the vision these two Latin fathers raised before his imagination, he 'read them as being the religion of the primitive Christians'.[10] The result was that 'the first centuries were his *beau idéal* of Christianity'.[11] Thus antiquity, as he called those centuries, intruded itself as 'the true exponent of the doctrines of Christianity and the basis of the Church of England'.[12]

His Early Writing Influenced by the Fathers

What he composed and wrote in the 1820s was composed and written under the influence of his newfound 'great theologians'. Henry Tristram lists what Newman actually did. He published an argument for strict Sunday observance derived from Chrysostom and the fathers in 1823; in 1826 a life of Apollonius of Tyana and the *Essay on Miracles*; in 1826 a plan to write a history of the first three centuries of Christianity for the *Encyclopaedia Metropolitana*; and in 1827 a defence of infant baptism from patristic testimonies. The more he reads the more he discovers 'that fresh vigorous power'[13] of the first centuries shown in the fathers. And in 1828 he began systematically to read them.[14] Already in 1827 his colleague, E.B. Pusey purchased several volumes of the fathers in Germany, 'I wish you could see them, they fit into my bookcases capitally ... huge fellows they are, but very cheap – *one* folio costs a shilling.'[15] In 1831 grateful pupils purchased further volumes, so that he now feels well and truly 'set up in the patristical line'.[16]

Still, as with most discoveries by John Henry Newman, this discovery of 'the paradise of delight' of the fathers was not without hiccup. Two difficulties, in fact, intruded themselves: 'the shadow of liberalism' and the Evangelical preconceptions with which he began. By liberalism here Newman means the theological variety, not the educational! Under the influence of this theological liberalism which consists in the view that religious doctrines are 'expressions merely of emotion, imagination, or will',[17] and which imperceptibly influenced him from 1825 onwards, Newman had been drifting towards preferring intellectual excellence to moral excellence. Two events shook him out of this danger: illness in 1827 due to overwork, and bereavement at the death of his youngest sister, Mary, a short while later. She was only nineteen years old. Thinking of her parting he wrote to his sister Jemima, 'What a veil and curtain this world of sense is! Beautiful, but still a veil!'[18]

The Return of the Early Interest

The difficulty of liberalism safely and gratefully overcome, Newman's early devotion to the fathers returned and in the Long Vacation of 1829 he 'set about reading them chronologically, beginning with St Ignatius and St Justin'.[19] But now the second difficulty intruded itself: he read them from a Protestant perspective. He explains what he meant in this passage: 'When years afterwards I first began to read their works with attention and on system, I busied myself much in analysing them, and in cataloguing their doctrines and principles', only to discover, on looking back over his work, that he 'had scarcely done anything at all', and he came to the conclusion that the fathers that he had been analysing, who 'were exclusively the ante-Nicene period, had very little in them'. His 'headings ran, "justification by faith only", "Sanctification", and the like'. Only later did he discover the reason for this result: 'I had read them simply on Protestant ideas, analysed and catalogued them on

Protestant principles of division, and hunted for Protestant doctrines and usages in them.'[20]

In a letter to a friend he wrote, 'I read Justin very careful(ly) in
1828 – and made most copious notes – but I conceive most of my
time was thrown away. I was like a sailor landed at Athens or grand
Cairo, who stares about – does not know what to admire, what to
examine – makes random remarks, and forgets all about it when he
has gone.'[21] This was a searingly painful realisation for him: 'it was
unprofitable to try and read the fathers "without an object", or
rather, "without a previous knowledge of controversies which are
built upon them".'[22] It was simply a case of not knowing what to
look for in them. However, this early unfruitful excursion had one
important effect, 'I rose from their perusal with a vivid perception
of the divine institution, the prerogatives, and the gifts of the episcopate; that is, with an implicit aversion to the Erastian principle',[23]
which makes the church subject to the state. The church could not
be in bondage to any temporal power, since she has her own divine
constitution and mission.

Researching the First Ecumenical Council
About 1830 a proposal was made to him to the effect that he should
compose a history of the principal councils. 'I accepted it', he writes
in the *Apologia*, 'and at once set to work on the Council of Nicaea. It
was to launch myself on an ocean with currents innumerable; and I
was drifted back first to the ante-Nicene history, and then to the
church of Alexandria.'[24] This historical orientation, coupled with an
aversion to theological liberalism, led him to a new and refreshing
refinding of the fathers. His response to this request grew into the
(for its time) monumental work, *The Arians of the Fourth Century*.
His encounter with history led him to the discovery of tradition,
and tradition to the discovery of a pre-Nicene church which was
dogmatic, sacramental and hierarchical, that is non-Protestant. 'The
wholehearted patristic study thus begun enabled Newman gradually to complete his recovery of the full Christian revelation. He had
already studied Holy Scripture, and knew much of it by heart: now
the other great treasure house was laid open to him.'[25]

II. THE DIFFICULTY OF READING THE FATHERS
The reading of the fathers, then, is not an easy enterprise assured of
success. In an article, 'The Theology of the Seven Epistles of St
Ignatius', written in 1838, he claims that 'with our modern notions
and modern ignorance' it is likely that the unprepared reader will

consider Justin an Arian or Cyprian a papist. The underlying problem is that many approaching the fathers rely heavily on
'antecedent reasoning' in the form of certain modern ideas. In that
way 'the ancient church', whose mouthpiece the fathers are, 'cannot
speak for herself'. The fathers are then called 'venerable', that is, out
of date and useless! To come to the fathers with preconceived, modern hermeneutical tools was like trying 'to criticise Gothic architecture by the proportions of Italian, or to attempt the mysterious
strains of Beethoven on the flute or guitar'.[26] Worse still, a very general theory about them is sometimes employed 'to measure the
nature and value of their contents'. For instance, it is common to say
that pagans, Jews and philosophers so far infiltrated the fathers as
to dilute their teaching.

How to Read the Fathers

How, then, should one read a particular father to advantage?
Newman's answer is full of that wisdom that is gained by struggle
and suffering, as when he realised that his early reading was 'time
thrown away'. He writes, 'We must, as a preliminary, do these two
things – divest ourselves of modern ideas and prejudices, and study
theology.'[27] To illustrate his point, he then lists key expressions in
the Seven Epistles such as 'perfect man' (*teleios anthrôpos*); 'flesh-
bearing' (*sarkophoros*); 'begotten and unbegotten' (*gennetos kai agen-
netos*); 'from Mary and from God' (*ek Marias kai ek Theou*). Now,
according as one knows the fathers' usage of these terms in general,
one will not impose one's own sense on them, and in the process
pervert rather than unpack Ignatius' sense. Thus in the *Letter to the
Smyrnians* St Ignatius writes, 'What availeth it me, if any one
praiseth me, but blasphemeth my Lord, not confessing that he bore
flesh (*sarkophoron*)' (Smyrnians, 5). Thus Newman translates the
word *sarkophoros*.[28] Newman comments on Ignatius' usage, 'This
word is of a dogmatic character on the face of the passage; and it is
notoriously such in after-controversy. It is also used by Clement of
Alexandria, Athanasius, and in the Confessions of the Emperors
Valentinian, Valens and Gratian. It was used both in the
Apollinarian and Nestorian controversies; by the Catholics against
Nestorius, who asserted that our Lord was not 'flesh-bearing God'
(*Theos sarkophoros*) but 'God-bearing man' (*anthrôpos theophoros*),
and by the Apollinarians as imputing to the Catholics what was the
Nestorian tenet.'[29]

Newman's approach to the Fathers reminds one of his attitude
to religious belief in general: 'if a man begins by summoning them

before him, instead of betaking himself to them, – by seeking to make them evidence for modern dogmas, instead of throwing his mind upon their text, and drawing from them their own doctrines, – he will to a certainty miss their sense.'[30]

A Special Sensitivity

Thus Newman wrote while still an Anglican (1839). He also discovered that one needed a special sensitivity to understand the world to which a father gave access and from which he lived. One may illustrate this from his original work called *Lectures on Justification*, written in 1838 and still esteemed in our times by theologians as different as Louis Bouyer and Hans Küng. Of course this subtle and profound investigation also illustrates his ability to go beyond clashing positions, in this case, the Protestant and popular Catholic theology of justification, and reach into what he calls that 'more elegant and fruitful teaching which is moulded after the image of erudite antiquity', that is, the fathers.[31] To this work we will now direct our attention since it is a splendid instance of his ability to enliven and transcend existing conflicts by means of skilful return to the fathers, the first systematic expositors of revelation.

III. AN ILLUSTRATION: THE FATHERS ON JUSTIFICATION

In the *Lectures on Justification*, composed in 1837-38, he strikes out 'to steer a "*Via Media*" (middle way) between Protestantism and Romanism, between the "erroneous" idea of justification by "faith only" and the "defective" theory of "justification by obedience".'[32] The combat between these two views had seen a major separation of Protestant and Catholic since the Reformation. The former, 'justification by faith', Newman adjudged to be 'beside the truth', the latter, 'justification by works', to fall 'short of the truth'. Of course, one ought to remember the stage of his personal journey which he is travelling at this point: the high spring of the *Via Media* when he was trying to bring out, in substantive form, an Anglican *Via Media* founded on distinct principles of its own and steering a middle course between the Scylla (as he then saw it) of the Reformers' errors and the Charybdis of Roman exaggerations through additions to the apostolic faith of antiquity. Always convinced of St Ambrose's dictum, '*Non in dialectica complacuit Deo salvum facere populum suum*', ('It has not pleased God to save his people by means of logic'),[33] Newman now shows that both the Lutheran and Catholic view, at least in this popular aspect, are both partially right. The truth is that both faith and good works are essential to our justification, and a balanced theology will include both. He defends his position in the clearest terms: the idea that 'we are absolutely saved by obedience, that is, by what we are, has introduced the proper merit of good works; that we are absolutely saved by faith, *or by what Christ is*, the notion that good works are not conditions of our salvation'.[34] The full truth Newman locates in the teaching of the fathers on the matter, in particular that of Athanasius, Augustine and Leo.[35]

The fathers show that we are not primarily justified by either faith or good works, but rather by the indwelling in us of the Holy Spirit, who is 'the characteristic gift of the New Testament'. And so he writes: '… for it (our justification and sanctification) is nothing short of the indwelling in us of God the Father and the Word incarnate through the Holy Ghost … *This* is to be justified, to receive the Divine Presence within us, and be made a temple of the Holy Ghost'.[36] And again, '… the cross must be brought home to us, not in word, but in power, and this is the work of the Spirit. This is justification; but when imparted to the soul, it draws blood, it heals, it purifies, it glorifies'.[37] This is the key, the source, the very heart of justification. Both the Reformers' idea of 'justification by faith only' and the popular school theology of Catholics must be corrected by it: the former by major reformulation so that faith is seen both to spring from the indwelling Spirit of the crucified and risen Christ, and issue in holiness and good works; the latter by way of completion: the indwelling Spirit is the source of that 'faith that works through charity' (Gal 5:6).

The Higher Viewpoint in the Fathers
Now what is of interest here is that Newman corrects both positions by an appeal in each case to the fathers. When dealing with the Lutheran axiom, 'justification by faith', he explains,

> … here perhaps we may see somewhat of the meaning and depth of the doctrine of justification by faith when rightly understood. If justification, or the imparting of righteousness, be a work of the Holy Ghost, a spiritual gift or presence in the heart, it is plain that faith, and faith alone, can discern it and prepare the mind for it, as the Spirit alone can give it. Faith is the correlative, the natural instrument of the things of the Spirit.[38]

The last sentence is a quotation from St Augustine to which explicit reference is made. Secondly, when filling in the lacunae in the

Catholic position he refers to St Athanasius.[39] Writing of our Lord's resurrection as the source of our righteousness Newman says, '(our Lord) was raised again and justified by the Spirit; and what was wrought in him is repeated in us who are his brethren, and the complement and ratification of his work ... The divine life which raised him, flowed over and availed unto our rising again from sin and condemnation. It wrought a change in his sacred manhood, which became spiritual, without his ceasing to be man, and was in a wonderful way imparted to us as a new-creating, transforming power in our hearts.'[40] He also calls on St Augustine in the same context to support his view.[41]

In that way, then, Newman deals with a major controversy which began with the Reformation, continued for generations, and has given a coloration to the Catholic and Protestant views of the redemption. Two comments can be made before leaving it. First, his solution is not a compromise between two diametrically opposing views, 'but rather a wholly new perspective which actually changes the nature of the problem ... Opposing positions are undercut by being circumvented'. In that respect the *Lectures* are a pioneering classic in genuine ecumenical theology, which is not simply eirenic for its own sake.[42]

A More Elegant and Fruitful Teaching

The second comment is the more important in this chapter on Newman and the fathers. As we saw, Newman grew in the conviction that patristic teaching was both more 'elegant' and more 'fruitful' than anything else around. What was the key to the fruitfulness of the fathers' teaching? He is explicit in his answer, 'All theological definitions come short of concrete life. Science is not devotion or literature. If the fathers are not cold, and the schoolmen are, this is because the former write in their own persons and the latter as logicians or disputants. St Athanasius or St Augustine has a life which a system of theology has not.'[43] Perhaps here if anywhere we find a real clue to Newman and his view of the fathers. The fathers write out of fullness, out of a life of faith, of living hope and of active charity. This faith-life Newman identifies as the key to their elegance and fruitfulness. And since they write in their own persons they tell us what they have seen and heard and touched, just as the apostles do (I Jn 1:1-4). Their words 'deal with things, not with words'.[44] They enable us 'to get through and beyond the letter into the spirit'.

The Fathers Reading the Scriptures

And so Newman is led on, as by a natural progression, to recognise their particular contribution to the reading of scripture. 'Here is the especial use of the fathers as expositors of scripture; they do what no examination of the particular context can do satisfactorily, acquaint us with the *things* scripture speaks of. They tell us not what words mean in their etymological, or philosophical, or classical, or scholastic sense, but what they do mean actually, what they do mean in the Christian Church and in theology.'[45] The main reason for Newman's admiration lay in the fact that their attention was not diverted from the object of faith by the demands, or interests, of a system. Thus when he comes to the writing of the *Essay on Development* seven years later in 1845 he sees in scripture an inexhaustible reservoir of light and truth. 'It (scripture) cannot, as it were, be mapped or its contents catalogued; but after all our diligence, to the end of our lives and the end of the church it must be an unexplored and unsubdued land, with heights and valleys, forests and streams on the right and left of our path and close about us, full of concealed wonders and choice treasures.'[46] The whole of the church's history will be needed to unpack these treasures. The patristic interpretation of scripture wins Newman's acceptance and guides his own reading of scripture. It sets him in a clearly Augustinian context, as has been recently and imaginatively shown.[47]

It would be a major misapprehension to think that Newman is here proposing a method of naming to account for the meanings which expressions bear. To remove even the slightest tinge of such an illusion, it is enough to read even a page of the *Lectures*. For example, he describes justification in these terms: 'Justification comes *through* the sacraments; is received *by* faith; *consists* in God's inward presence; and *lives* in obedience.' He seems to have actually reproduced the style and tone of the fathers who enchant him.[48]

IV. THE FATHERS, THE KEY TO NEWMAN'S DISCOVERY
OF THE CHURCH CATHOLIC

It should be remembered that, with the launch of the Oxford Movement upon Keble's Assize sermon in July 1833, a principle preoccupation of Newman and the other authors of *The Tracts for the Times* was the prevention of the liberalisation of the church. The Movement would be in fact 'a second reformation,'[49] he wrote, and the Tractarians set out to inculcate into the church the principles of Athanasius and Augustine, of Chrysostom and Gregory Nazianzen.

In this endeavour they were convinced, at least initially, that the great seventeenth century Anglican divines were both their guides and their justification.

The Church of Alexandria

While writing the *Arians* he 'drifted back first to the ante-Nicene church and then to the church of Alexandria'. Here he learned and imbibed the principles of Clement, of Origen, of Dionysius and of Athanasius.

> Some portions of their teaching, magnificent in themselves, came like music to my inward ear, as if the response to ideas, which, with little external to encourage them, I had cherished so long. These were based on the mystical or sacramental principle, and spoke of the various Economies or Dispensations of the Eternal. I understood these passages to mean that the exterior world, physical and historical, was but a manifestation to our senses of realities greater than itself. Nature was a parable ... In the fullness of time both Judaism and Paganism had come to nought; the outward framework, which concealed yet suggested the Living Truth, had never been intended to last, and it was dissolving under the beams of the Sun of Justice which shone behind it and through it ... Holy church in her sacraments and her hierarchical appointments, will remain, even to the end of the world, after all but a symbol of those heavenly facts which fill eternity. Her mysteries are but the expressions in human language of truths to which the human mind is unequal.[50]

Here Newman has discovered the sacramental principle in its broadest sense. Revelation for its part had this same sacramental structure. The external may contain the internal, the visible contain the invisible, the historical contain the eternal, the tangible and the human contain the intangible divine.

The Christianity of Antiquity

In a review of a reductionist history of the church, Milman's *History of the Church* in 1841, Newman wrote, 'All that is seen – the world, the bible, the church, the civil polity, man himself – are types, and, in their degree and place, representatives and organs of an unseen world, truer and higher than themselves. The only difference between them is, that some things bear their supernatural character upon their surface, are historically creations of the supernatural system, or are perceptibly instrumental, or obviously symbolical.'[51]

Here he was sure that he learned the most authentic and, at the same time, thrilling Christianity of antiquity. However, it was no mere unseen religion he had found. As he loved to stress, we do not contemplate Christianity in conclusions drawn from dumb documents, but as a living energising reality to be appropriated ever anew in each generation. This enables him to understand the church as the fathers understood it.

In his 'final view' of the church, set out in the *Preface to the Third Edition of the Via Media* of the Anglican Church, itself written when he was still convinced that 'the Church of England was substantially founded on the fathers and that the fathers could never lead on to Rome',[52] Newman sees the church as Christ continuing in history as prophet, priest and pastor of humankind. The church, then, was a prophecy, a priesthood and a polity, so that it represented, contained and communicated to humankind the truth, the life and the love of the blessed Trinity, all made visible in the sacrament of Christ. Thus Newman tells a congregation in St Mary the Virgin in the 1830s, 'Christ has shown us, that to come to him for life is a literally bodily action; not a mere figure, not a mere movement of the heart towards him, but an action of the visible limb; not a mere secret faith, but a coming to church, a passing on along the aisle to his holy table'.[53]

The Catholicity of the Fathers

Newman had discovered the catholicity and universalism of the fathers. In fact, G. Dragas is of the opinion that 'the catholicity of the fathers is extremely important for understanding Newman properly … It was in the fathers – existing and acting concretely in history as Catholic persons – that Newman met the real force of Catholic reality … They were imbued with the life-giving power of God who in Christ has taken up human weakness, redeemed it and perfected it … He found in the fathers the Christ of the apostles as the life-giving Spirit active in the history of mankind and leading it to conformity with his spiritual and perfect form'.[54]

Catholicity Means Fullness

Newman also saw of course the fathers' practical rule-of-thumb by which they guided people when travelling in any unknown area to look always for the Catholic Church. Newman saw that catholicity was not a question of geography, however, for the church was already catholic on Pentecost day. Catholicity rather consisted in the fullness of revelation, expressed in the mystery of faith and articulated into an apostolic doctrine, a holy worship, and a unified polity tracing direct descent from the apostles. He increasingly perceived in the fathers the reality of catholicity as 'the catholic truth of the risen Lord with all its implications for Christian life and growth in history'. All during the Oxford Movement he wanted this catholicity to influence his church more and more, and for a time he was more than confident of success in that enterprise. The Church Catholic of the fathers was the blueprint, the model and the inspiration for the enterprise undertaken in the Oxford Movement. This also explains the volume of thumbnail sketches of the fathers of the early church which he published in 1840 in order to provide a model and inspiration for the work of the Oxford Movement.

Roman Catholicism not Patristic

All during the 1830s he felt that Rome had betrayed the Catholic reality both by introducing new dogmas and being tolerant of devotions not found in antiquity. She had undermined any kind of seeming apostolicity by her deviation from apostolic truth. Undoubtedly, Rome enjoyed a certain 'geographical catholicity' and that in contrast to the Anglican church. But Rome undermined and compromised this very catholicity by introducing or countenancing new doctrines and practices not present in antiquity. These doctrines and practices consisted in the main in the teachings of the Council of Trent, in devotions surrounding Our Lady, and in the role of the papacy.

Two Great Blows

All this time he had been reading the fathers from Anglican perspectives. The Roman Catholic Church keeps the fathers 'around her to ask their advice when it happens to agree with their own'.[55] This very selectivity was further evidence of Rome's departure from the church of the fathers and its teachings, and so justification for Newman's opposition. However, he was to make two discoveries which came as great blows to him.

The Monophysite Controversy

During the Long Vacation of 1839 he launched himself into the fathers of the fifth century, especially those involved in the Monophysite controversy. He read the circumstances and transactions of the Council of Chalcedon (451 AD). His reading implanted a first doubt in his mind as 'to the tenableness of the fundamental principle of Anglicanism'.[56] Absorbed in the doctrinal question of monophysitism, he discovered Pope Leo I, as the theologian of the council. But also he saw, in the middle of the fifth century, that

Christendom had a centre, a focus of unity acting with authority to protect the church's authentic faith in Christ against the Mono-physites, and that centre was personified in Leo. He noticed as well that during the crisis and after the Council of Chalcedon only those churches remaining in communion with the see of Rome continued in the faith, while communities who rejected Chalcedon fell into equivocation and even heresy in spite of their protestations to the contrary and their frequent appeals to scripture and to the fathers themselves. We shall have to address this matter in greater detail in our next chapter on tradition.

The Existing or the Prior Church?

Already alarmed by what he was discovering, Newman made a further discovery only a month later. An article in the *Dublin Review* for August 1839 by Nicholas Wiseman dealt with the Donatists with 'an application to Anglicanism'.[57] One of the extracts in the article carried the words of St Augustine, '*Securus judicat orbis ter-rarum*': the whole church judges without any fear of error. These words kept ringing in his ears.[58] Here Newman saw a simpler, clearer rule than that of antiquity for the settling of disputes in the church. 'St Augustine,' he wrote in the *Apologia*, 'was one of the prime oracles of antiquity; here then antiquity was deciding against itself.'[59] As Avery Dulles has perceptively commented, 'The *existing* church, and not simply the prior church, was the oracle of truth.'[60] And so the fathers started to rise up against Newman's notion and design of a *Via Media*.

Although his cherished *Via Media* was now pulverised, he tried to carry on as usual, though his animosity towards, and suspicion of, Rome attenuated considerably. He continued with the new view of things gained from his patristic studies of 1839 two years later when he gave 'himself to the translation of the doctrinal treatises of St Athanasius'.[61] These treatises brought up again before him the whole question of the Arian controversy and Nicene Council, and he clearly saw in that history what he had not perceived on the first study of it at the time of writing the *Arians*, namely, the same phe-nomenon which had already startled him in the history of Leo and the Monophysites, and of St Augustine and the Donatists. The fathers were beginning to make him a Catholic, a Roman Catholic!

V. SOME CONCLUSIONS

Newman may be legitimately regarded as a great student of the fathers, and as 'an heir to their way of thought' (de Lubac). As a 'paradise of delight to him', they guided his way. They were the ladder of his ascent into 'Catholic fullness'. In that way they had made him a Catholic.

Second, it is arguable that the Oxford Movement, or at least Newman's presence in it, was guided by the fathers. Their principles were its guiding lights. According as Newman discovered them, he was fascinated by them. But as this fascination grew, his desire grew to infiltrate their principles into the Anglican Church of his day.

Third, 'the history of their times never became an old almanac to him'.[62] Thus as a Catholic he found their 'elegant' and 'more fruitful' teaching very helpful. In his defence of the dogma of the Immaculate Conception in his *Letter to Pusey* one finds a skilful employment of the fathers like Justin, Irenaeus and Tertullian in order to recommend to his former friend and colleague the truth of Pope Pius IX's definition.

Fourth, and more significantly perhaps, Newman interprets the fathers in terms of their most daring initiatives, convinced they were authors of original minds who produced exciting and original works.[63] He avoids both an antiquarian adulation of them which would fossilise them, and on the other hand, an anachronistic employment of them for later times. As we have seen, he showed in his study of the theology of St Ignatius that this latter attitude was doomed to failure. Instead, Newman noticed the abiding power of the fathers and their teaching to stimulate later and fresh thought. For example, an early original work as a Catholic, *On Consulting the Faithful in Matters of Doctrine*, develops a theology of the lay faithful which has clear links with the Athanasian idea of the 'eccesiastical sense'.[64]

Finally, Newman received not only inspiration from the ideas of the fathers, but also models for living and for his many projects. In Chrysostom he saw the ideal of the pastor, while in Athanasius and Nazianzen his theological ideals or prototypes stood out.[65] And if it is true, as Augustine argues in the fifth century and Bonaventure in the thirteenth, that we become like those whom we love most, then perhaps Newman reflects for our later times something of the attraction of these fathers, their pastoral quality and their theological excellence.[66] Our next chapter, in fact, will show their influence as he outlines the way by which revelation is to be appropriated.

CHAPTER 3

Discerning the Power of Revelation
in the Present

'Newman gives us colossal fragments, but he does not usually construct a finished edifice. He is like Homer from whom the Greek philosophers took their texts, as St Thomas culls the principles of his science from scripture.'[1] This was the judgement of his friend, Richard Simpson, in 1858 when Simpson was editor of the controversial Catholic review, *The Rambler*. History has shown that he has given the world 'colossal fragments' which have been an inspiration for the many in this generation who have fallen under the spell and influence of the man. Pope Paul VI has said that this is so much Newman's hour that he is a 'beacon for all who are seeking an informed orientation and sure guidance amid the uncertainties of the modern world'.[2]

In this chapter my objective is to deal with just one of these 'colossal fragments', his thinking on the way in which a sincere Christian makes Christian revelation his own, appropriating the unfathomable riches of Christ and living up to these new discoveries. In 1870 he lamented that

> some persons speak of Christianity as if it were a thing of history, with only indirect bearings upon modern times; I cannot allow that it is a mere historical religion. Certainly, it has its foundations in past and glorious memories, but its power is in the present. It is no dreary matter of antiquarianism; we do not contemplate it in conclusions drawn from dumb documents and dead events, but by faith exercised in ever-living objects, and by the appropriation and use of ever-recurring gifts.[3]

These words come out of the abundance of Newman's heart. All during his long life he tried to help believers to narrow the gap, as it were, between themselves and the living objects confronting them in the world of faith. We already referred to this central concern of Newman in the opening chapter on the nature of revelation. God wishes to be known and loved. It is precisely to this end that he has revealed his life and communicated his love to humankind. In this chapter, then, we will look at the way Newman attempted to help people realise what they believed, hoped in and loved. This pastoral and apostolic programme guided his work for souls, directed his reading and writing, and, as we hope to show, stimulated some of his most original insights.

The Problem of Creeds
Newman worried about those who recited the Creed without thinking about what they professed. 'The problem of Creeds with their increasingly scientised expressions, capable of glib repetition and even more glib mental assent, and the slow economy of living growth in understanding, plagued his thinking incessantly.'[4] In August 1835 he wrote to his aunt, Elizabeth, that 'the most religiously-minded men are ready to give up important doctrinal truths because they do not *understand their value* ... In my present line of reading, then, I am doing what I can to remedy this defect in myself, and (if so be) in some others. And it is a very joyful thought which comes to me with a great force of confidence to believe that, in doing so, I am one of the instruments which our gracious Lord is employing.'[5] The full appropriation of the content of faith is a subject of great pastoral and pedagogical importance, and, what is immediately important, is a subject that engaged Newman's brilliance at great and laborious lengths.[6]

The Dimensions of Christianity
First of all we need to look at the briefest summary of what Newman sees as the component dimensions of Christianity. His 'method of inquiry was to leap in *medias res*'.[7] We must follow him in our investigation of his method of appropriating the riches of revelation. His subject is Christianity. It is a subject at once personal, social, historical, complex and, above all, of transcendent beginning, dimensions each of which will engage us presently. Christianity is a personal reality, because it engages the whole person. It is not a mere theory in the mind, nor a moral rule for living, nor is it only a form of spirituality. No, it engages the whole of the person, spirit, will and heart, because 'true Christianity is the presence of Persons – to know Christ and through him the Father. Obedience, not a frame of mind, is the test.'[8] One could become a Christian only in terms of an unconditional surrender to Christ and by coming, through him, into a communion of life with the Father and the Holy Spirit. So much is Christianity a 'presence of Persons' that Newman

strongly contends that the 'doctrine of the Trinity is not proposed in scripture as a mystery,'[9] but rather as a saving reality, a divine plan on the part of the Triune God to draw men and women into the divine company of the Three. 'Frail man requires pardon and sanctification; can he do otherwise than devote himself to, and trust implicitly in, his Redeemer and his Sanctifier?'[10]

A Social Reality

Christianity is also a social reality in that it is a visible body of Christians living in the world. Christianity is a church, which

> is a collection of souls, brought together in one by God's secret grace, though that grace comes to them through visible instruments, and unites them to a visible hierarchy ... The kingdom of God spreads externally over the earth, because it has an internal hold upon us, because, in the words of the text, 'it is within us', in the hearts of its individual members. Bystanders marvel; strangers try to analyse what it is that does the work; they imagine all manner of human reasons and natural causes to account for it, because they cannot see, and do not feel, and will not believe, what is in truth a supernatural influence.[11]

An Historical Religion

Christianity, thirdly, is an historical religion. In writing the *Essay on Development* Newman categorically states that 'Christianity has been long enough in the world to justify us in dealing with it as a fact in the world's history. Its genius and character, its doctrines, precepts, and objects cannot be treated as matters of private opinion or deduction, unless we may reasonably so regard the Spartan institutions or the religion of Mahomet ... Christianity has long since passed beyond the letter of the documents and the reasonings of individual minds, and has become public property. Its "sound has gone out into all lands" and its "words unto the ends of the world" ... Its home is in the world; and to know what it is we must seek it in the world and hear the world's witness of it.'[12] Christianity, then, for Newman is an obvious fact on the stage of world history. It is even more, it is history, a living tradition of faith and morals and worship. In St Athanasius, his 'great theologian', Newman saw a man who took for granted a permanent, living stream of truth and life. Of him he writes:

> The fundamental idea with which he starts in the controversy

is a deep sense of the authority of tradition, which he considers to have a definite jurisdiction even in the interpretation of scripture ... According to him, opposition to the witness of the church, separation from its communion, private judgement overbearing the authorised catechetical teaching, the fact of a denomination, as men now speak, this is a self-condemnation.[13]

Anyone who wished to study Christianity would thus have to deal with realities which 'are not placed in a void, but in a crowded world'.[14]

A Complex Reality

Christianity is also a complex reality in the sense that its principles, doctrines, sacraments and history are deep and intricate. They weave together to form a unique whole, one living idea, and so they make up a body, a living organism.[15] In the *Preface to the Third Edition* of the *Via Media* written in 1877, some forty years after the first appearance of this work, Newman provides an outline of this complexity. One quotation may suffice: 'Christianity, then, is at once a philosophy, a political power, and a religious rite: as a religion, it is holy; as a philosophy, it is apostolic; as a political power, it is imperial, that is, One and Catholic. As a religion, its special centre of action is pastor and flock; as a philosophy, the schools; as a rule, the papacy and its curia.'[16] This does not mean that the Christian faith is vague and cloudy. But it does mean that Christian revelation, in scripture and tradition, brings before the mind of the serious inquirer distinct principles and doctrines, which combine deftly into the Christian system.

Revealed Reality

Finally, Christianity is a revealed religion. It comes from beyond history. It is in history, yes, but is not of history, like its Founder (Jn 17:13-5). 'Revealed religion,' Newman writes in 1829, 'brings us into a new world – a world of overpowering interest, of the sublimest views.'[17] In 1836 he wrote that 'the Catholic Church has ever taught, as in her Creeds, that there are facts revealed to us, not of this world, not of time but of eternity, and that absolutely and independently ... primary objects of our faith and essential in themselves.'[18] In 1835 Newman wrote one of the 'Tracts for the Times' against rationalism in revealed religion.[19] Near the end of his life, in 1879, he wrote that for fifty years he had resisted to the best of his powers the spirit of rationalism and liberalism in religion.[20]

Christianity, he claims in the Grammar, 'is a *revelatio revelata*; it is a definite message from God to man distinctly conveyed by his chosen instruments, and to be received as such a message; and therefore to be positively acknowledged, embraced, and maintained as true, on the ground of its being divine.'[21]

Journey into 'Catholic Fullness': Conversion

Those, then, are what we may call 'the dimensions' of Christianity. Newman only gradually became aware of them. Even more slowly did he make his own the fullness of Catholic truth.[22] We are now going to look at Newman's own personal discovery of these dimensions. The process of discovery was a great spiritual and ecclesiological journey, 'the most toilsome, but also the greatest, the most meaningful, the most conclusive, that human thought ever travelled during the last century, indeed one might say during the modern era'.[23] It was a journey that set out from a profound conversion. As an explorer sets out into the unknown drawn by adventure and eager for discovery, so Newman, guided by a spirit of obedience to the light and in fidelity to the voice of conscience, made his own the treasures of revelation. In 1845 he finished the *Essay on the Development of Christian Doctrine* with words that are perhaps more apt to describe the feelings of a modern mineral diviner discovering a rare ore than a Christian suddenly aware for the first time of the full treasures of the faith.

> (The Church) pauses in her course and almost suspends her functions; she rises again, and she is herself once more, all things are in their place and ready for action. Doctrine is where it was, and usage, and precedence and principle, and policy; there may be changes but they are consolidations or adaptations; all is unequivocal and determinate, with an identity which there is no disputing ... Such were the thoughts concerning the 'Blessed Vision of Peace' of one whose long-continued petition had been that the Most Merciful would not despise the work of his own hands ... And, now dear reader, time is short, eternity is long.[24]

Conversion Not Logic

It was a conversion, not a piece of research or logic only, which had led him to this 'Blessed Vision of Peace'. This, however, was his third conversion. The first had taken place at the age of 15 years,[25] the second at the age of 28 years. With each interior change his horizon broadened. His journey, in fact, took him from Evangelism to

Anglicanism, and from Anglicanism increasingly towards Roman Catholicism. At the age of 79 he wrote these remarkable words: '... there is a certain ethical character, one and the same, a system of first principles, sentiments and tastes, a mode of viewing the question and of arguing, which is formally and normally, naturally and divinely, the *organum investigandi* given us for gaining religious truth, and which would lead the mind by an infallible succession from the rejection of atheism to theism, and from theism to Christianity, and from Christianity to Evangelical Religion and from these to Catholicity. And again when a Catholic is seriously wanting in his system of thought, we cannot be surprised if he leaves the Catholic Church, and then in due time gives up religion altogether'.[26]

It was easy, then, for Newman to see that it was inner change and growth, an interiority, which opened the door for him into the riches of Christ. It was not history, theology, logic, nor any combination of these. True, all of these were useful, each one in its own way. And this helps us to understand the following idea of Newman: 'I had a great dislike of paper logic. For myself, it was not logic then that carried me on; as well might one say that the quicksilver in the barometer changes the weather. *It is the concrete being that reasons*; pass a number of years, and I find my mind in a new place; how? the whole man moves; paper logic is but the record of it.'[27]

But much earlier in 'The Tamworth Reading Room Articles', written in 1841 in response to the educational ideas of Sir Robert Peel and Lord Brougham, Newman stated that it was a perfect fallacy to hope to make people religious by information and reasoning or logic on their own. 'Logic makes but a sorry rhetoric with multitude; first shoot around corners, and you may not despair of converting by a syllogism ... Logicians are more set upon concluding rightly than on drawing right conclusions. They cannot see the end for the process.'[28] The way to the truth is a concrete, individual journey that passes through the heart of the individual believer. It is the way of interior, personal growth, at once more complex, more comprehensive and more personal than the reductionist approach of abstract reasoning.

Fr Bernard Lonergan, S.J., best states the originality of Newman's insight in this vital area of theology and catechetics: 'Basically the issue is a transition from the abstract logic of classicism to the concreteness of method. On the former view what is basic is proof. On the latter view what is basic is conversion. Proof appeals to an abstraction named right reason. Conversion transforms the con-

crete individual to make him capable of grasping not merely conclusions but principles as well.'[29] Newman was convinced that men
could grow in their appreciation of the faith but not by means of
knowledge on its own, nor by the impact of facts and information
and evidences alone. The heart had to be reached and corrected, the
intellect purified of its pride and obstinacy, and the will redirected
into pathways of virtuous living.

The appropriation of the depths of Christ in his church depended,
then, on a right moral, spiritual and intellectual state much more
than on 'the rude operation of syllogistic treatment.'[30] This explains
why in 1846, shortly after his becoming a Catholic, he wrote in connection with the *Development*:

> It is unreasonable in anyone to object that the grounds a per-
> son gives for his conversion cannot be expressed in a formula,
> but require some little time and consideration to master;
> which seems to be your correspondent's complaint of my
> volume (*Development*). If I could express them in a formula,
> they would not really be the more intelligible or comprehen-
> sible ... You must consent to think – and you must exercise
> such resignation to the Divine Hand which leads you as to
> follow it any whither ... Moral proofs are grown into, not
> learnt by heart.[31]

For Newman 'life is not long enough for a religion of inferences. We
shall never have done beginning, if we determine to begin with
proof. We shall ever be laying our foundations; we shall turn theology
into evidences, and divines into textuaries.'[32] It would be a mistake,
of course, to jump to the conclusion that Newman was careless
about evidence or little interested in the texts and authorities per-
taining to any particular point of faith or theology. It is enough to
peruse the principal theological compositions, such as the *Essay on
Development, Tracts Theological and Ecclesiastical*, the *Letter to Pusey*
and the *Letter to the Duke of Norfolk* to see the sheer variety of
authors consulted, texts assembled and arguments marshalled by
Newman.

The Basis of a Personal Christianity

Still, 'the basis of personal Christianity' cannot be scientific knowledge nor argumentative proof. These tools are hopelessly inadequate to cope with 'those giants, the passion and pride of man'.[33] In
the final analysis, a naïve understanding of the human person as
rational animal would produce an inadequate and naïve theological

method. 'After all, man is *not* a reasoning animal; he is a seeing, feeling, contemplating, acting animal. He is influenced by what is direct and precise.'[34] It is this insight which ultimately guided Newman in all his thinking and writing on the vital questions under consideration. And this insight he derived from within his own experience of an ongoing conversion. Ian Ker has shown how the providential course of Newman's journey took him through what Ker calls 'the main varieties of Christianity'. Ker's conclusion is that 'through his (Newman's) appropriation of the positive elements and through his criticism of the negative elements in the main varieties of Christianity, Newman offers not only a unique approach to the fullness of Christianity in Catholicism, but also an invaluable critique of the present state of the Catholic Church'.[35]

What, then, is the way to appropriate the riches of revelation? It is high time to see if Newman *actually* outlines a method of appropriation. The *Grammar of Assent* is a primary statement of that method. To it we now turn our attention.

The Grammar of Assent: the way of Appropriation

Etienne Gilson, who wrote the introduction for a 1955 edition of the work, has this to say. 'More than eighty years after its publication, the *Grammar of Assent* has preserved intact its power of suggestion, its actuality and its fecundity as a method of investigation whose potentialities are far from being exhausted.'[36] In claiming so much for the *Grammar* he is but reaffirming what Newman himself wrote in 1880, ten years after completing the volume: 'I will add that a main reason for my writing this *Essay on Assent*, to which I am adding these last words, was, as far as I could, to describe the *Organum Investigandi* which I thought the true one.'[37] While the actual origins of the *Grammar* are deep and subtle,[38] we may look to it as his magisterial treatment of the way in which the believer penetrates to the heart of his faith, appropriating its riches and then putting them to work in his life.

As Francis Bacchus has carefully noticed, the key to the *Grammar* is the difference between inference and assent,[39] 'inferential method' and 'illative method',[40] syllogistic method and cumulative method. Michael Novak has clearly shown that Newman always wrestled with the elusive difference between formal, logical ways of knowing, on the one hand, and living self-involving ones, on the other.[41] That wrestling runs the whole span of Newman's life. In the *Grammar*, however, he succeeded in doing what he never did before, namely, stating the actual process by which the

Christian realises,[42] or assents in a personal manner, to the objects of faith. *The Grammar* well merits the praise of being his masterpiece in the field of epistemology.[43] When he finished it he had the feeling that his life's work was largely done.

The Path to Knowledge

Perhaps the following passage more than any other summarises the contrast between 'the analytical method of verbal influence' and the real method: 'As to logic, its chain of conclusions hangs loose at both ends; both the point from which the proof should start, and the points at which it should arrive are beyond its reach; it comes short both of first principles and of concrete issues ... Thought is too keen and manifold, its source are too remote and hidden, its path too personal, delicate, and circuitous, its subject-matter too various and intricate, to admit of the trammels of any language, of whatever subtlety and of whatever compass.' Thus for Newman 'logic ... does not really prove ... for genuine proof in concrete matter we require an *organ* on more delicate, versatile, and elastic than verbal argumentation'.[44] Analysing carefully this quotation it is possible to find the following elements: first, the sources of thought; next, the subject-matter which will vary from subject to subject, science to science; thirdly, the path of reasoning, and finally, the point of arrival of the reasoning process. A brief word needs to be said on each aspect of the thought process.

The Sources of Thought

First, there are the sources of thought. Newman wisely points out that 'every thinker is his own centre' when it comes to thinking on practical or moral questions.[45] This means that a particular horizon is already in place in each inquirer, and with it a particular set of 'first principles', implicit but influential on one's way of thinking and acting. As each person has within himself 'a depth unfathomable, an infinite abyss of existence',[46] it is wrong to pretend that he is fully alive to the deepest derivation of his thought: in these first principles it largely escapes him. This will be particularly the case with Christianity.

Unique Subject-Matter

Next, the subject-matter of any area of inquiry always determines the nature of the method to be followed. In the area of theology and belief, the 'method of investigation' will have to be commensurate with Christianity, a subject at once personal, social, historical, complex and mysterious. At the beginning of this article we underlined the dimensions of Christianity in order to highlight fully the great and sacred issue engaging Newman. The way of appropriation of our faith must fit the nature of our faith.[47]

The Personal and Delicate Path to Knowledge

Thirdly, the path to certitude, and to the personal appropriation of the faith (which is our present concern and interest), is 'personal, delicate and circuitous'. This pathway is never travelled in isolation from the personality and character, spiritual, moral and intellectual, of the traveller.[48] First principles play a major part in a person's concrete thinking. 'As a man's portrait differs from a sketch of him, in having, not merely a continuous outline, but all its details filled in, and shades and colours laid and harmonised together, such is the multiform and intricate process of ratiocination, necessary for reaching him as a concrete fact, compared with the rude operation of syllogistic treatment.'[49]

Not Inference but the Illative Sense

Fourthly and finally, strict inference cannot, of itself, lead to certitude. As Newman time and time again repeats, the conclusions of an inference are conditional on the premises. Logicians, he says, are far more interested in concluding rightly than in right conclusions! A conclusion is held, not for itself, but in dependence on its antecedent. The way to certitude is the way of cumulation and convergence of probabilities under the direction of the illative sense.[50] The illative sense is the level of judgement in the mind's movement towards truth. It enables one to know what is so, and so reach the truth in the concrete real order. It is able to gather the many evidences, and assemble the various probabilities, and make both converge on the truth. It is 'a grand word for a common thing',[51] being the mind's power of judging in the concrete.

Making the Faith one's own

We are now in a position to show the full bearing of the foregoing comments on one's personal appropriation of the faith and its realities. The personal 'realisation' of what one believes is a slow journey, a testing pilgrimage but a rewarding arrival. It is in miniature somewhat like the journey of God's people in the bible and under the guiding hand of God who gradually manifested to them, in 'the fullness of time', his Son, who 'is the radiant light of God's glory and the perfect copy of his nature'.[52] Each person moves, delicately and circuitously, sometimes with speed, often more slowly, under the influence of motives and influences sometimes but vaguely felt, drawn and attracted by a growing vision of religious dogma and under its growing impact, until in the end, shadows become substances, notions become realities, and the heart of the Saviour speaks to the heart of the believer.

This process is thus carried on in the heart and mind of the believer, 'not *ex opere operato* (by the very activity itself), by a scientific necessity independent of ourselves, but by the action of our own minds, by our own individual perception of the truth in question, under a sense of duty to those conclusions, and with an intellectual conscientiousness'.[53] In this way, further, the mere notional grasp of the dogmas of the faith is transformed into a real, living grasp, and notional assent becomes a real assent. The Athanasian Creed becomes, in time, a 'hymn of praise, of confession, and of profound, self-prostrating homage, parallel to the canticles of the elect in the Apocalypse'.[54] The gap so easily separating the believer from the God manifested in Jesus Christ is narrowed, and like Newman, the believer catches a glimpse of the blessed Vision of Peace.[55] His attention is focused on the reality indicated by the dogma, so that the dogma makes a deep impression on him. The whole of the reality in the dogma is present, and not just an aspect or a part. The dogma imprints itself as a living portrait on his religious imagination. It becomes his.

Lutgart Govaert has provided an object lesson and clear illustration of such appropriation in Newman's own gradual understanding of the figure of Mary.[56] Many of the devotional manifestations in honour of Our Lady had been his great crux as regards Roman Catholicism. But through his conversions Newman came to see that 'the idea of the Blessed Virgin was as it were *magnified* in the Church of Rome, as time went on – but so were all the Christian ideas; as that of the Blessed Eucharist'.[57]

Appropriation in the great Trilogy of Development, Apologia and Grammar
As already pointed out, the key to all of Newman's originality lies in his own interior experience of conversion, development and the concomitant appropriation on his part of the dogmas of the Catholic faith. This experience puts him in a privileged position of insight with regard to the subject we are now considering. In his *Essay on the Development of Christian Doctrine* we find his doctrinal appropriation of Catholic dogma, that dogma that he described as 'one, absolute, integral, indissoluble, while the world lasts'.[58]

Nineteen years later the assault of Charles Kingsley necessitated a more personal statement of 'his meaning': the *Apologia* stands as his *personal* appropriation of his authenticity in Christ. Finally, in the *Grammar* he provides a *philosophical* treatment of the precise form of insight and assent that is involved in the religious faith of the believer. This work, then, is the philosophical appropriation of Catholic authenticity in Christ.[59]

Concluding Remarks

Certain aspects of Newman's thinking stand out in sharp relief, so stark as to amount to what one might call 'Newman peculiarities'. We can now look at some of these idiosyncrasies and, in the light of what has been already said in the course of this chapter, attempt an explanation.

Firstly, Newman did not consider himself a theologian. He was thinking, however, of the type of theologian generally in vogue in his day.

> A theologian is one who has mastered theology – who can say how many opinions there are on every point, what authors have taken which, and which is the best – who can discriminate exactly between proposition and proposition, argument and argument, who can pronounce which are safe, which allowable, which dangerous – who can trace the history of doctrines in successive centuries, and apply the principles of former times to the conditions of the present.[60]

His own description disqualifies him as a theologian, perhaps because he was interested primarily in helping people to make their faith a conscious and personal possession. All his works were written with this pastoral end in view. It is no paradox that, in the very letter just quoted, he proceeds to name St Gregory Nazianzen as his model, a man who, alone with the evangelist John, enjoys the radiant title of *Theologus* in the Eastern Church! 'Like St Gregory Nazianzen I like going my own way.'[61]

Next, Newman's apologetic for the faith lays down two preconditions, one of preference, the other of exclusion. 'I am suspicious then of scientific demonstrations in a question of concrete fact, in a discussion between fallible men. However, let those demonstrate who have the gift, *'unusquisque in suo sensu abundet'* (Let each one excel in his own area) ... I prefer to rely on the argument of an accumulation of various possibilities.'[62] He knew the power in the combination of cumulative probabilities and the illative sense from his own personal itinerary. But he was also aware that no argument, however powerful, can overcome 'those giants, the pride and passion of man'. Accordingly, he demands conversion from a large section of people before they can fruitfully enter 'upon what are called the evidences of Christianity'. He both describes the deep-seated attitudes, and lists the hidden principles, which simply render some people incapable of hearing the evidences. He demands from such people a conversion of heart, or at least that 'class of sentiments, intellectual and moral, which constitute the formal preparation' for the true assessment of the evidences for Christianity.[63]

Finally, there is his striking statement in the *Apologia*: 'I came to the conclusion that there was no medium, in true philosophy, between atheism and catholicity, and that a perfectly consistent mind, under those circumstances in which it finds itself here below, must embrace either the one or the other.'[64] This passing statement was quickly and easily misunderstood as an abandonment, in principle and in practice, on Newman's part of 'any thought of bringing arguments from reason to bear upon the question of the truth of the Catholic faith'. Some saw in his statement a reduction of his defence of the Catholic Creed to the proposition that 'it is the only possible alternative to atheism'. In 1880 Newman wrote a vigorous and enlightening explanation of his statement as a note appended to a new edition of the *Grammar*.[65] It is perhaps one of the most significant pieces he ever wrote. He explained his point in the light of his own gradual growth into the fullness of Catholic truth. The statement was verified, in Newman's experience, in the case of each person who discovered Catholic faith after long and painful searching. Newman's was a practical principle derived from his deep insight into the progressive, or what he often called the accumulative, force of the reasons and evidences for Christianity. He saw that people either grew towards deep Christian faith, or else gradually fell back into agnosticism. Perhaps it is not too much to contend that our times have seen the verification of Newman's prophetic insight?

Part Two: Shoots

'... nor is religion ever in greater danger than when in consequence of national or international troubles the Schools of Theology have been broken up and ceased to be ... Theology is the fundamental and regulating principle of the whole church system.'
(Via Media, *I, xlvii*)

CHAPTER 4

The Vigour and Vitality of Sacred Tradition

Where is the Faith?
People who want to know 'the faith' and who wish to deepen their understanding and grasp of it in our times frequently come face to face with two approaches or methods. These approaches are at one in that they both set out to indicate the whereabouts of 'the faith' and the way thereto. However, they diverge, and may even conflict, in that they seem to be based upon opposing understandings of 'the faith'. According to the first method, 'the faith' is a definite deposit which is articulated in creed, sacrament and commandment. To know it one has only to familiarise oneself with its credal formulae, its order of worship in the liturgy, and its code of behaviour in commandment and precept of the church. In creed, cult and code one learns at once the essential content of 'the faith' as well as its abiding outline. In this perspective, the fact of revelation is of the first importance, since revelation provides the substance of the creed, the life given for the world (Jn 6:50) in liturgy, and the guarantee and model of 'the way' of life that is pleasing to the Father of our Lord Jesus Christ.

The second approach, now in the ascendancy in many quarters, does not see 'the faith' as a definite deposit. Rather it is an unknown to be discovered. This discovery can be made from scripture or with the assistance of religious experience and the help of the more prestigious theologians in the church. In this perspective 'the faith' is not a given. It is an unknown to be sought. Revelation, though central to the content of 'the faith', is not a definite given so much as an incipient inspiration or vision that still requires a patient search for a central content.

Not for the First Time
Newman was well aware of the issue. In 1836 he gave this version of it: 'We exult in what we think our indefeasible right and glorious privilege to choose and settle our religion for ourselves; and we stigmatise it as a bondage to be obliged to accept what the wise, the

good, and the many of former times have made over to us, nay, even to submit to what God himself has revealed.' Newman does not conceal his anxiety at the prospects it opens up, 'this strange preference ... of enquiry to belief'. When in 1870 he published the *Grammar of Assent* he was equally forceful: 'We cannot without absurdity call ourselves at once believers and inquirers also.'[1] Clearly, 'inquiry' here cannot have the meaning of that investigation of 'the faith' which Newman not only lauds, but also names as both the evidence of a living faith and as poignantly illustrated in the case of the Blessed Virgin who 'does not think it enough to accept, but dwells upon it; not enough to possess, she uses it; not enough to assent, she develops it; ... from love and reverence, reasoning after believing'.[2]

The Deposit of Faith

In Newman's vision of faith,[3] there is a not surprising emphasis on the concept of 'the deposit of faith'. The first 'impressions of dogma' of the 1816 conversion were to prove lasting. The remainder of his life was to draw on this deposit. When in 1836 he wrote his first major piece on apostolical tradition he expressed himself on tradition in these striking terms. '"Those things which thou hast heard from me through many witnesses," says St Paul to Timothy, "commit these same to faithful men, who shall be able to teach others also." This body of truth was in consequence called the *depositum* as being substantive teaching, not a mere accidental deduction from scripture. Thus St Paul says to his disciple and successor Timothy, "Keep the deposit, hold fast the form of sound words, guard the noble deposit" ... What is the deposit? That which has been entrusted to you, not which thou hast discovered; what thou hast received, not what thou hast thought out; not a matter of cleverness, but of teaching; not of private handling, but of public tradition.'[4]

In Newman's day the attribution of Pauline authorship to the fourteen letters, including the Letter to the Hebrews, was unquestioned. Scholars today, for reasons which it is not necessary to mention here, generally prefer to speak of three categories of letter, those which are definitely Pauline, those which are doubtfully Pauline, and those which are pseudonymous. This subdivision of the letters, however, has but little bearing upon the point which Newman is here making, namely, that the reality of 'the deposit of faith' was vital to the early apostolic church.[5]

In the School of Calvin

Now all this was in 1836, precisely twenty years after Newman's first conversion. It must be remembered that such a clear and lucid exposition of the ideal sacred tradition did not emerge for him immediately upon his conversion. On the contrary, he was certain that the dogmatic truths vividly and indelibly impressed upon his mind on that occasion were adequately testified to in scripture. They stood on or near its surface, and one could pick them from it as easily as apples from a tree. As is well known, the books read by Newman at that stage of his life were 'all of the school of Calvin'.[6] They were put into his hands by Walter Mayers, his school principal. The effect of this was to turn him to the scriptures from which he made a collection of texts in proof of the doctrine of the Trinity and 'in support of each verse of the Athanasian creed'.[7] Here he found a particular manifestation of the Reformer's doctrine of 'scripture only'.

With the Help of Friends

As with many of the discoveries made by Newman in the course of his remarkable itinerary of mind and heart, it was often the province of encounter with different people which paved the way of discovery. This was especially so in the case of his unexpected discovery of tradition. Edward Hawkins (1789-1882), Provost of Newman's college of Oriel (1828-1874) and his immediate predecessor as the vicar of St Mary the Virgin, was 'the means of great additions to my belief'. He loaned Newman Sumner's *Treatise on Apostolical Preaching* and helped Newman realise the impending attack on the scriptures of the New Testament. This fact must have made Newman have first doubts about the tenableness of the Reformers' principle of 'scripture only'. But it was Hawkins' sermon on tradition, published in 1819 and which Newman heard Hawkins preach, that made the deepest impression of all on him. 'Impression' is a semi-technical term for Newman who adopted it from David Hume. In Newman's usage it means that which enters the intellect vividly and so with impact. Hawkins' sermon on tradition made this impact on Newman's mind, and 'opened upon Newman a large field of thought'.

The Anglican Doctrine of Tradition

Hawkins set out to present the High Anglican doctrine on the subject. His thesis was that 'the sacred text (of scripture) was never intended to teach doctrine, but only to prove it, and that, if we would learn doctrine, we must have recourse to the formularies of the church; for instance to the catechism, and to the creeds'.[8] This principle removed the foundation principle of the Bible Society and led the young Newman to discontinue his subscription. His fresh insight into the place and operation of tradition in the transmission of 'the faith' was to affect radically Newman's spiritual and theological journey. One can see this in the case of *Tract 85* on 'Holy Scripture in its relation to the Catholic Creed', itself one of the finest theological compositions of the author.[9] One may also see it in *The Prophetical Office of the Church*, which is an attempt to avoid the extremism of both the Protestants and the Romans as he then perceived them.

Turning Towards the Arena of History

The discovery of the idea of tradition at the tender age of eighteen must be the factor responsible for his turning towards the early centuries and even towards the medieval church as seen through the eyes of Hurrell Froude. Having begun to read the fathers a second time in 1828, as we saw, after 'the shadow of liberalism' began to lift from him under the double blow of illness and bereavement, he began research on the Council of Nicaea for a projected history of the principal councils. Reading widely in this field, he was convinced that 'antiquity was the true exponent of the doctrines of Christianity and the basis of the Church of England'.[10] Writing many years later in 1881 he could declare, 'I yield to no-one still in special devotion to those centuries of the Catholic Church which the holy fathers represent.'[11]

The Arians of the Fourth Century

Eventually *The Arians of the Fourth Century* appeared. Only a small section of some twenty pages dealt with the actual council. The greater part of the work focuses on the history and theology of the times. Newman immersed himself in the school of Alexandria where he encountered Dionysius and Clement, Origen and Athanasius 'and others who were the glory of it, its see, or its school'.[12] As we have seen in the chapter on the fathers, these early luminaries of the church impressed him greatly, even more by their philosophical, than by their theological, doctrine. They gave him a context and a critique with which to understand the causes and the course of Arianism. Since Newman's time the phenomenon of Arianism has been the object of further investigation.[13] Still Newman's study of the heresy, in the context of the school of

Alexandria, the Council of Nicaea and the struggle of Athanasius, was of major importance for his discovery of the church and, in particular, of tradition. The *Arians* volume was itself, he felt, 'inexact in thought and incorrect in language', but 'with all its defects', it had 'good points in it, and in parts some originality'.[14]

More than ever he was convinced that to be deep in this early and formative phase of the church's history was to discover the genuine face of the faith. 'The primitive church in spite of the corruptions which disfigured it from the first, still in its collective holiness may be considered to make as near an approach to the pattern of Christ as fallen men ever will attain.'[15] This was in 1832.

A Collective Holiness

The notion of 'collective holiness' is significant. It highlights the fact that Christianity is a way of life, indeed a way of holiness, not only for the individual, but for the community of believers. It is as an idea harmonious with, and illustrative of, the fact that the first believers in the post-Pentecost church were called 'followers of the way'.[16] And these first Christians were 'one mind and one heart' (Acts 4:32). Newman's plunging into the history of the ante-Nicene church was the happy discovery that the adventure of holiness was alive and well in the church of the fourth century. This discovery confirmed his confidence in the dignity, indeed the pre-eminence, of the witness of the Nicene church. This portion of ecclesiastical history was to yield up major and further insights destined to fill out his understanding of tradition. It is time to make an inventory of these elements.

I. DISCOVERY OF THE LAY FAITHFUL

What amazed Newman in the fourth century was the fact that the teaching of Nicaea on the absolute divinity of Christ was sustained after the council not primarily by the bishops, but by the great mass of lay faithful. The battle of Arianism was conducted in Alexandria between the Arians and Athanasius. Apart from the two Gregories, Basil of Caesarea, Hilary of Poitiers and a few other bishops, the time after the great council was one of devastating confusion with one local synod after another either reneging on, or reversing, the defined teaching of the *homoousion* ('of one substance with the Father'). St Jerome could write after the Council of Rimini in 359, 'The whole world groaned in astonishment to find itself Arian.'[17]

If the greatest crisis the church ever had to cope with was Arianism, the true champions of the revealed truth were the lay faithful.[18] This discovery of the role of the laity in the transmission and protection of the truth about Christ at the time of the Arian storm imprinted itself deeply on Newman's imagination. Among other things, it taught him that personal influence is the means *par excellence* of propagating the truth in the world. In the University Sermon bearing this title and delivered in 1832, he stated his thesis vigorously: 'It (the truth) has been upheld in the world not as a system, not by books, not by argument, not by temporal power, but by the personal influence of such men as ... are at once the teachers and patterns of it.'[19]

In his controversial article *On Consulting the Faithful in Matters of Doctrine* written in 1859 he described this 'intimate understanding', this 'contemplation and study', as the *consensus fidelium*.[20] He saw Pope Pius IX consulting the laity in relation to their perception of Our Lady's immaculate beginning in 1848 before the Pope solemnly defined the doctrine six years later. In 'consulting', the Pope showed 'trust' and 'deference' to the faith of the laity, but not 'submission'. The Holy See treats them 'with attention and consideration'. The reason for this attention is that 'the body of the faithful is one of the witnesses to the fact of the tradition of revealed doctrine'.[21]

The subsequent misunderstanding of Newman's position, as well as the furore let loose by his opponents, are now a matter of history. Newman is 'the most dangerous Catholic in England'! He explained himself by copious reference to the Roman theologians, Perrone and Passaglia. In the third edition of the *Arians* in 1873 he republished the article as Appendix V with the fresh title, 'The Orthodoxy of the Body of the Faithful during the Supremacy of Arianism.'[22] It effectively cleared up the basic misunderstandings.

II. THE DISCOVERY OF THE APOSTOLIC ORIGIN OF THE EPISCOPATE

In his study of the church at the times preceding and following Nicaea, Newman saw a church that was not only governed by bishops, but bishops who claimed apostolical descent. In the very year in which the *Arians* was presented, the Oxford Movement began with Keble's sermon on 'National Apostasy'. The context of the sermon was the Bill to suppress some Anglican bishoprics in Ireland. Newman saw in the initiative the direct interference of the state in the internal life of the church and the denial of the church's independent identity and sovereignty. For the rest of his life he was going to resist this tendency to subject the church to the state, what he called Erastianism.

This movement began as a spontaneous response to 'the peril

into which the church has come'. Its protagonists wrote pamphlets or tracts on key areas of the church's faith, doctrine, worship and order. Newman wrote the first. Its theme was the apostolic character of the episcopate.

Newman feared the forgetting of 'the real grounds on which our authority is built – our apostolical descent'. It is the apostolic succession of the episcopate that constitutes 'the claim of the church upon the attention of men'. The implications of this truth are paramount. 'We have been born, not of blood, nor of the will of the flesh, nor of the will of man, but of God. The Lord Jesus Christ gave his Spirit to his apostles; they in turn laid their hands on those who would succeed them; and these again on others; and so the sacred gift had been handed down to our present bishops, who have appointed us as their assistants, and in some sense representatives.'[23] The remainder of this short exposition tries to bring home to readers the fact, the reality and the pastoral imperatives that flow from the truth of 'the doctrine of apostolical succession'. In a passage of high rhetoric he concludes, 'Exalt our holy fathers, the bishops, as the representatives of the apostles, and the angels of the churches; and magnify your office as being ordained by them to take part in their ministry.'[24]

III. THE DISCOVERY OF THE CENTRAL PRINCIPLES OF ANCIENT CHRISTIANITY

Newman's study of the fathers was a veritable 'paradise of delight' for him. This we have seen in the second chapter. The fathers manifested to him the face of primitive Christianity. This face so attracted him that he set about a 'second reformation'[25] of the church in the light of these same principles. This was the guiding orientation of the Oxford Movement: could the principles of Ambrose and Augustine, of Athanasius and Gregory Nazianzen be actualised and given fresh currency, in the church of the nineteenth century? Newman was supremely confident that they could. To this end he wrote *The Church of the Fathers*.[26] Three principles in particular stood out for him in the life of this church. They were the dogmatic, sacramental and hierarchical principles. They deserve a brief treatment, especially since they are central to our theme of tradition.

Firstly, there is the *dogmatic* principle. The conversion of 1816 impressed the great dogmas of God, Christ, the Holy Spirit, the heinousness of sin, the redemption, the reality of eternal life on the young Newman. Christianity consists in a definite message communicated to humanity. Consequently, 'dogma has been the funda-

mental principle of my religion'.[27] If the religion of the great doctors of the primitive church was dogmatic, so must the religion of
the Anglican Church be.

Secondly, there was the principle of the *sacraments*. Since
Christianity is not only the divine truth, but also the divine life
given in revelation, this life must be available to humankind. 'Our
Lord, by becoming a man, has found a way whereby to sanctify
that nature, of which his own manhood is the pattern specimen. He
inhabits us personally, and this inhabitation is effected by the channel of the sacraments.'[28] As 'the means and the pledges of grace, the
keys which open the treasure house of mercy', the sacraments are
the assurance of his personal love, his presence and 'the pledge that
he will change our hearts'.[29] He was never to change his opinion in
this respect. The church becomes visible in her sacramental worship
of God and in the sanctification of her members. He believed this
position to be the teaching of scripture, the faith of the primitive
church, the theology of the Caroline Divines Laud, Stillingfleet and
Bramhall and the teaching of the Anglican Prayer Book.

Thirdly, there was the *episcopal* principle, which we have just
seen. 'What to me was pure *divino* was the voice of my bishop in his
own person. My own bishop was my Pope; I knew no other, the
successor of the apostles, the Vicar of Christ.'[30]

Apostolic Tradition

By the year 1836 Newman's views on the handing on of divine revelation had attained a clarity that inspired him to write a lengthy
tract on the subject of apostolic tradition.[31] This composition represents a watershed in his unfolding views. He rejects the idea of the
liberal dogmatic theologian, Dr Hampden, claiming that 'tradition
is *nothing more* than expositions of scripture, *reasoned* out by the
church, and embodied in a code of doctrine'.[32] His irony is palpable
as he comments on this contention. 'We had fancied that St Paul
"*delivered*" to his converts "that which he had also received"; we
had fancied that St Irenaeus enumerated the succession of bishops,
through whom the tradition of gospel doctrine had come down to
his day, and that Tertullian testified to a like tradition, and that
Vincent of Lérins had even gained a name in theological history by
appealing to the testimony, not of scripture, but of antiquity and
catholicity, as the warrant for the creed of his day, but it seems, after
all, that the celebrated "*Quod semper, quod ubique, quod ab omnibus*",
means nothing more than "The bible, and the bible only, is the religion of Protestants".' And then he proceeds to state unequivocally

his own view. 'Had scripture never been written, tradition would have existed still; it has an intrinsic substantive authority, and a use collateral to scripture.' And if the truth be told, the millions 'realise the world unseen' by 'creeds and catechisms, liturgies and a theological system'.[33]

Tradition at Nicaea

To illustrate the point Newman now employs the phenomenon of the First Ecumenical Council. That council banishes the idea that the Son was not God. He is not made, but he is 'begotten from the Father'. Most important of all, he is of 'one substance' (*homoousios*) with the Father.

Now the word *homoousios* is not found in scripture, but 'it has the sanction of various fathers in foregoing centuries'. Newman noticed that Athanasius reminded his contemporaries that the word had been used 'by ancient bishops, about 130 years since', and that, while the word had been proposed at the Council of Antioch which in 268 AD deposed Paul of Samosata, bishop of that city, for his denial of the Son's divinity, the fathers eventually decided to withdraw it 'as if capable of an objectionable sense'.[34] However, with the passing of time the fathers of Nicaea were able to adopt the term in order to express the numerical identity of the substance of Father and Son.

This adoption was not particularly surprising in view of the fact that 'a body of doctrine had been delivered by the apostles to their first successors, and by them in turn to the next generation, and then to the next ... "The things that thou hast heard from me through many witnesses", says St Paul to Timothy, "the same commit thou to faithful men, who shall be able to teach others also" (2 Tim 2:2)'.[35] 'Scripture alone' was 'a principle that allowed revelation to be measured by the recipient and not by the revealer'.[36] This was its most radical defect. The result is, further, that 'though all sects agree together as to the standard of faith, viz. the Bible, yet no two agree as to the interpreter of the Bible'.[37]

Anglican Tradition versus Roman Authority

The Church of England, then, proceeds via scripture and tradition. As such she keeps away from the religion of Protestantism. But what of the Church of Rome? Rome bases herself on the threefold of scripture, tradition and magisterium. To take a later formulation of the Catholic view, a formulation representing a major advance over those of the nineteenth century, it may be appropriate to turn to the

Dogmatic Constitution on Divine Revelation of the Second Vatican Council. It states, 'Sacred tradition, sacred scripture, and the teaching authority of the church, in accord with God's most wise design, are so linked and joined together that one cannot stand without the others, and that altogether and each in its own way under the action of one Holy Spirit contribute effectively to the salvation of souls.'[38] It would seem that Newman's notion of tradition, which comprises the fact of the apostolic succession, means that he must now look with kinder eyes towards Rome.

At least this is what some observers of the scene in the mid 1830s felt. It made him feel self-conscious.[39] 'All the world was astounded at what Froude and I were saying,' he wrote, 'men said that it was sheer Popery.'[40] However, he was emotionally set against Rome from tenderest years. 'My feeling was something like that of a man who is obliged in a court of justice to bear witness against a friend.' The truth was that he 'felt it to be a duty to protest against the Church of Rome'.[41]

Between Reformers and Romanists

But how? Apart from the underlining of her offences, consisting as they did 'in the honours which she paid to the Blessed Virgin and the saints',[42] he would have to develop the *Via Media*. 'The glory of the English Church is that it has taken the *Via Media*, as it has been called. It lives *between* the (so-called) Reformers and Romanists.'[43] He was aware, though, of the difficulty of his project. 'I considered that to make the *Via Media* concrete and substantive, it must be much more than it was in outline; that the Anglican Church must have a ceremonial, a ritual and a fullness of doctrine and devotion, which it had not at present, if it were to compete with the Roman Church with any prospect of success.'[44]

Enter the Theology of Tradition!

Central to his strategy was the need for a theology of tradition! 'Rome can be answered with an adequate theory of tradition.'[45] The result is that he has to attempt 'to work out a theory of tradition which will keep him from Rome'.[46] The outcome was the outstanding volume, *Lectures on the Prophetical Office of the Church, Viewed Relatively to Romanism and Popular Protestantism*. 'It was to be his principal contribution to a distinctively Anglican divinity, as it sought to define the peculiar theological position of the Church of England and to provide a justification for her existence as a separate Christian communion beside the churches of the Reformation and

Rome.'[47] As a composition, it was to cost him 'an immense deal of trouble'.[48]

This work at this vital point in the Oxford Movement, and in Newman's personal journey, represents a fresh height in his gradual appropriation of the meaning of sacred tradition. His research would be an organising and unifying inventory drawn from a vast inheritance in scripture, the fathers, the early councils, tradition and the Caroline Divines who constituted the golden age of Anglican theology. What is the nearest approximation to that primitive truth which Ignatius and Polycarp enjoyed and which the nineteenth century has virtually lost?[49] *The Prophetical Office* is the answer.

Two Types of Tradition

Newman distinguishes two forms of tradition, episcopal and prophetical. As the name suggests, episcopal tradition is that which comes from the apostles along the line of the apostolic succession of bishops and which is destined to continue through history until the glorious return of the Lord of history. Anglo-Catholics do not in fact object to tradition in either mould. They only protest that Rome 'substitutes the authority of the church for that of antiquity'. As for the fathers, she keeps them 'around her neck to ask their advice when it happens to agree with her own'. Genuine and reliable tradition is attested to by 'Catholicity, antiquity and the consent of the fathers'.[50] If Protestants may invoke private judgement to interpret scripture, they cannot do so in the case of these witnesses of tradition. 'History is a record of facts' and the fathers 'are far too ample to allow' selective interpretation.[51]

Episcopal Tradition

Episcopal tradition is, as might readily be expected, particularly bound up with the handing on of the creed from generation to generation by the apostolical line of bishops, and with the celebration of the church's liturgy by the same bishops. Now this tradition 'is delineated and recognised in scripture itself, where it is called the *Hypotyposis*, or "outline of sound words".'[52] Here Newman is clearly at pains both not to damage the unique authority of scripture and to resist 'what he takes to be the Roman Catholic view that tradition provides an extra and independent source of revelation'.[53]

Prophetical Tradition

There is also 'prophetical tradition'. 'Almighty God placed in his church first apostles, or bishops, secondarily prophets. Apostles rule and preach, prophets expound. Prophets or doctors are the interpreters of the revelation.'[54] This tradition is a 'vast system', 'existing primarily in the bosom of the church', 'pervading the church like an atmosphere'. It is witnessed to sometimes in writings, sometimes in liturgies, in controversial works, in local customs, and in all the myriad media composing ecclesiastical life and history. Given its vastness of content and its subtlety of expression, prophetical tradition 'may easily' be 'corrupted in its details, in spite of its general accuracy and its agreement with episcopal'.[55] The decrees of the Council of Trent could claim, in the light of this notion of prophetical tradition, to be 'apostolic' and so revealed. The truth, however, is that 'they are the ruins and perversions of primitive tradition'.[56] Thus Newman in 1836.

An aspect of his treatment of tradition, scripture and revelation deserving attention is the fact that he defines both scripture and tradition, in both its modes, in the light of revelation. This is a most helpful and insightful perspective, it seems, and rather unique in its time. Scripture and tradition both witness to revelation each in its own measure, and not independently of each other, nor in the same degree since scripture has the higher dignity, and tradition is polymorphic in outline while unitary in substance and so difficult to determine, particularly in its prophetical mode.

Fresh Shocks

Supremely certain of the Anglican Church's credentials and equally convinced of the distortions of the Church of Rome, Newman entered the Long Vacation of 1839.[57] He turned into the course of reading which he had many years before chosen as especially his own. This course was the history of the early church, in particular the councils, with special attention being given to the fathers' writings. This time he 'began to study and master the history of the Monophysites'. What he learned was going to be dramatic.[58]

The issue was the christological heresy of Monophysitism. Once again Newman saw how the Council of Ephesus of 449, now gone into history as the *Latrocinium Ephesinum*, supported the archheretic, Eutyches. A second council two years later had to be called. Again the bishops hesitated until Pope Leo of Rome intervened. His intervention was to prove decisive. The correct doctrine about the person and natures in Christ, and their relationship, was rescued and promulgated. The threatening heresy was overcome. But most of all, Newman realised the authority of the Bishop of Rome: his intervention was simply accepted. He was clearly the focus of unity and the guarantor of authentic faith. Six years earlier Newman had

highlighted the importance of 'the apostolical descent' of the
Anglican bishops. That was the theme of the first *Tract for the Times*.
He had demonstrated three years later in the *Prophetical Office* the
role of the successors of the apostles in the handing on of apostolic
tradition. But now, in Leo, Bishop of Rome, he has found the focal
bishop, so to speak, and the See with which all other Sees must be in
harmony in order to persevere in 'the faith given once for all to the
saints' (Jude 3).

In a letter written five years later Newman states succinctly the
impact of this discovery upon himself. 'I found more matter for
serious thought in the history (of the Monophysites) than in anything I had read ... I found the Eastern Church under the superin-
tendence of (as I may call it) Pope Leo. I found that he had made the
fathers of the council unsay their decree and pass another, so that
(humanly speaking) we owe it to Pope Leo at this day that the
Catholic Church holds the true doctrine. I found that Leo based his
authority on St Peter.'[59]

Athanasius *Contra Arianos: Further Light on Tradition*

Two years later, in 1841, Newman set himself down to the translation of St Athanasius, the 'much-enduring'[60] opponent of Arians.
This launched him for the second time into the century of Nicaea
and Arius and Athanasius. He had already visited this dramatic
portion of church history in his *Arians*. Much later, in fact in 1881,
he would compile an appendix volume of theological annotations
covering the themes of the theology of the great Alexandrian. He
devotes four pages to the idea of tradition in the thinking of
Athanasius. In the process he refers to contemporary and earlier
fathers. 'The fundamental idea with which Athanasius starts in the
controversy is a deep sense of the authority of tradition, which he
considers to have a definite jurisdiction even in the interpretation of
scripture, though at the same time he seems to consider that scripture, thus interpreted, is a document of final appeal in inquiry and
in disputation.'[61] 'See,' says Athanasius, 'we are proving that this
view has been transmitted from fathers to fathers ... The devil persuades you (the Arians) to slander the Ecumenical Council for com-
mitting to writing, not your doctrines, but that which "from the
beginning those who were eye-witnesses and ministers of the
word" have handed down to us. For the faith which the council has
confessed in writing, that is the faith of the Catholic Church.'[62]

In the *Orations*, Athanasius cries out, 'Who heard in his first cat-
echisings that God had a Son, without understanding it in our

sense? Who, on the rise of this odious heresy, was not at once startled at what he heard as being strange to him?' Newman understands Athanasius as teaching that scripture and tradition 'constitute one rule of faith, and that, sometimes as a composite rule, sometimes as a double and co-ordinate, sometimes as an alternative, under the magisterium, of course, of the church, and without an appeal to the private judgement of individuals'.[64]

Nor is it possible for 'some Protestants' to reduce tradition to scripture, identifying 'evangelical tradition' with the gospels and 'apostolic tradition' with the letters. Newman quotes numerous passages from the fathers to show that this will not stand up to scrutiny. Perhaps the one from St Irenaeus is enough: 'Polycarp ... whom we have seen in our first years, ... was taught these lessons which he learned from the apostles, *which the church also transmits, which alone are true. All the churches of Asia bear witness* to them; and *the successors* of Polycarp, down to this day, who is a much more trustworthy and *sure witness* of truth than Valentinus.'[65] Theodoret says that the word *Theotokos* was used 'according to apostolic tradition' and 'no one would say *Theotokos* was in scripture'.[66]

Athanasius in the fourth century simply assumes that there is a substantive body of teaching, originating from the apostles, transmitted in the life of the church from generation to generation, and for which the episcopate is responsible. Leo, a century later, acts as a trustworthy teacher and authoritative custodian of this same tradition. His authority as Bishop of Rome is responsible for the excising of the heresy of Monophysitism and for the strengthening of the whole church in the faith at a time when the oscillation and prevarication of sections of the episcopate seem to have compromised the truth.

Scripture: The Document of Proof in the Early Church?
In the second last of the discourses composing the *Prophetical Office* Newman had set out to present the early church's practice and view of the role of holy scripture in deciding points of faith

> When a novel doctrine was published in any quarter, the first question which the neighbouring bishops asked each other was, 'Is this part of the rule of faith? Has this come down to us?' The prevailing opinion of the church was a sufficient, even overpowering, objection against it ... When, however, the matter came before a council, when it was discussed, when the fathers reasoned, proved, and decided, they never went in matters of saving faith by tradition only, but they

guided themselves by the notices of the written word as by
landmarks in their course.[67]

All this was in 1837.

By the early 1840s, however, his study of the fathers in closer detail,
especially his study of Athanasius, the father especially associated
with Nicaea, and of Leo, who is the towering figure of the Council
of Chalcedon, led him to shift his perspective drastically from the
view that attributed exclusive authority to holy scripture in preference to tradition in matters of faith. He now saw a different scenario.

> At Ephesus, for example, the general council did not refer to
> a single passage of scripture before condemning Nestorius,
> but principally to the creed of Nicaea, and to ten or twelve
> passages from the fathers. And in the fourth general Council
> of Chalcedon the language of its members was, first to last, to
> keep to the faith of Nicaea, of Constantinople, of Athanasius,
> Cyril, Hilary, Basil, etc., scripture being hardly once men-
> tioned.[68]

So much for the ecumenical councils, as for the fathers' own views
on the role of scripture in the proof of doctrine. Newman sees with
increasing clarity that the fathers honour scripture and use tradition. However, they often cite scripture in a mystical or sacramental
manner.[69] Accordingly, they prove not in a manner that attempts to
force the assent of the mind, but rather in a manner that seeks to
unfold the hidden treasures of truth and wisdom in the inspired
word. They are in fact overwhelmed by the profundity and inex-
haustibility of the word.

The Sufficiency of Holy Scripture

All his life long Newman held to the view that the whole of the faith
is contained in, and witnessed to, by scripture. He also held, since
his encounter with Hawkins in 1818, that the church teaches the
creed even if scripture and tradition must prove the articles of the
creed.[70] And then ecclesiastical history, especially during the time
of the church of the fathers, convinced him of the indispensable
place of tradition, both episcopal and prophetical.

Scripture, however, is always a unique witness to revelation and
a record of our Lord's teaching. As the inspired expression of this
divine revelation, scripture contains the whole of Christian faith.[71]
Anglicans hold the same position, any differences being merely
verbal.

> Catholics and Anglicans (I do not say Protestants) attach different meanings to the word 'proof', in the controversy as to whether the whole faith is, or is not, contained in scripture. We mean that not every article of faith is so contained there that it may thence be logically proved, *independently* of the teaching and authority of tradition; but Anglicans mean that every article of faith is so contained there, that it may thence be proved, *provided* there be added the illustrations and compensations supplied by the tradition.[72]

And he immediately goes on to adduce by way of example his 'great theologian',[73] St Athanasius, who employs tradition at times to determine the meaning of scripture passages, which then become documents of final appeal in the proof and definition of doctrine.[74]

One Apostolical Tradition in Many 'Channels'

Apostolic tradition has many 'media', 'instruments' or, as Newman more frequently writes, 'channels'. It is highly informative to look a little at those channels. In the famous article *On Consulting* he lists them in a sparkling passage.

> I think I am right in saying that the tradition of the apostles, committed to the whole church in its various constituents and functions *per modum unius*, manifests itself variously at various times: sometimes by the mouth of the episcopacy, sometimes by the doctors, sometimes by the people, sometimes by liturgies, rites, ceremonies, and customs, by events, disputes, movements, and all those other phenomena which are comprised under the name of history. It follows that none of these channels of tradition may be treated with disrespect; granting at the same time fully, that the gift of discerning, discriminating, defining, promulgating, and enforcing any portion of that tradition resides solely in the *ecclesia docens*.[75]

The list of channels is as comprehensive as it is impressive. It suggests both episcopal and prophetical tradition, as Newman explained these distinctions in 1836 in *The Prophetical Office*. In fact, the first two channels are precisely the two mentioned in the well-known passage on prophetical tradition quoted earlier.

As for the people, this is Newman's famous teaching on the faithful as a medium of apostolic tradition. His study of the fourth century convinced him of the existence of such tradition. In *On Consulting* he spells out the precise nature of this 'fidelium sensus and consensus'.[76] He lists its characteristics as follows. 'Its consensus is to be regarded: 1. as a testimony to the fact of the apostolical dogma; 2. as a sort of instrument, or *phronema*, deep in the bosom of the mystical body of Christ; 3. as a direction of the Holy Ghost; 4. as an answer to its prayer; 5. as a jealousy of error, which it at once feels as a scandal.'[77] This instinct is no doubt parallel in Newman's mind to the illative sense by which the mind can judge truly and so reach concrete reality reliably.[78]

Newman's attention was drawn to the 'sensus fidelium' by a recent fact in ecclesiastical history. Pope Pius IX had investigated the belief of the lay faithful in the whole Catholic world only a short while earlier with regard to the sinlessness of the Blessed Virgin. He did this 'because the body of the faithful is one of the witnesses to the fact of the tradition of revealed doctrine, and their consensus throughout Christendom is the voice of the infallible church'.[79]

An Illustration: How could the Church teach the Immaculate Conception?
The defining of the immaculate beginning of Our Lady's life by Pius IX in 1854[80] deeply disturbed many of Newman's old friends and cherished colleagues from his Oxford days. Among these was E. B. Pusey. Pusey wrote a response which he described as an *Irenikon* but which stung Newman, particularly with regard to the truthfulness of the new dogma. In Pusey's mind it was a gratuitous teaching of the Church of Rome, without any justification in theology or foundation in revelation.

Newman undertook to show that the new dogma was contained in revelation. As we observe him showing how this dogma is in divine revelation, we will see his understanding of tradition on trial, as it were, since it is to apostolic tradition that he will turn as his source.

Since apostolic tradition is 'the great source of doctrine',[81] it might be expected to provide the evidence for the new dogma. The Pope had, among others, 'consulted' the faithful, and they are a particular 'channel' of apostolic tradition. Newman's own pointing out of this truth in *On Consulting* had generated such controversy that he felt well advised to steer clear of that channel. He looked instead to the channel of the fathers. But first he stated, in crystal clear terms, the ground rules for recourse to apostolic tradition in general.

Firstly, it had to be clear *how* the church determines an apostolic tradition. 'There are at least two ways ... 1. When credible witnesses declare that it is apostolical; as when three hundred fathers at Nicaea stopped their ears at Arius' blasphemies. 2. When, in various places, independent witnesses enunciate one and the same doctrine, as St Irenaeus, St Cyprian, and Eusebius assert that the "apostles founded a church, Catholic and one".'[82]

The second ground rule stipulates that, besides the apostolic source or form of the tradition, the tradition had also to be 'a belief which, be it *affirmative* or *negative*, is *positive*'. In other words, the mere absence of a tradition in a country, is not a tradition the other way. Newman brings forward examples of an affirmative tradition in the proposition, 'Christ is God', and of a negative tradition, the proposition, 'no one born of woman, is born in God's favour'.[83]

Thirdly, no tradition carries with it its own interpretation: 'it does but land (so to say) a proposition at the feet of the apostles, and its interpretation has still to be determined – as the apostles' words in scripture, however much theirs, need an interpretation.'[84] Newman puts forward the proposition, 'No one born of woman is born in God's favour.' He then questions its universality, and justifies this criticism by adding the instance of our Lord being born of woman. And he was sinless!

Fourthly, there are explicit and implicit traditions. The former are doctrines contained in the letter of the doctrine handed down, the latter in 'the force and vigour' of the word of the proposition.

Then Newman proceeds to apply these ground rules to Mary's immaculate conception. First of all, he asks, 'What is the great rudimental teaching of antiquity from its earliest date concerning her? … She is the Second Eve.'[85] He immediately puts forward three fathers who, in different places, taught this truth unequivocally. They are St Justin Martyr representing Palestine, St Irenaeus representing Asia Minor and Gaul, and Tertullian representing Rome and North Africa. Each of these fathers repeatedly teach that Our Lady is the 'Second Eve'.[86] The proposition 'Mary is the new Eve' passes the second test of an apostolical tradition since 'St Justin, St Irenaeus, and Tertullian are witnesses of an apostolical tradition, because in three distinct parts of the world they enunciate one and the same definite doctrine'.[87]

It is an explicit tradition. But from this explicit tradition two other implicit traditions follow. 'First (considering the condition of Eve in paradise), that Mary had no part in sin, and indefinitely large measures of grace; secondly (considering the doctrine of merits), that she had been exalted to glory proportionate to grace.'[88] Newman explains the inference in this way. 'If Eve was raised above human nature by that indwelling moral gift which we call grace, is it rash to say that Mary had even a greater grace? … And if Eve had this supernatural inward gift given to her from the first moment of her personal existence, is it possible to deny that Mary too had this gift from the first moment of her personal existence?'[89]

In Conclusion
Our concern has been to outline Newman's discovery of tradition and his growth into its riches. As a result of the exciting itinerary of his life, he came to a deep and critical sense of the nature of tradition and its indispensable place in the transmission of divine revelation. Now this is all the more striking when one remembers that he had to start out with the Calvinist doctrine of 'scripture alone'. At that time he had an aversion to any notion of tradition, seeing it as a most serious derogation from the dignity and authority of the written revealed word.

His encounter with Edward Hawkins in the Oriel Common Room, and, in particular, his hearing of 'the famous sermon' on the 31st May 1818 on the subject of tradition set Newman thinking about the significance of the church's own life as a carrier of, and witness to, divine revelation. Later when he began to discover the fathers, his initial Protestant perspective prevented him perceiving their Catholicity. Through his research of the Arian controversy he discovered the School of Alexandria and its great doctor, Athanasius, who championed the *'homoousion'* teaching of the First Ecumenical Council and struggled against the Arians with the weapons both of the church's living tradition and scripture.

As the adventure of the Oxford Movement progressed, Newman felt called upon to show how the Anglican position avoided the extremes of the Reformers and the Romanists. This was going to require an adequate theology of tradition to correct the former and resist the latter.[90] He set about providing this theology in *The Prophetical Office of the Church*. He felt supremely confident that this elaboration of tradition would be a perfect protection against Rome and consistent with the patristic and Caroline witness to the church's Catholic form.

However, he had not adverted to the significance of other discoveries which he had made in his detailed study of the church's history, particularly the early centuries, such as the apostolic origin of the episcopate and its responsibility in each century for the received doctrine of faith, as well as the part played by the lay faithful after Nicaea in the reception and defence of that council's teaching. These two aspects, however, suddenly struck him in 1839 and again in 1841 as he realised the Catholicity of the church in St Augustine and in its apostolic principle of unity in faith as personitied in the then Bishop of Rome, Leo the Great. He now understood the principle of episcopal and prophetical tradition, and the many channels of the latter, which altogether and with scripture, 'conspire' to hand on 'the Catholic fullness' of revelation.

His acquisition of this dynamic understanding of tradition, an understanding both subtle and discriminating, enabled him to work out a theology of the laity as well as a justification for Marian dogmas which until recently he had considered 'the great crux' with the whole Catholic system. This theology of sacred tradition seems particularly apposite for our own later times. Of the validity of this claim we shall have further evidence in the next chapter.

CHAPTER 5

The Flowering of Newman's Theology
of Tradition in the Second Vatican Council

Tradition: Variations on the Theme
The last chapter attempted to draw out Newman's deepening discovery of tradition as an indispensable category of Christianity. This chapter, however, will show how Newman's understanding of tradition received significant affirmation in Vatican II. That acceptance may serve as an ideal launching pad for fruitful dialogue with the council. This goal, however, requires that we turn aside for a while from the relentless exposition of Newman to the exposition of conciliar teaching. This turning aside should have the effect of highlighting the warm reception of Newman's theology of tradition by the Catholic world.

It is a commonplace to say that the Second Vatican Council was a watershed in Catholic theology. The pioneering work of the pre-conciliar scripture scholars, theologians, historians and liturgists bore fruit in the council. One area of Catholic theology that benefited enormously from this scholarship and from the council was our understanding of tradition. Although a constitutive factor of Christianity, tradition was poorly understood in recent centuries. The theology of tradition has now been happily renewed. The first part of this article will attempt to trace the course of this renewal.

Theology, however, is faith seeking understanding. This puts the onus on us to go in search of a contemporary understanding of tradition. It is not enough to rest on the great achievement of recent decades. Development is the only sign of life. My guides in this search will be John Henry Newman, whose thought influenced the council powerfully, and Eric Voegelin, the well-known philosopher of history. In the second half of the chapter 1 will try to show how the thinking of these two men can deepen and expand our theological understanding of Christian tradition. Basing myself on their insights I will conclude the article with a descriptive statement of tradition as historical *anamnesis* and pastoral *diakonia*.

A New Testament Emphasis: Fidelity to the Gospel

What strikes one very powerfully as one reads the New Testament is the emphasis put on fidelity to the gospel. The words of Paul at the opening of Galatians are a good instance: 'I am astonished at the promptness with which you have turned away from the one who called you and have decided to follow a different version of the good news. Not that there can be more than one good news; it is merely that some troublemakers among you want to change the good news of Christ; and let me warn you that if anyone preaches a version of the good news different from the one we have already preached to you, whether it be ourselves or an angel from heaven, he is to be condemned' (1:6-8). The same emphasis on fidelity to the gospel is presented in other places in the shape of little creeds, short statements of faith. Perhaps two of the most typical are I Corinthians 11:23-26 on the Eucharist, and 1 Corinthians 15:3-8 on the resurrection. In both cases Paul explains that he is only teaching what he has been taught himself. He is a link in the chain handing on the faith, a faith that existed before him, is now passed on by Paul, and will continue after him because it is God's saving truth and as such, God intends it to reach every heart.

The strength of emphasis placed on fidelity to the handing on of the gospel, 'the good news of Jesus Christ, the Son of God' (Mk 1:1), in New Testament literature is striking, to say the least. It is an obvious fact. One does not have to go searching for it. It is on the surface of the inspired text. Like the other apostles, Paul is consumed with the desire to carry out his mandate, received from the risen Lord, to bring the message of Christ to the ends of the earth (Acts 9:15-16; 22:15; 26:17; Rom 1:5; 11:13; Gal 2:2, 8, 9; see also the Pauline Eph 3:8; Col 1:27; 1 Tm 2:7). However, the fidelity of the apostle flows as an effect from the fidelity of God demonstrated in the incarnation, life, death and resurrection of the Son of God, who, as Paul loves to proclaim, 'loved me and sacrificed himself for my sake' (Gal 2:20). Fidelity to the gospel is a response to the fidelity of God to his people. Paul and the other apostles are faithful because God has been faithful to them first (1 Jn 4:19).

The Inner Being of God is Faithful Love

This idea of fidelity as response to the God, who has loved them to the end, (Jn 13:1), is well worded in the creed-hymn in 2 Timothy 2:11-13:

> If we have died with him, then we shall live with him.
> If we hold firm, then we shall live with him.

If we disown him, then he will disown us.
We may be unfaithful, but he is always faithful,
for he cannot disown his own self.

The inner being of God is faithful love. After all, he is the God of the
Covenant with Abraham and Moses, the God who, in 'the fullness
of time' (Mk 1:15; 1 Cor 10:11; Gal 4:4; Eph 1:10; Heb 1:2; 9:26; 1 Pt
1:20), has sent his only-begotten Son, his beloved Son, as a man like
us in all things but sin (Heb 4:15-16; 5:9-10). This faithful love of the
God of Israel has been beautifully described in a kind of anamnetic
reflection at the very opening of the Letter to the Hebrews: 'At various times in the past and in various different ways, God spoke to
our ancestors through the prophets; but in our own time, the last
days, he has spoken to us through his Son, the Son he has appointed
to inherit everything and through whom he made everything there
is. He is the radiant light of God's glory and the perfect copy of his
nature' (1:1-3).[1]

The radiant fidelity of God in Christ has been accurately, even if
a little poetically perhaps, painted by Nicholas of Cusa, a fifteenth
century author: 'Such is this loud voice, echoing in the depths of our
being, a voice which reaches us through the prophets, urging us to
adore the one Creator, to practice virtue, to seek refuge in our
Saviour, in whom we find the strength to rise above the life of the
senses. For centuries this voice has sent forth its sound; its volume
grew unceasingly till the time of John the Baptist, himself the voice
of one crying in the wilderness and pointing to the Saviour; finally
this great voice was made flesh. Then it gave utterance with ever
greater clearness and force to many expressions – doctrines and
miracles – and in the end, to show that for the sake of truth even the
most terrible fate of all – the death of the body – must be chosen,
with a loud cry it gave up the ghost.'[2] Nicholas brilliantly over-
views the whole sweep of revelation and salvation history. He sees
the faithful love of God coming down the ages of Israel until, in the
end, that love becomes flesh and hands itself over on the wood of
the cross. Jesus Christ is, according to St Paul, 'the love of God
made visible' (Rom 8:39). St John's gospel speaks of the very same
faithful love:

The word was made flesh, he lived among us, and we saw his
glory, the glory that is his as the only Son of the Father, full of
grace and truth (*pléres káritos kai alethéias*) (Jn 1:14).

Christ the Embodiment of the Father's Faithfulness
Christ is the embodiment of the Father's loving kindness, the

enfleshment of this rocklike faithfulness.[4] Christ is the divine *hesed* and *emeth* placed henceforth at the very centre of history. He is not only the eternal exemplar of this fidelity of God, but also the infinite source of the church's consequent fidelity. Being the incarnation of the Father's loving kindness and rocklike fidelity towards men, Christ reveals the great heart of the Father unconditionally set on men: 'No one has ever seen God; it is the only Son, who is nearest to the Father's heart, who has made him known' (1:18).

So What is Tradition?

I am now in a position to suggest a preliminary idea of tradition. Tradition is Christ's fidelity to us in the church, the historical blossoming of the people of Israel (Gal 6:16), and the church's effort in consequence to respond to that love. Tradition, then, consists in the process by which the risen Christ remains with his people, touching the lives of individual men and women in the church until the end of time. 'Know that I am with you always, yes, to the end of time' (Mt 28:20).

There is a good illustration of this process of tradition in the history of the apostolic community described in the opening pages of Acts: 'These remained faithful to the teaching of the apostles, to the brotherhood, to the breaking of bread and to the prayers' (2:42). This 'remaining faithful' involves two entwined aspects, one of process, the other of content. Tradition, then, is both process and content. As process, it is the actual handing down of the elements that constitute Christianity as a living system of truth, life and love. As content, tradition includes the elements of doctrine, brotherhood, the breaking of bread and prayers. Nicholas Lash states the importance of tradition in strong terms: 'The conviction of Christian belief (is) that the message proclaimed in the life, death and resurrection of Jesus Christ is God's definitive word to mankind. Therefore unless the word proclaimed to men of every generation, age and culture is, in some significant sense, the same word, God's promise is not fulfilled.'[5] The request of the two disciples on the first Easter Day to the Risen Lord 'to stay with them' (Lk 24:28) as together they walked the road from Jerusalem to Emmaus, is not merely historical: it is above all typical of Christians down the centuries. It expresses a longing deep in the heart of the community founded by Christ. Along the roads of Christian history this partnership has been sought, found and cherished.

This Chapter Before the Council!

If I had been trying to write this chapter in 1960, and not in 1995, my themes would have been predictable. Scripture and tradition would have been clearly distinguished, if not actually separated as two parallel but independent sources of revelation. A subsection would have tackled the question of how much of the original revelation was in each source. What is in which documents? Such treatment presupposes a definite and limited understanding of revelation as knowledge communicated to man in clear propositions, revelation as the provision of information from God for men. In all of this the normative role of the church's magisterium would assume preponderance. Being put almost outside and above the concrete process of the church's life, the magisterium would be seen as the external authority interpreting scripture and using tradition for her own purposes. So much for content.

Not only the content, but also the style or tone of the article would have to be different. The differing standpoints of the Christian churches would have demanded an apologetical approach, an approach that would justify the Roman Catholic positions against the Protestant positions. I would have to be more dogmatic, and so less historical, than is now in order. And the whole debate would have to be conducted at some distance from the key category of revelation, and the light it throws on the respective authority of scripture, tradition and magisterium. However, in the last decades we have come far. Vatican II has occurred. The work of biblical scholars, historians of theology and dogmatic theologians has been taken, sifted and turned out, purified by the Holy Spirit, in the literature emanating from the council. Progress in the work of ecumenism has made all Christians more sensitive to the sources in revelation of the church's life, worship and faith. All this means that it is now possible to deal with the topic of tradition more biblically, more historically and more ecumenically. It is possible to seek what unites us, and finding it to grow in deeper mutual understanding.

The Struggle in Vatican II: A Context for Understanding Tradition

The constitution of Vatican II on divine revelation is a splendid illustration of the new style evident in Roman Catholic theology at the present. 'There is a respectable theological view that, outstanding as is the importance of the much larger dogmatic constitution on the church, the *Constitution on Divine Revelation* may prove to be the supreme achievement of this council.'[6] The questions and issues debated and written on in this constitution are increasingly recognised 'as being among the most fundamental problems for contemporary Christian belief and doctrine'.[7] As tradition is one such issue dealt with in the document, we may now turn to the document itself.

Not surprisingly, the subject of revelation spanned practically the whole course of the council from 1962 until 1965, the first draft being presented in 1962 and the final in 1965. The fact that it took fully five attempts to arrive at an agreeable statement is an indication of the great change of viewpoint that came about over the four years. The original draft was entitled 'On the Sources of Revelation', a title that speaks for itself. The first two chapters bore the titles, 'The Souble Source of Revelation' and 'The Inspiration, Inerrancy and Literary Form of Scripture'. By November 1964 a consensus had emerged. There are three notable features of this consensus which deserve our attention and throw light at once on the theme of this chapter.

Revelation as Interpersonal Dialogue

Firstly, revelation is no longer conceived of as simply information communicated by God in his Son made flesh. Rather it is portrayed as an *interpersonal dialogue* in which 'it pleased God, in his goodness and wisdom, to reveal himself and to make known the mystery of his will ... By this revelation, then, the invisible God (cf. Col 1:5, 1 Tim 1:17), from the fullness of his love, addresses men as his friends (cf. Ex 33:11, Jn 15:14-15), and moves among them (cf. Bar 3:38), in order to invite them and receive them into his own company.'[8] The contrast between this theology of revelation and that originally proposed may be expressed in terms of the difference between making a 'declaration of love' to someone, and simply providing him with information. 'This plan of revelation is realised by deeds and words having an inner unity.'[9] Revelation, then, consists not in mere words but in deeds as well. Revelation is thus 'interpreted activity'. That is, certain events are understood to be 'the words of God' to man, better, to be his self-gift to man. This means that the whole concrete history of Israel is the very stuff of revelation. In the closing phrases of the article Christ is declared to be the fullness of revelation. Christ is the unlimited love of God revealed to men, a love in which the 'deepest truth about God and the salvation of man is made clear to us'.[10] This great shift of perspective has enormous repercussions for the meaning of scripture and tradition, as we shall see later.

Scripture and Tradition: The Media of Revelation

Next, the discussion of the relationship between scripture and tradition has been recast. Originally the question was: What is in which documents? How much revelation is in scripture and/or how much in tradition? But now a new idea altogether of tradition has emerged, an idea derived from scripture and from the history of the church. The new question is, What are the forms in which the fullness of revelation comes to us? What are the media for the transmission of revelation? This shift means that tradition is to be seen in a new and broader context.

The Magisterium as Servant of the Word of God
Thirdly and finally, the function of the magisterium is seen in a newer light, re-evaluated. Especially since the First Vatican Council, the magisterium of the church was focused in the papacy, and put above scripture and tradition, and almost outside the living stream of the church's faith and practice. Of course, it was presented as the faithful watchman of what was going on. Vatican II, however, takes an entirely newer approach: the magisterium has the duty of 'hearing the word of God with reverence'. 'This magisterium is not superior to the word of God, but is its servant.'[11]

The Achievement of the Council: The Recovery of the Historical Concept
What has been happening during the council? The historical perspective on tradition was recovered and brought to bear on the subsequent discussion. If we want to get to the council's underlying, but guiding, idea of tradition, we must now take a look at the history of the concept. Besides providing the true key to the understanding of the document, the study of the history of the concept should itself throw light on both the nature and function of tradition.

Already by the time of the rabbinical writings there was constant reference to the 'tradition of the fathers'. This means that the Old Testament had a fairly clear awareness of tradition. 'Earlier experience gave meaning to the later event which in turn threw light on the earlier experience.'[12] These events and their meanings were taught by the elders. In the ancient world a teacher was usually called 'father' and his pupil or disciple 'son'. The Christian teachers were also called 'fathers' in the first Christian centuries. By the fourth century the expression, 'father of the church', had achieved a distinct meaning. The 'fathers of the church' are the bishops who in the first centuries handed down, in their preaching, catechisms and in their celebration of Christian imitation, the apostolic kerygma, as this was given by the apostles themselves.[13] In its content tradition is the same as the apostolic teaching written in the 'inspired scripture'.

The Battle of Athanasius

The case of Athanasius is a good illustration. The struggle of the church with the Arian heresy began in Alexandria, the see of Athanasius. It seems important to refresh our memories of the last chapter. Athanasius, the champion of the truth, writes his great *Orations against the Arians* in defence of the creed of Nicaea. 'The fundamental idea with which he starts in the controversy is a deep sense of the authority of tradition, which he considers to have a definite jurisdiction even in the interpretation of scripture, though at the same time he seems to consider that scripture, thus interpreted, is a document of final appeal in inquiry and in disputation. He assumes that there is a tradition, substantive, independent and authoritative, such as to supply for us the true sense of scripture in doctrinal matters – a tradition carried on from generation to generation by the practice of catechising and by the other ministrations of holy church.'[14] Thus Edward Schillebeeckx can say: 'From the time of Athanasius onwards, it was therefore becoming less common to refer directly to scripture and more common to refer directly to the "authority of the fathers". There was a firm conviction of the responsibility of the episcopate in each generation for the "received doctrine" which, having been clarified in the light of contemporary problems, was handed down to the next generation. The fathers, who were the teaching bishops of previous generations, formed the link between the apostolic faith and the later generations.'[15]

The Life of the Communities the Bearer of the Tradition

But it was not only the fathers who transmitted the word of God. The Christians themselves, in their families and in their worship, handed on the gospel. The early Christian communities were thus the bearers of the tradition. For the first three centuries the extent to which the whole life of the church is seen as the bearer of the tradition 'is affirmed so emphatically that it can only be translated into images taken from the biological order'.[16] In the very next century, the century of Athanasius and Ambrose and Augustine, Basil and Chrysostom, and the two Gregories, the apostolic faith in the divinity of Christ, which was defined in Nicaea, was proclaimed, maintained and defended as much, if not more, by the faithful than by the bishops.

This historical fact led Newman, writing in 1859, to see in the laity one of the media or instruments of apostolic tradition. His words are worth recalling: 'The body of the laity is one of the witnesses to the fact of the tradition of revealed doctrine ... their consensus through Christendom is the voice of the infallible church.'

And Newman continues in these striking lines: 'I think I am right in saying that the tradition of the apostles, committed to the whole church in its various constituents and function *per modum unius*, manifests itself variously at various times: sometimes by the mouth of the episcopacy, sometimes by the doctors, sometimes by the people, sometimes by liturgies, rites, ceremonies and customs, by events, disputes, movements, and all those other phenomena which are comprised under the name of history. It follows that none of these channels of tradition may be treated with disrespect; granting at the same time fully, that the gift of discerning, discriminating, defining, promulgating, and enforcing any portion of that tradition resides solely in the *ecclesia docens*.'[17]

The Patristic View of Tradition: Broad, Rich and Encompassing

This broad, rich and encompassing view of tradition held sway from the patristic age until the end of the thirteenth century. 'In other words, before events caused the emergence of normative criteriological questions, the particular components of the total reality – bible, bishops, theologians, faithful – are not seen as rival "authorities". Rather they are considered to be complementary con-stituents of one complex whole: the process whereby the apostolic tradition is sustained and enlightened by the Spirit of the Risen Christ.'[18] It was a period in which there was not only faithful memory, but also a deepening of insight.[19] Christ, 'who is the full-ness of revelation', was considered to be present in the totality of the tradition.

The Battle Cries that will soon tear Apart

In the twelfth century, however, the reforms of Pope Gregory VII (Hildebrand) change the scene and prepare the way for the emer-gence of authority. The theological results were considerable. Two such results are relevant to our present concern. First, there is a shrinkage in the idea of church: whereas for twelve centuries, the church was seen as the whole community, the idea of church now shrinks to the clergy. In the second place, there is a transition from one idea of episcopal authority to another. Ministry is no longer seen as the exercise of a service in which Christ is present, but as the processing of personal rights and claims. Already a certain separa-tion appears and a wedge is driven between bishops and people, and between tradition and scripture. Towards the end of the thirt-eenth century the fateful question is asked by Henry of Ghent, 'Must we rather believe the authority of this doctrine (sacred scrip-ture) than those of the church, or the other way round?' It is only a short step to the battle cries that will soon tear Christendom apart, the battle cries of 'scripture alone', 'the church alone', or 'tradition alone'.

The Achievement of Dei Verbum

We are now in a position to appreciate the originality of *Dei Verbum*. We can appreciate why Karl Barth was thrilled by this product of the council. '*Si jamais il y a eu un concile de réforme, c'était bien celui là* (If ever there was a council of reform, it was certainly this one).'[20] This may be considered a positive acknowledgement of the overall content of the document. It is not a suggestion that all is now well and that all questions are now answered. Another look at the council's specific treatment of tradition and its importance will bring this out.

Perhaps the most important section is article 8 of the constitution: 'And so the apostolic preaching, which is expressed in a special way in the inspired books, was to be preserved by a continuous succession of preachers until the end of time. Therefore the apostles, handing on what they themselves had received, warn the faithful to hold fast to the traditions which they had learned by word of mouth or by letter (2 Thess 2:15), and to fight in defence of the faith handed on once and for all. Now what was handed on by the apostles includes everything which contributes to the holiness of life, and the increase in faith of the People of God; and so the church in her teaching, life, and worship, perpetuates and hands on to all generations all that she herself is, all that she believes.'[21] It is clear that this is a recovery of the broad patristic understanding of tradition.

But there is even more in the recovery of the balanced truth. Scripture, tradition and magisterium are interrelated. Their interdependence is underlined. We will let the document speak for itself. 'It is clear, therefore, that sacred tradition, sacred scripture, and the teaching authority of the church, in accord with God's most wise design, are so linked and joined together that one cannot stand without the other and that all together and each in its own way under the action of the Holy Spirit, contribute effectively to the salvation of souls.'[22] A burning concern of the council was to put scripture, tradition and magisterium together as facets or components in the church's transmission of revelation, which was seen as a saving message.

Thirdly, the magisterium is declared explicitly to be not above the word of God, but to be its servant. It must first listen to the word in scripture and tradition. This put an end to a situation in which, in practice, curial directives and papal teachings came to be considered as immune from biblical research, historians, theologians, and the consensus of the believing community. The authority of scripture and tradition have been vindicated, while the competence of the magisterium has been asserted ('the task of authentically interpreting the word of God, whether written or handed on, has been entrusted exclusively to the living teaching office of the church').

Finally, *Dei Verbum* does not answer the question, What is the ultimate supreme norm for the guidance of the faithful? The council leaves this question open. However, in section 21 it says: 'Like the Christian religion itself, all the preaching of the church must be nourished and ruled by sacred scripture.' The council, and Catholic theology today generally are much more concerned to preserve the component elements in the transmission of revelation, the saving word of God, than to solve a question that has divided Christians historically, and fascinated Christians theologically. The attitude of Catholic theologians today is to ascribe exclusive authority to neither 'scripture alone', nor 'tradition alone' (the idolatry of history), nor 'to what has been done for a long time'. The life of Christ, who is the revelation, flows through scripture *and* tradition *and* the authoritative voice of the church.

As Catholics, we have tended in recent centuries, in the direction of 'tradition alone' and 'today alone'. Our current need is to shift the emphasis in the direction of scripture. As Walter Kasper has written:

> Vatican II certainly emphasises the interconnection of scripture, tradition and magisterium, but the interrelation is no longer a one way process. It is no longer a question of interpreting scripture in the light of tradition and dogma, but the biblical scholar is now expected to make his contribution to the church's judgement. This means that the process may be inverted so that dogma must be understood in the light of scripture.[23]

We began with the idea of fidelity in our discussion of Christian tradition. The sustained emphasis in the literature of the New Testament on God's fidelity to his people in Christ and in the church (Eph 3:20-1) is summarised in the formula: 'God is always faithful' (2 Tim 2:13).[24] This fidelity on God's part is both the inspiration and the norm for the fidelity of the church to God. Fidelity is a New Testament idea that opens the way for us into a deeper and more personal grasp of the meaning of tradition in the lifestream of the church. Most of all, an approach to tradition via fidelity helps us to understand Christian tradition in a new light.

Tradition as Fidelity

It has been well said that the key to any issue consists in asking the right question. Tradition can only be understood if we first ask the right questions. The key question in the church must be: How are we to be faithful Christians in this twentieth century? What does Christ ask of us, both as individuals and as a church? How can we both faithfully remember 'the infinite treasure of Christ' (Eph 3:8) and serve one another and our non-believing brothers and sisters in such a way that they 'will know that we are Christ's disciples' (Jn 13:35)? These are the real questions.

The immediate value of these questions is that they expand the question of tradition and fidelity. They easily show that tradition as fidelity is a question not only of 'the truth', but also of 'the life'. Orthodoxy must include the reality of orthopraxis. This shifts our consideration of tradition on to the broader basis of the whole of church life, and this squares with the point made earlier that tradition as a process involves the whole of the church's life, doctrinal and devotional, sacramental and scriptural, moral and institutional. The daily life of the church of the apostles is described in the pages of the Acts of the Apostles. One section of the work captures the tone of the apostolic community and now requires a fuller consideration.

> The whole group of believers was united, heart and soul; no one claimed for his own use anything he had, as everything they owned was held in common ... None of their members was ever in want, as all those who owned land or houses would sell them ... (These) remained faithful to the teaching of the apostles, to the brotherhood, to the breaking of bread and to the prayers ... Day by day the Lord added to their community those destined to be saved (4:32, 34; 2:42, 47).

The life of the community is like a plant sown in the soil of a people one in mind and in heart, nourished by the Eucharist, given light by the apostolic teachings, and unified by the daily prayers. This community draws into itself all those who are being saved. The attraction of its lifestyle is irresistible. Filled with the scent of the Risen Christ and with the power of the Holy Spirit to witness, the church both builds up its members and wins new ones at one and the same time. Living she grows and this same growth is the evidence of the life of the Lord and the Holy Spirit within her total system of sacrament and apostle, teaching and prayer, charity and mission. Her whole system was the medium of revelation simply because her whole system communicated Christ, 'who is the fullness of revelation'.[25] Her persevering together resulted in the faithful handing on of the riches of Christ her Lord. In the words of Ignatius of Antioch, 'In your unanimity and concordant charity Jesus Christ is sung.'[26]

When the Second Vatican Council considers the church, it is not surprising that the Jerusalem community influences her deliberations very powerfully. The *Dogmatic Constitution on the Church*, perhaps the *Magna Carta* of the council, loves to describe the church as 'a people made one with the unity of the Father, the Son and the Holy Spirit'.[27] The council describes the concrete life of the church in terms of the triple mission of her prophetical role in teaching, her priestly role in the celebration of the sacraments, and her kingly or shepherding role in terms of the guidance of the hierarchy and the charity animating the specific vocations of all her members. It is a refreshing vision of the church as the community of the Incarnate Word celebrating the gifts of her great Redeemer and attempting to meet the needs of her members and those not within her fold. It is no wonder, then, that the council is in an enlightened position when she comes to describe both the content and process of tradition in her *Dogmatic Constitution on Divine Revelation*.

Light from the Philosophy of History: Eric Voegelin

The work of a great modern philosopher might be very helpful at this point in our efforts to penetrate even more deeply within the theological reality of tradition which, like all realities in revelation, is greater than anything we can ever say of it.[28]

This philosopher's work is rich in insight and erudite in its recovery of the wisdom of the great civilisations, revelational and philosophical, that have built up our world but which are now largely lost. His work is original in its understanding of the various wisdoms thus assembled, and extremely relevant to the task of appreciating the way in which any great society constitutes and maintains her being in the course of history. I am referring to the work of Eric Voegelin, whose monumental many volumed 'Order and History' stands as a decisive contribution in this century to man's ongoing attempt to understand God, himself, his history and contemporary society.[29]

It would be an insult to the depth of Voegelin's work to try to summarise in the short space available here his thought on tradition. Fortunately he has written several articles touching on the theme using the deep insight gained in his Herculean labours in the field of the philosophy of history. He helps us to see with striking clarity the meaning and purpose of tradition in general and in the particular case of the Christian community emanating from Judaeo-Christian revelation. His thesis may be stated as follows: every nation is born from a deep experience.

An Originating Experience

This experience is an originating experience in the sense that its meaning gathers a people whose subsequent direction along the roads of history it illuminates and guides. This founding experience is both understood and articulated by the particular society which it founds. Voegelin speaks of symbolisation which includes both basic texts, key rituals and ordering structure which hand on the originating deep experiences to the later generations.

Need to Relive the Originating Experience

The meaning of the symbols depends, from the nature of the case, on the experience which engendered them. 'The symbols intend to convey a truth experienced.'[30] They come from this experience, they convey the meaning of this experience, and so they can only be grasped in the light of this experience. This means that the community must relive the originating deep experiences, in order to know what the symbols are truly saying. This reliving is very demanding existentially, because it requires that the community should live the original standards but it is indispensable if the community is to maintain contact with the originating experience which gave it birth.

If the originating experiences are not attained, things happen to the symbols whose only *raison d'être* is to carry and convey the truth experienced at the outset and origin of the community. The first is the routine repetition of the symbols which generates a superficial piosity. The ritual is gone through but the life has been betrayed. The people honour their origins with their lips, but their hearts are far away. They are left without roots.

The second effect of failing to live the originating deep experiences consists in the reaction of scepticism. The routine repetition of what has become mere externalised cliché provokes scepticism. To quote Voegelin: 'We have spoken, therefore, of a truth experienced rather than of a truth attaching to the symbols. As a consequence, when the experience engendering the symbol ceases to be a presence located in the man who has it, the reality from which the symbols derive their meaning has disappeared. The symbols in the sense of a spoken or written word, it is true, are left as traces in the world of sense perception, but their meaning can be understood only if they evoke, and through evocation reconstitute, the engendering reality in the listener or reader.'[31]

The possibility of this sceptical reaction is only increased by the fact that the basic symbols by which we pass on our grasp of revelation are not concepts referring to objects located in space and time. They are rather the carriers of truth about invisible and transcendent reality. Just as 'faith is the substance of things hoped for, and the evidence of things unseen' (Heb 11:1), so too Christian symbols are the substance of things hoped for and the evidence of things unseen, but they are this only for those who have experienced the truth and love which generates them.

In an analysis reminiscent of Newman's explanation of the Christian 'idea' becoming Christian doctrine, Voegelin outlines the process by which the engendering or originating experience is expressed in an original account which gradually becomes an arsenal of doctrinal truths. Without contact with the original experience, the doctrines are cut off from their source. They are dead symbols, and so cannot fail to cause a sceptical reaction. In this way Voegelin suggests 'the phenomena of original account, dogmatic exposition and sceptical argument, as a sequence that can attach itself to every experience of non-existent (transcendent) reality when it becomes articulate and, through its symbols, enters society as an ordering force'.[32] Perhaps the members of the Christian community wish to be faithful to the faith of their fathers. In that case, however, their living can only be piously superficial because they have not experienced the truth and life which produced the symbols.

In illustration of the point, one might quote Hans Urs von Balthasar's fascinating description of the Dominican Order as the contemplation of Dominic spread out in space and time. Citing Bernanos, von Balthasar sees all Dominicans as participants in the contemplative charity of Dominic: 'The Order of Preachers is presented to us as the charity of St Dominic spread out in space and time, his contemplation become visible.'[33] It is this experience of Dominic which gives the true sense to all that is involved in being a member of the Dominican Order. Without such an experience an individual Dominican will be quite unable to see the point of the various rules and time-honoured practices of his community. He will not be able to see the wood for the trees. In a similar way, it is contact with the originating experience of Christianity in the ministry, passion, death and resurrection of Christ, and in the sending of the Holy Spirit, as written down in the New Testament, which makes full sense of the Christian community and its life.

Contact with a Living Christianity

Without such an experience of living Christianity an intelligent Christian will end up either a pious conservative or else a sceptic ever ready to challenge the witness to the faith with the vulgar agnostic questions, 'How do you know?' and 'How can you prove it?', questions every teacher of religion knows from his classroom. Common to both conservative and sceptic is lack of contact with a living Christianity. The sceptic will recover a living faith, and the conservative will deepen his shallow discipleship, the day they meet a community where Jesus lives in people who are venturing all on his word and so make him present in the midst of men and reveal him to those who know him poorly or not at all (see Jn 13:34-5; 15:12; 17:21f; Mt 18:20). In other words, the fundamental hermeneutic of all church doctrine and ritual and order is the quality of the lived Christianity of its professed adherents.

Further Light: John Henry Newman

In 1843 Newman completed his *Oxford University Sermons* whose theme was the survival of faith in the individual and in the church. After years of struggle, after volumes of reading and sustained reflection on the experience of faith in himself and in his contemporaries, Newman concluded that the strength of the church resides in the witness, often unnoticed, of the mass of faithful Christians. They are the key medium in the handing on of the faith. His words are strong and clear: 'The truth has been upheld in the world not as a system, not by books, not by argument, nor by temporal power, but by the personal influence of such men as have already been described, who are at once the teachers and patterns of it.' The recurring theme of holiness makes its appearance again.

Though instances of great holiness are rare, yet they are enough to win God's silent battles and to impress his Kingdom upon society. He explains his conviction in the light of the intrinsic power of the witness of holiness. 'The men commonly held in popular estimation are greatest at a distance; they become small as they are approached, but the attraction, exerted by unconscious holiness, is of an urgent and irresistible nature; it persuades the weak, the timid, the wavering and the inquiring; it draws forth the affection and loyalty of all who are in a measure like-minded; and over the thoughtless or perverse multitude it exercises a sovereign compulsory sway, bidding them fear and keep silence, on the ground of its own divine right to rule them – its hereditary claim on their obedience, though they understand not the principles or counsels of that spirit, which is "born, not of blood, nor of the will of the flesh, not of the will of man, but of God".'[34]

Why the Lay Faithful may be Consulted

In 1859 he returned again to the same idea in his seminal composition *On Consulting the Laity in Matters of Doctrine*. He focused on the performance of the Catholic laity after the Council of Nicaea (325 AD) in defending the council's teaching on the divinity of Our Lord against the Arians. Quoting passage after passage from the fathers of both the Greek and Latin Church of that century, he illustrated the point made earlier in the *Oxford Sermons* that it is the body of the faithful who, endowed with a special sense of the faith or *phronesis* as he called it, are key transmitters of divine revelation. Underlining the fact that Pius IX carefully consulted the *consensus fidelium* before defining the dogma of the Immaculate Conception of Mary in 1854, Newman sees in this but the exhibition of a truth always present, even if often overlooked, in the history of Christian truth and its transmission down the centuries. His words speak for themselves:

> As to the particular doctrine of which I have here been directing my view (the Immaculate Conception) and the passage in history by which I have been illustrating it (the Arian controversy), I am not supposing that such times as the Arian will ever come again. As to the present, certainly if there ever was an age which might dispense with the testimony of the faithful, and leave the maintenance of the truth to the pastors of the church, it is the age in which we live. Never was the episcopate of Christendom so devoted to the Holy See, so religious, so earnest in the discharges of its special duties, so little disposed to innovate, so superior to the temptation of theological sophistry. And perhaps this is the reason why the *consensus fidelium* has, in the minds of many, fallen into the background. Yet each constituent portion of the church has its proper functions, and no portion can safely be neglected.

Here we see Newman pressing into service the comprehensive insight he gained in his toilsome learning of the true idea of tradition, in particular, of the set of channels that witness to revelation. The fact that the faithful possess a 'sensus fidei' makes them one such channel. This truth explains Pope Pius IX 'consulting' them in the matter of their perception of Our Lady's holiness. 'Though the laity be but the reflection or echo of the clergy in matters of faith, yet there is something in the *pastorum et fidelium conspiratio*, which is not in the pastors alone. The history of the definition of the Immaculate Conception shows us this; and it will be one among the blessings which the Holy Mother, who is the subject of it, will gain for us, in repayment of the definition, that by that very definition we are all reminded of the part which the laity have had in the pre-liminaries of its promulgation. Pope Pius has given us a pattern, in his manner of defining, of the duty of considering the sentiments of the laity upon a point of tradition, in spite of whatever fullness of evidence the bishops had already thrown upon it.'[35]

Much of Newman's life was devoted to the task of recovering the riches of the Christian tradition. He read the fathers right through on two occasions. He wrote extensively on many of them. The *Orations against the Arians* of Athanasius he translated, produc-ing a volume of explanatory 'Annotations', in themselves a trea-sure-house of patristic thought and research. As he wrote, there arose before him the vision of 'the church of the fathers'. This living community provided him with the inspiration he needed at the time of the Oxford Movement. As we have seen in chapter three, it made him a Roman Catholic: 'The fathers made me a Catholic', he wrote in 1864 in his *Letter to Pusey* explaining Pope Pius IX's recent definition of the dogma of the Immaculate Conception. His careful research, and especially his attempt to live a life founded on Christ's teaching in the New Testament, had given him experiences indispensable for understanding the Catholic Church of his own day.

Newman's conclusive itinerary[36] into the fullness of the Catholic faith began, then, with his own encounter with the Christianity of the apostles and the fathers. They provided him with the original account of the great event of Christ. The experience of conversion at the age of fifteen and again at the age of twenty-seven impressed indelibly on his soul the image of the early church, which is in any case the normative portion of the church history. Most of all, it equipped him to understand, and finally to embrace, the whole phenomenon of Catholic dogma and worship, which developed in later centuries, especially since the twelfth century. It saved him from becoming a sceptic, or a 'liberal' as he preferred to call the

Christian of his day who could not see the meaning, harmony and splendour of the Christian dogmas. 'The most religiously minded men are ready to give up important doctrinal truths because they do not understand their value. A cry is raised that the creeds are unnecessarily minute, and even those who could defend them, through ignorance, cannot ... What is most painful is that the clergy are so utterly ignorant on the subject. We have no theological education.'[37]

His Task: Helping Catholics realise their Faith

His providential journey into the Catholic faith along an itinerary that took him from the edges of liberalism or scepticism through personal interiorisation of the originating experience of the Christian community, as these are articulated in the inspired literature of the New Testament and the authoritative texts of the fathers, also helped him to realise the job he had to do to help his contemporaries. He had to help them 'realise' the meaning of the creeds and dogmas they easily professed with their lips, but which they might have easily dismissed as unmeaningful or irrelevant to the business of living. This pastoral focus gives Newman's life its unity. He tried in tract and sermon and letter, to reveal to his hearers and readers the real content of the Catholic faith, the faith given once and for all to the saints. He strove to help them 'realise' this faith, being convinced of the twofold threat posed by the rising tide of scepticism, on the one hand, and shallow religiosity, on the other. He wanted people to have a 'real apprehension' as opposed to a merely 'notional apprehension' or grasp of their faith. He wished to lead them towards a 'real assent' or commitment to Christ. In the words of the apostle, he strove to help people 'know him in whom they believed'. This is the key to the *Grammar of Assent*, explaining both its content and purpose.

Newman knew what he was doing. He knew from his personal experience, as well as from his studies, that Catholic dogma and church life and worship are food and drink for the Christian who has made contact with Christ and his mystery. Without this experience they mean little or nothing to believers. From the abundance of his own heart Newman strove to raise a people for Christ. A measure of his success may be gauged from these words written many years later by one who heard Newman preach from the pulpit of St Mary's in Oxford: 'Newman's sermons came down like a new revelation. He had the wondrous, the supernatural power of raising the mind to God, and of rooting deeply in us a personal conviction of

God, and a sense of his presence. He compelled us to an intuitive perception of moral obligation – of that natural law of right, which is written in the mind by the word and wisdom of God.'[38]

A Striking Convergence

The parallel between Newman and Voegelin is striking. Both agree in their analysis of Christian history as a sequence of originating experiences, original account, and dogmatic exposition. Both underline the fact that when the originating deep experiences are not reached or lived, a twofold danger emerges: scepticism or fideistic piosity. Thirdly, they are one in pointing out the way of renewal: recover the original experiences and the original accounts, and then live them. Voegelin might well have been thinking of Newman when he wrote:

> … the experiences of transcendence are being recaptured in a peculiarly backhanded manner. For the experiences which had been reduced to shadows by dogmatic incrustations, and seemed to be removed from the reach of the living by the successive attacks of antitheologism and antimetaphysicism, have returned from limbo by the back door of historical knowledge. To a field that apparently had been cleared of them so that they would not disturb the futuristic dreams of *paradis artificiels*, they are being introduced as 'facts of history' – through the exploration of myth, of the Old and New Testaments, of apocalyptic and gnostic movements, through comparative religion, Assyriology, Egyptology, classical philology, and so forth.[39]

Fourthly, the living of the originating experiences means that one must be converted anew every day. To try to live as the apostles did, and as the fathers prescribe, is very demanding in everyday life. It requires conversion. Thus conversion is the personal and social key to the fruitful grasp of the church's life, worship and teaching in this latter part of the twentieth century. Finally, the authentic living of Christians is the key element or ingredient in the work of handing on the faith to the generations yet to be born, 'and so the church, in her teaching, life, and worship, perpetuates and hands on to all generations all that she herself is, all that she believes'.[40] Under Christ, who is the Lord of history, and in the church he founded on Peter and the twelve, the witness of authentic Christians hands on the faith quietly, yet effectively.

Covering the Facts

Theology is a reflection on faith and in faith. It attempts to understand and to express the faith of holy church. An immediate test of
how well it has done that might be its ability to throw some light on
key facts in the life of the church. The foregoing reflection on
Christian tradition seems to account for the following phenomena
in the church today.

1. The *Decree on Priestly Formation* of Vatican II reforms radically
the way dogmatic theology has been taught for centuries. Once the
professor began with the dogmas of the church and then proceeded
to justify them by appropriate citation of scripture and father and
council. The council proposes a complete reversal of this process:
'Dogmatic theology should be so arranged that the biblical themes
are presented first. Students should be shown what the fathers of
the Eastern and Western Church contributed to the fruitful transmission and illumination of the individual truths of revelation and
also the later history of dogma and its relationship to the general
history of the church.'[41]

2. The tone of the Second Vatican Council is in sharp contrast
with that of the First Vatican Council. The later council is biblical,
patristic and pastoral in tone. Its deliberations were guided by the
fruits of about sixty years of sustained biblical, patristic and historical and liturgical scholarship which had done much to recover the
balanced truth concerning the founding experiences of Christianity,
as well as by the gospel urge to preach the gospel effectively to the
whole of humanity, an urge personified so attractively in Pope John
XXIII.

3. The council was a call to conversion and to renewal *in capite et
in membris*. It proclaimed the call of Christ to all Christians to aim at
holiness of life and to live the gospel (Mk 1:14). Chapter five of
Lumen Gentium is a fine expression of this gospel call. On the
response of the people of God to this urgent summons will depend
the quality of presence of the church, and the measure of her influence on the world generally. It was the clear conviction of the council that only a lived Christianity will speak to our contemporaries.
'Modern man tends to believe witnesses more easily than he
believes teachers,' wrote Pope Paul VI.

4. There exists the phenomenon of an ecumenical movement.
This is a living proof that Christians are abandoning the battle cries
that have divided them for centuries. 'The church alone', or 'scripture alone', or 'today alone' are seen to be hopelessly inadequate
expressions of Christian authority. Instead of pointing the finger,

each Christian church is now renewing its fidelity to the Lord and his one gospel, and is seeking to consider dispassionately the possibility that, over centuries, it may have either lost or played down vital components of the originating revelation. Once again tradition, as the creative reliving of the original experiences in scripture and the fathers, fits well with the genuine spirit of the modern ecumenical movement.

5. The power and evangelising force of certain pathways in the church today should make the theologian think. The Focolare Movement puts primary emphasis on living the 'word of God', especially the words that have to do with mutual love as the new commandment of Jesus. A regular feature of this spirituality is the sharing of experiences of Jesus in the midst of those united in his name (Mt 18:20) and present in his word when lived. The Charismatic Movement emphasises the role of the Holy Spirit in prayer leading people into the experience of the lordship of the Risen Christ. These two movements, examples of the many that could be mentioned in the church today, highlight the necessity of the lived gospel as the key to the church's creative *anamnesis* of the past and loving *diakonia* in the present. Yet again the experience of these pathways of gospel living in the church of today seems to square with the view of tradition which we tried to develop in this chapter.

Come, Lord Jesus (Rev 22:20)

The symbol of marriage provides a concrete image or analogy for our grasp of tradition. In the light of this analogy it is easy to see tradition as the bride's fidelity to her Lord and to her children. In being faithful to her Lord and to her children she has to remember the promises of the covenant signed in the blood of his cross (Eph 2:11-18) and to transmit all his gifts to her children. Tradition demands this twofold fidelity. Tradition, then, is both *anamnesis* and *diakonia*, the creative reliving of the once for all experience that has made her, and the imaginative communication of her riches to the ever varying situations and needs of her children through the centuries. She loves to relive the romance of her youth by which she became his beloved bride. She longs to nourish her children today and always with all that Christ, who is her life (Col 3:4),[42] has given her. Or, to use the words of *Dei Verbum*, 'This sacred tradition, therefore, and sacred scripture of both the Old and New Testaments are like a mirror in which the pilgrim church on earth looks at God, from whom she has received everything, until she is brought finally to see him as he is, face to face (1 Jn 3:2)'.[43] She is conscious that the whole lifestyle of the family is what makes the family, and is the key factor in the formation and education of each of her children.

CHAPTER 6

In the Lists with the Doctrinal Liberals: the Strategy and the Struggle

There is much of that narrow spirit of that slothful servant (who buried his master's talent) at the present day, in which is strangely combined a profession of knowing everything, with an assertion that there is nothing to know concerning the Incarnation.[1]

The previous chapter made the point that Newman's understanding of tradition flowed into the theology of the council, in particular, the *Dogmatic Constitution on Divine Revelation*. This fact shows how influential the great cardinal's thinking has been. At the same time as he was discovering this insight, however, he saw all about him another fact – the rising tide of infidelity, an infidelity not motivated by crass immorality but by a gradual closure of the mind against the invisible and by a weakening of faith in the unseen world which revelation manifests. We will now present both Newman's struggle with this new world and his strategy for the transmission of the treasure of revelation in an age of reason and revolt.

In 1864, at the conclusion of his enforced autobiography, John Henry Newman expressed admiration for the great French 'liberal' Catholics, the Dominican Fr Lacordaire and Count Montalembert. 'The only singularity,' says Montalembert in his biography of the great Dominican, 'was his liberalism. By a phenomenon, at that time unheard of, this convert, this seminarist, this confessor of nuns, was just as stubborn a liberal as in the days when he was a student and a barrister'.[2] Newman declares that he is unable to differ in any important matter from these two men: 'In their general line of thought and conduct I enthusiastically concur, and consider them to be before their age.'[3] In spite of his adulation for these liberals, however, he refrains from using their language about liberalism, explaining that his rejection of the language is based on some differences between him and them 'in the use of words or in the circumstances of country'.[4]

The One Great Mischief

He not only rejects that language as the accurate account of his own line of thought and conduct, he also employs the word 'liberalism' to describe the 'one great mischief' of his times. In writing to a friend in March 1831 he expressed the view that the majority of the persons you meet generally are liberals. In saying they are liberals he realises he is 'saying almost as bad of them as can be said of anyone.'[5] Many years later, on the occasion of his becoming a cardinal, he repeated his protest against liberalism in religion: 'I rejoice to say, to one great mischief I have from the first opposed myself. For thirty, forty, fifty years I have resisted to the best of my powers the spirit of liberalism in religion. Never did holy church need champions against it more sorely than now, when, alas! it is an error overspreading, as a snare, the whole earth.'[6] On his own admission, then, it is legitimate to see Newman's life and work as a struggle against liberalism in religion.

Defining the Term

It seems that it was with real deliberation that Newman chose the word 'battle' to describe his struggle against liberalism: 'My battle was with liberalism; by liberalism I mean the anti-dogmatic principle and its developments.'[7] He saw it 'reducing the awesome mystery of God to the level of human understanding, human feeling and human convenience'.[8] Acknowledging that a description of liberalism as essentially the 'anti-dogmatic principle' tells us very little about it, he defines the phenomenon in a passage of considerable theoretic penetration.

> Now by liberalism I mean false liberty of thought, or the exercise of thought upon matters, in which, from the constitution of the human mind, thought cannot be brought to any successful issue, and therefore is out of place. Among such matters are first principles of whatever kind; and of these the most sacred and momentous are especially to be reckoned the truths of revelation. Liberalism then is the mistake of subjecting to human judgement those revealed doctrines which are in their nature beyond and independent of it, and of claiming to determine on intrinsic grounds the truth and value of propositions which rest for their reception simply on the external authority of the divine word.[9]

In other words, liberalism is rationalism in the field of religion, and it consists in making 'our reason the standard and measure of the doctrines revealed'. Earlier in the Essay on *The Development of Christian Doctrine* he offers the following description of liberalism:

> That truth and falsehood in religion are but matter of opinion; that one doctrine is as good as another; that the Governor of the world does not intend that we should gain the truth; that there is no truth; that we are not more acceptable to God by believing this than by believing that; that no one is answerable for his opinions; that they are a matter of necessity or accident; that it is enough if we sincerely hold what we profess; that our merit lies in seeking, not in possessing; that it is a duty to follow what seems to us true, without a fear lest it should not be true ... that we may safely trust to ourselves in matters of faith – this is the principle of philosophies and heresies, which is very weakness.[10]

Newman challenged this principle all his life long or at least from his well known experience of conversion at the age of fifteen. 'From the age of fifteen, dogma has been the fundamental principle of my religion: I know no other religion; I cannot enter into the idea of any other sort of religion; religion as a mere sentiment, is to me a dream and a mockery. As well can there be filial love without the fact of a father, as devotion without the fact of a Supreme Being.'[11] Decisive for his whole life was this conversion in 1816 when he 'fell under the influence of a definite creed, and received into his intellect impressions of dogma, which, through God's mercy, have never been effaced or obscured'.[12] His religion was dogmatic in the strict sense:[13] the great realities of God's gracious and loving self-communication were offered to men. 'Revealed religion,' he wrote in 1828, 'brings us into a new world – a world of overpowering interest,'[14] especially because Christianity is the presence of Persons, as he loved to repeat.[15]

Revelation a New World

The new world that revelation opens up and introduces to the sincere believer, brings before us the unfathomable riches of Christ and therefore demands our total obedience of faith.[16] This explains why Newman in his Anglican preaching insisted so much upon obedience to the word of God. 'Obedience, not a frame of mind, is the test,'[17] or, as he puts it in only his second sermon, 'I want a man on the one hand to confess his immortality with his lips, and on the other, to live as if he tried to understand his own words, and then he is on the way of salvation.'[18] He set out, particularly in those early homilies, to underline the claims of duty and the details of obedience.[19] It is not an exaggeration to say that the principal part of his mission in the Anglican Church consisted in the retrieval of the complete circle of the truths of revelation in scripture and in the fathers. This theological and apostolic goal inspired both the beginnings and subsequent development of the Oxford Movement.

First Principles of Liberalism
Perceptive commentators like Thomas Vargish point to the correlation between religious questions and philosophy of mind in Newman.[20] This is the key to the neatness with which he is able to encapsulate in clear propositions the central positions of the all-pervading, but equally elusive, spirit of liberal thinking in a note appended to the *Apologia*. It is worth quoting the first four of these propositions, which were familiar to Newman as far back as 1834.

> 1. No religious tenet is important, unless reason shows it to be so. Therefore, e.g. the doctrine of the Athanasian creed is not to be insisted on, unless it tends to convert the soul; and the doctrine of the atonement is to be insisted on, if it does convert the soul.
> 2. No one can believe what he does not understand.
> Therefore, e.g. there are no mysteries in true religion.
> 3. No theological doctrine is anything more than an opinion which happens to be held by bodies of men.
> Therefore, e.g. no creed as such is necessary for salvation.
> 4. It is dishonest in a man to make an act of faith in what he has not had brought home to him by actual proof.
> Therefore, e.g. the mass of men ought not absolutely to believe in the divine authority of the bible.[21]

Newman saw in these principles the seeds that would devastate the very heart of revealed religion. They constituted an inexorable and relentless philosophico-theological sequence leading from Anglicanism to Protestantism, from Protestantism to latitudinarianism, to liberalism and, finally, to atheism, as we will soon see.

Dogma mere Sentiment and Opinion
The 'march-of-mind'[22] represented by the rampant liberalism which Newman saw developing all around him is nowhere more clearly formulated than in the discourses on university education delivered between 1852-3 in Dublin. One of these discourses, 'A form of infidelity of the day,' portrays the sentiments and policy of liberalism in relation to the scientific nature of revealed religion and its study in theology. The liberals' 'fundamental dogma is, that

nothing can be known for certain about the unseen world'.[23] The pursuit of theological studies is the pursuit of a mirage. 'Christianity has been the bane of true knowledge, for it has turned the intellect away from what it can know, and occupied it with what it cannot.'[24]

It follows, as clearly as day the night, that Christianity lacks the credentials necessary for inclusion in the university curriculum. 'Religion is not the subject-matter of a science.'[25] Newman puts the following accusation against the Christian faith on the lips of the typical liberal, 'You may have opinions in religion, you may have theories, you may have arguments, you may have probabilities; you may have anything but demonstration, and therefore you cannot have science.'[26] This text is very revealing indeed, not only of the basic stance of the liberals towards religion and theology in the university, but also of the liberals' model of knowing, what might be called their epistemology.

This model consists in demonstration or in formal explicit reasoning 'from sure premises to sure conclusions'.[27] This model of scientific knowledge, inspired by Aristotelian logic and applied in the world of physics and mechanics since the time of Newton and Bacon, seemed simply to annihilate Christianity's claim to recognition in the general concerns of a university in the modern world. It also engendered 'a feeling, not merely of contempt, but of absolute hatred towards the Catholic theologian and the dogmatic teacher'.[28] As dogma, then, has no substance and Christianity in consequence no content, Christianity has no vital role to play in human living, and ought to be replaced by more substantial and scientific realities like economics and physics.[29] 'Thanks to the new philosophy, sight is able to contest the field with faith. The medieval philosopher had no weapon against revelation but metaphysics; physical science has a better temper, if not a keener edge for the purpose.'[30]

Not Without a Past

Such a radical standpoint did not emerge overnight. The liberal party in the Church of England began from insignificant elements about the turn of the eighteenth into the nineteenth century. A small elite group in four or five of the Oxford Colleges set about the renewal of the university, and began to exert 'an influence which made men of religious seriousness shrink into themselves'.[31] They did not put reason before faith, nor knowledge before devotion, but 'they unconsciously encouraged and successfully introduced into Oxford a licence of opinion which went far beyond them'.[32] They began in good faith to promote principles and practices but were not aware of the implications of their own chosen principles. In 1836 Renn Dickson Hampden was appointed Regius Professor of Divinity in Oxford and he sent Newman a copy of his pamphlet, 'The Scholastic Philosophy, considered in relation to Christian Theology'. What alarmed its reader was the distinction drawn between 'the simple religion of Christ' and theological opinion. Hampden included the doctrine of the Divine Trinity in theological opinion and contended that the Church of England was not yet liberal in its spirit.[33]

Still the atmosphere of the university was not yet liberal in its theology, and the genius of Keble, Froude, Pusey and the other leaders of the Oxford Movement temporarily turned the tide against the still uninfluential liberal party. When the liberals eventually succeeded in orchestrating the rejection of Newman's *Tract 90*, where he attempted to show the harmony between the Thirty-nine Articles and the basic doctrines of the church of the fathers, thereby pointing towards a possible Catholic interpretation of the Articles, he saw the cause of the liberals beginning to make real headway.[34] By the 1860s what had begun imperceptibly with a handful had become a popular movement of national proportions. 'Phaeton has got into the chariot of the sun; we, alas! can only look on, and watch him down the steep of heaven. Meanwhile, the lands, which he is passing over, suffer from his driving.'[35] By the time he writes his *Apologia* it is relatively easy for Newman to streamline the basic tenets of the liberal methods in theology.

Replacing Religion, Deforming Reason

The leader of the Oxford Movement saw in this liberalism both an evil and a tragic error. It was an evil in that it replaced God by man, the church by the state, and the laws of God by the traditions of men. It was an error in that it amounted to a massive deformation of human reason and relegated conscience, our true connection with God. The new philosophy was a stab near the heart of the truth, the ultimate abyss of God's counsels disclosed to us in Christ and made present in his church. Its basic position was that the church might be correct in theology but wrong scientifically. Or as Chesterton, re-echoing Newman, will put it years later, 'While we are being naturalists, we can suppose that Christianity is all nonsense; but then, when we remember that we are Christians, we must admit that Christianity is true even if it is nonsense.'[36]

The Christian faith is no longer anthropologically significant. It has nothing to say, and even less to offer, to men and women in the modern world when it comes to 'the more universal and eternal questions, (such as) the secrets of the human heart and conscience, the confrontation between life and death, the triumph over spiritual sorrow, the laws in the history of mankind that were born in the depths of time immemorial and that will cease to exist only when the sun ceases to shine'.[37] The Christian mysteries are 'words which make nonsense'.[38] The Christian anthropologist, historian, psychologist, sociologist, economist or scientist may safely assume that his Christian faith is meaningless while he is plying his trade, but when he remembers that he is a Christian, he must remember that his faith is true even if it is nonsense, for 'there is no positive truth in Christianity' and 'one creed is as good as another'.[39] And this explains yet another of the tenets of liberalism which he lists in 1864. 'No revealed doctrines or precepts may reasonably stand in the way of scientific conclusions. Therefore, e.g. political economy may reverse Our Lord's declarations about poverty and riches, or a system of ethics may teach that the highest condition of body is ordinarily essential to the highest state of mind.'[40]

In the Field of Education

A striking illustration of this 'march-of-mind' was exhibited in the field of education. Sir Robert Peel, leader of the Conservative party, and an orthodox churchman, unwittingly aired the liberals' view of education and disparaged Christian teaching in a speech at the opening of a reading room in Tamworth on 19th January 1841. He proclaimed the views of Jeremy Bentham's utilitarianism and of Bentham's disciple, Lord Brougham, for whom 'useful knowledge' became a substitute for religion.[41] Science and literature are to be the new curriculum of education. Religion has played out its part, and its function in the formation of the individual and the regeneration of English society can be morally catered for by science and literature.

Peel has expressed the typical liberal viewpoint on education that 'in becoming wiser a man will become better', meaning by wiser more conversant with the facts and theories of physical science; and that such a person will 'rise at once in the scale of intellectual and *moral* excellence'.[42] Virtue was the child of knowledge, vice of ignorance. The new ideal of education was secular: it did not openly reject Christianity, but simply substituted it as irrelevant because obsolete in the new world now emerging. In the pages of *The Times* Newman penned in reply seven sparkling 'Letters of

Catholicus', the last one appearing on February 27, 1841, the same day as *Tract 90*.[43]

The Fault of our Nature

He stoutly resists the view that such an education would make people moral or religious. He insists, 'To know is one thing, to do is another; the two things are altogether distinct.' Sir Robert Peel 'makes no pretence of subduing the giant nature, in which we were born'. Newman makes the comparison, 'When a child cries, the nursery maid dances it about, or points to the pretty black horses out of window, or shows how ashamed poll-parrot or poor puss must be of its tantrums.' The idea of useful knowledge as the new method and content of education 'is the new art of living, offered to the labouring classes, we will say, for instance, in a severe winter, snow on the ground, glass falling, bread rising, coal at 20d the cwt. and no work'. All that was in the second letter. In the third we find, 'Glory, science, knowledge, and whatever other fine names we use, never healed a wounded heart, nor changed a sinful one ... You do not get rid of vice by human expedients ... You must go to a higher source for renovation of heart and will. You do but play a sort of "hunt the slipper" with the fault of our nature, till you go to Christianity.'[44] The letters must be read to appreciate their humour and incisiveness.[45]

Exposing a Fallacy

As science reflects physical nature and literature 'is the life and remains of the *natural* man, innocent or guilty', they can neither cope with 'those giants, the pride and passion of man', nor supply the medicine for 'the fault of our nature'.[46] They are quite unable to provide a religion, a morality or an ethics. Peel 'offers to bribe the foe'.[47] 'Strong liquors, indeed, do for a time succeed in their object; but who was ever consoled in real trouble by the small beer of literature or science?' Literature and science cannot rise higher than their sources, and those sources are in the natural man and physical science respectively. To attempt to do by means of these instruments what was once done by Christian faith and sacrament is to be quite 'unreal'.[49] His words clinch the issue:

> People say to me, that it is but a dream to suppose Christianity should regain the organic power in human society which once it possessed. I cannot help that; I never said it could. I am not a politician; I am proposing no measures, but exposing a fallacy, and resisting a pretence. Let Benthamism reign, if men have no aspirations; ... do not attempt by phil-

osophy what was once done by religion. The ascendancy of faith may be impracticable, but the reign of knowledge is incomprehensible. The problem for statesmen of this age is how to educate the masses, and literature and science cannot give the solution.[50]

Thirty-eight years later, in his *Biglietto* Address, on the occasion of receiving the cardinal's hat from Pope Leo XIII, Newman will return to this theme, but with tones that correspond to the tragic progress and destructive inroads of liberalistic philosophy into the fabric of church and state in England. 'There is much in the liberalistic theory which is good and true; e.g. not to say more, the precepts of justice, truthfulness, sobriety, self-command, benevolence, which, as I have already noted, are among its avowed principles, and the natural laws of society.'[51] But these principles and laws have totalitarian claims made for them such that they supplant the revealed principles of the faith, and the fundamental laws of life and love in the church. What does Newman think of this usurpation? 'It is not till we find that this array of principles is intended to supersede, to block out religion, that we pronounce it to be evil.'[52] Educational liberalism shows up literature in its true colours as a straightforward assault on revelation and Christian faith. It is not only an error but, more seriously, an evil. 'There never was a device of the enemy so clearly framed and with such promise of success.'[53] The logic of his analysis seems to justify both this assessment and prognosis of the future course of liberalism. Not only would the growth of civilisation have a bearing on the faith, it would necessarily modify it.[54]

Newman's Struggle: Relativising the Relativisers
'I wrote against most of the propositions of liberalism in some part or other of my Anglican works', Newman declared in the *Apologia*. He also contributed to joint works such as the *Lyra Apostolica* which was published in 1836 and has a poem on liberalism. 'The Age to Come' defines 'the position and prospects of liberalism':

> When I would search the truths that in me burn,
> And mould them into rule and argument,
> A hundred reasoners cried – 'Hast thou to learn
> Those dreams are settled now, those fires are spent?'
> And did I mount to simpler thoughts, and try
> Some theme of peace, 'twas still the same reply.
>
> Perplexed, I hoped my heart was pure of guile,

> But judged me weak in wit, to disagree;
> But now I see, that men are mad awhile,
> And joy the age to come will think of me;
> 'Tis the old history: Truth without a home,
> Despised and slain; then rising from the tomb.[55]

The challenge posed by the liberals drew from Newman a lifelong response which we will now describe. The principal strands in that response are his recovery of the doctrinal and liturgical riches of the early centuries, his articulation of the truth about the human mind and knowing, and his tentative outline of a *organon investigandi* for Catholic theology.

I. RECOVERING THE FULL CIRCLE OF REVEALED TRUTHS

The only real question for Newman after his conversion in 1816 and again in 1827[56] was, where can we discover the truth revealed by God? Where is revealed Christianity in all its fullness? In 1831 a request, destined to be providential, was made to him to write a book on the early councils of the church to be part of a series for a theological library. He completed the work in only fifteen months. *The Arians of the Fourth Century* focuses on the first ecumenical council. 'As he proceeded he became more and more convinced that the early church was the true exponent of the revealed teaching of Christianity,'[57] as we have seen. Praised later by Döllinger as a 'work which will be read and studied in future generations as a model of its kind,'[58] it deals with the reasons for the definition of Our Lord's divinity in terms of the *homoousion*. The process of definition and defence of the scriptural truth would be necessary with the passing of time when the voices of the apostles were no longer heard in the church and the contrary voices of heresy were raised as in the case of Arius of Alexandria. By the end of 1832 he had recovered in substantial completeness the full circle of truths.

Living the Truth

The use he made of these truths was extraordinary: while revealed religion won the allegiance of his mind, the call to holiness fascinated him. 'Holiness before peace,' became his motto. He tried to base his whole life on the truths of revelation, while his preaching was an attempt to provide the students of Oxford and the people of his parish with real foundations for Christian living. The lasting power and quite extraordinary beauty of *The Parochial and Plain Sermons* are proof that Newman's religion was neither a dull dogmatism nor a harping moralism, but rather good news for those who heard him. 'The Holy Spirit dwells in body and soul, as in a temple. Evil spirits indeed have power to possess sinners, but his indwelling is able to search into all our thoughts, and penetrate into every motive of the heart. Therefore, he pervades us (if it may be so said) as light pervades a building, as a sweet perfume the folds of some honourable robe; so that in scripture language, we are said to be in him and he in us. It is plain that such an inhabitation brings the Christian into a state altogether new and marvellous.'[59] It was this recovery of, together with the ability to communicate, the truths of revelation that made him the inspiring leader of the Oxford Movement from 1833 onwards.

Liberal Amnesia
Newman simply indicted the liberals of a repudiation of this authoritative portion of the church's life. They conveniently ignored the importance of tradition and the councils. Given their guiding principles, of course, this was as understandable as it was devastating for the church. In the *University Sermons* he castigates the liberals' 'irreverence towards antiquity ... the profanation of the church, the bold transgression of the duty of ecclesiastical unity – the growing indifference to the Catholic creed, the sceptical objections'.[60]

No Museum Religion
It was no museum religion, however, which Newman wanted revived. The Christian faith, he loved to say, may have its origins in great and glorious events in the past, but its power is in the present. 'We do not contemplate it in conclusions drawn from dead events and dumb documents,' he once wrote, 'but by faith exercised in ever-living objects, and by the appropriation and use of ever-recurring gifts.'[61] In 1845 he wrote that he was the first writer who made life the mark of a true church.[62] And here we meet a theme in Newman's personal faith-itinerary that is characteristic, the development of doctrine.

A Religion for all Seasons
This aspect of the Christian faith struck him profoundly.[63] Not only was revealed religion for today, not only was it capable of changing sinful hearts and setting them on the road to holiness of life, it also displayed remarkable signs of vitality. Nicholas Lash is correct, it seems, in claiming that 'Newman was one of the first Catholic theologians seriously to hold in tension the demands of historical con-

sciousness and the Christian conviction that the gospel of Jesus Christ is irreplaceable and unchangeable.'[64] Newman insists that Catholic dogma 'is one, absolute, integral, indissoluble while the world lasts'.[65] 'The conviction of Christian belief is that the message proclaimed in the life, death and resurrection of Jesus Christ is God's definitive word to mankind' so that 'unless the word proclaimed to the men of every generation, age and culture is, in some significant sense, the same word, God's promise is not fulfilled'.[66] He gave his mind to the idea of doctrinal development in 1842, although 'it had been a favourite subject with (him) all along'.[67]

Growth the only Sign of Life

His great crux with Rome lay in her devotional excesses towards Mary and the saints, as well as emphasis on the role of the papacy in the life of the church, 'the variations of popery', as he once called them. These represented 'corruptions' and 'innovations' in the faith of the apostles and the fathers. But now beginning to realise that, on the one hand, revelation must develop in the mind of the church as the church appropriates this revelation, and that, on the other hand, the Anglican position was no longer tenable, he saw the hypothesis of doctrinal development as a likely explanation of the Roman 'corruptions'. 'The simple question (was), "*where*, what is this thing in this age, which in the first age was the Catholic Church?"'[68] The effort at verification of that hypothesis resulted in the *Essay on the Development of Christian Doctrine*. 'If that book is asked, why does its author join the (R) Catholic Church?, the answer is, because it is the church of St Athanasius and St Ambrose.'[69]

Permanence and Growth in Tension

But there was more: the principle of development of doctrine 'not only accounted for certain facts, but was in itself a remarkable philosophical phenomenon, giving a character to the whole course of Christian thought'.[70] It showed how the Catholic faith was permanent yet growing: permanent because 'the faith given once for all to the saints' (Jude 3), growing because in the life of the Christian and in the history of the church 'the abyss of God's counsels'[71] was capable of increasing assimilation. In particular, it demonstrated how the Roman Catholic Church combined and harmonised the ideas of continuity and development.

> The idea of the Blessed Virgin was, as it were, *magnified* in the Church of Rome, as time went on – but so were all the Christian ideas; as that of the Blessed Eucharist. The whole

scene of pale, faint, distant apostolic Christianity is seen in Rome, as through a telescope or magnifier. The harmony of the whole, however, is of course what it was. It is unfair then to take one Roman idea, that of the Blessed Virgin, out of what may be called its context.[72]

In his penetrating introduction to Newman's *Philosophical Notebook* E. Sillem devotes a lengthy section to Newman's 'personal liberalism', some principal tenets of which were the richness or mysteriousness of each person or thing before us, the intrinsically developmental nature of life, and the concreteness of all thought as 'the reasoning of the concrete being'.[73]

II. LIBERALISM AS THE DEFORMATION OF HUMAN REASON

As we have seen, the basic intellectual argument of the liberals against revealed religion was that it was unscientific because it lacked 'demonstration'.[74] It lacked the methodological techniques of inquiry, investigation and induction underpinning the new natural sciences. At best Christian faith and theology were only matters of taste and sentiment. The liberals tried to devise 'what cannot be, some sufficient science of reasoning which may compel certitude in concrete conclusions'.[75] In the attempt they ended up with a view of the mind and its operations that Newman describes as 'theoretical and unreal'.[76]

The liberals reduced all reasoning to the form of the syllogism. Unless one could begin with premises that were certain, there was no hope of reaching a certain conclusion. Only such conscious, 'scientific' and methodic argument led to the truth.

Newman challenged the reductionism in this position all the way from the *University Sermons* to the *Grammar* where he sets out 'the real and necessary method' of reasoning.[77] This work, hailed as 'the masterpiece in the field of epistemology',[78] shows how the conclusions of formal demonstrations are always probable, because dependent on the truthfulness of premises. Furthermore, this calculus of knowledge had distinct and limited provinces, and was quite inapplicable and irrelevant in the provinces of history, ethics and religion. In these provinces the method would have to fit the subject-matter under study.

The Way to the Truth

What, then, is the way to the truth? The *Grammar* maps the route. This route we have briefly looked at in chapter III. We saw that the key to that most original composition is the difference between

inference and assent, or between 'inferential' or 'syllogistic' method
and 'cumulative' method. 'The real and necessary method is ... the
cumulation of probabilities, independent of each other, arising out
of the nature and circumstances of the particular case which is
under review; probabilities too fine to avail separately, too subtle
and circuitous to be convertible into syllogisms, too numerous and
various for such conversion, even were they convertible.'[79] We can
reach the truth, that which is, by the act of assent or true judgement
which is precisely the mind's power of terminating a process of reasoning. True judgement, which the illative sense performs, thus
'determines what science cannot determine, the limit of converging
probabilities and the reasons sufficient for a proof'.[80]

Saving Reason from Reason

In elaborating the truth about our capacity to know truth, Newman
has exposed the high-sounding claims of the liberal view of the
mind for what these claims are in truth: a restrictive and narrowing
rationalism fitting the mind into moulds, and a consequent obstacle
closing off the human spirit from the discovery of vital truths in history, ethics, morality, religion and theology. His great achievement
consists in his liberation of the human mind from the shackles of
rationalism that claimed to be open and liberal, but which in fact
was closed to reality and limiting of the human person.[81] Eric
Voegelin claims that 'we do not live in a "post-Christian", "post-
philosophical", or "neo-pagan" age, or in the age of a "new myth",
or of "utopianism", but plainly in a period of massive deculturation
through the deformation of reason.'[82] With that verdict I believe
Newman would agree.

'Liberalism: A Half-way House tending towards Atheism'

It is a consensus among Newman scholars that he was very aware
of the galloping impact of the Enlightenment on Europe in general.
In particular, he saw how the Enlightenment weakened the Judaeo-
Christian view of life at the very time as it genuinely advanced the
natural and human sciences. The result was a shock to the culture of
Newman's time. That shock became increasingly manifest to him. It
expressed itself as a deepening polarisation between a religious
view of reality and a merely rational one, as if faith were the enemy
of reason and science, and science were the enemy of faith. In an
early letter he addressed himself to this 'current of the world'[83]
where he saw 'the most religiously-minded men ready to give up
important doctrinal truths because they do not *understand their*

value … what is most painful is the fact that the clergy are so utterly ignorant on the subject.'[84]

In 1873, many years later he is even more definite in a perceptive sermon. 'I think the trials which lie before us are such as would appal and make dizzy even such courageous hearts as St Athanasius and St Gregory, and they would confess that, dark as the prospect of their own day was to them severally, ours has a darkness different in kind from any that has been before it . Christianity has never yet had the experience of a world simply irreligious.'[85] Finally, towards the end of his life he wrote: 'From the time that I began to occupy my mind with theological subjects I have been troubled at the prospect, which I considered to lie before us, of an intellectual movement against religion, so special as to have a claim upon the attention of all educated Christians.'[86]

A Cultural Polarisation

The choice was going to be, in the ultimate analysis, between Catholicism and atheism as the two polarisations. 'There was no medium, in true philosophy, between atheism and Catholicity, and a perfectly consistent mind, under the circumstances in which it finds itself here below, must embrace either the one or the other.'[87] This comment, however, was easily misunderstood as an admission by Newman that he had no arguments for the truthfulness of the Catholic faith, or rather that the only argument he had was that Catholicism was the only genuinely complete alternative to atheism. He replied to this misrepresentation with two points.

First, he recalled his many writings in defence of revealed religion and refreshed his readers' minds on the range of evidence and argument he advanced on behalf of the one church of Christ. Then he explained that there is 'a certain *élan* of thought impelling some towards Christ, while another *élan* attracts in the opposite direction. There is a certain ethical character, one and the same, a system of first principles, sentiments and tastes, a mode of viewing the question and of arguing, which is formally and normally, naturally and divinely, the *organum investigandi* given us for gaining religious truth, and which would lead the mind by an infallible succession from the rejection of atheism to theism, and from theism to Christianity, and from Christianity to Evangelical religion, and from these to Catholicity.'[88]

Ascending and Descending

There is, then, an ascending movement of inquiry and faith, and there is a contrary descending movement as well. These two counter movements differentiate in terms of the character, moral, spiritual and intellectual, of the person, and so not in terms of the objective matter of revealed religion nor in terms of the evidences which are real and objective, but which are not capable of compelling acceptance. 'The multitude of men,' he explains, 'are not consistent, logical, or thorough; they obey no law in the course of their religious views; and while they cannot reason without premisses, and premisses demand first principles, and first principles must ultimately be (in one shape or another) assumptions, they do not recognise what this involves.'[89] It is the concrete being that reasons, and the concrete being is the sum of his 'first principles'.[90]

Love for the Truth leads to the Truth

A tragic flaw in the liberal outlook was the tacit assumption that the human person is a rational animal only, and not as well 'a seeing, feeling, contemplating, acting animal',[91] who will judge, decide and act according to the first principles that constitute his real being. What Newman identifies as central in the pursuit of truth is a love for the truth, a regard for the good combined with an aversion to evil. 'Logic makes but a sorry rhetoric with the multitude: first shoot around corners, and you may not despair of converting by a syllogism.'[92] Bernard Lonergan comments appositely, 'Basically the issue is a transition from the abstract logic of classicism to the concreteness of method. On the former view what is basic is proof. On the latter view what is basic is conversion. Proof appeals to an abstraction named right reason. Conversion transforms the concrete individual to make him capable of grasping not merely conclusions but principles as well.'[93] Newman is convinced that 'we judge for ourselves, by our own light, and on our own principles; and our criterion of truth is not so much the manipulation of propositions, as the intellectual and moral character of the person maintaining them, and the ultimate silent effect of his arguments or conclusions upon our minds'.[94]

This is Newman's final answer to the liberals who would sit at home and wait for God and his Christ to come to them and convince them. The assumption underlying this attitude derives from a liberal 'first principle' according to which man is the measure of God. The fact that the world 'thinks itself a judge of religious truth, without preparation of heart',[95] is the inevitable result of this first principle.

III. TOWARDS A SKETCH OF AN 'ORGANON INVESTIGANDI'

Newman's reply to the liberals, however, contained a positive alternative to their theological positions and not only a refutation. True, he preferred to address himself to particular issues and problems of his day and felt himself a little unreal whenever he set out to write treatises. Still, one of the abiding concerns of his life was the sketching of a 'new philosophy' for Christianity.

The new age of liberal civilisation would require a 'new theology'. In 1836 Newman wrote to Hurrell Froude that 'James Stephen wanted from him a new philosophy. He wanted Christianity developed to meet the age.'[96] The *Grammar of Assent* is his final response to this need which preoccupied him for the whole of his life. It attempts a sketch of the method of investigation Newman judged to be appropriate to theology in the broadest sense. This purpose is identified in a note which, ten years after its first printing, he appended to the *Grammar*. In it he says, 'A main reason for this *Essay on Assent* was, as far as I could, to describe the *organum investigandi* which I thought the true one.'[97]

Already upon the first publication of the *Grammar* one reader wrote in these enthusiastic tones: 'No-one, as far as I know, has ever done for theology what Bacon did for physical science, and since I saw the announcement of your essay, I have been looking for its appearance with great curiosity and interest, for there are many passages in your writings which indicate that you had given very much thought to many of the questions which would be illustrated in a theological *Novum Organon*.'[98] This verdict is surely exaggerated, since Newman sets out an *organon investigandi*, and not a *Novum Organon*, in the *Grammar*. His letter in reply puts the distinction beyond all doubt, 'You have truly said that we need a *Novum Organum* for theology – and I shall be truly glad if I shall be found to have made any suggestions which will aid the formation of such a calculus – but it must be the strong conception and the one work of a great genius, not the obiter attempt of a person like myself, who has already attempted many things, and is at the end of his day.'[99] The *Grammar of Assent* is not a *Novum Organon* for theology but the earnest suggestion of elements that might contribute to the eventual outline of such a calculus. Here, once again, Newman leaves us with 'colossal fragments', not 'finished edifices'.[100]

Part Three: Fruits

'That a thing is true, is no reason that it should be said, but that it should be done; that it should be acted upon; that it should be made our own inwardly.'

(Parochial and Plain Sermons, *V*, 45)

CHAPTER 7

Fidelity to Conscience: The Way to the Truth

The name of John Henry Newman is particularly associated with the reality of conscience.[1] The attention which his thinking on this theme continues to attract is proof of the seminal quality of his insight into the subject.[2] That the subject was uppermost in his life and thought can be seen at once in a comment like the following: 'Were it not for this voice speaking so clearly in my conscience and my heart, I should be an atheist, or a pantheist, or a polytheist when I looked into the world.' The context of this quotation, which is simultaneously arresting and provocative, is that of the proofs of the existence of God. 'These do not warm or enlighten me,'[3] he admits, though he is 'far from denying the real force of the arguments in proof of a God, drawn from the general facts of human society and the course of history.'[4]

The Way of Proof

Here he had in mind, almost certainly, the proofs, of a formal deductive kind, advanced by contemporaries like William Paley (1743-1805). 'This clearheaded and almost mathematical reasoner,' as Newman described him,[5] published his *View of the Evidences of Christianity* in 1794. His work became famous for its clarity of style, its 'clear, clever and powerful'[6] argument, and its appeal to the objective testimony of facts. Still, Newman did not warm to its method,[7] neither in the proofs for the existence of God nor in its validation of Christian revelation.

A Twofold Reserve

His reserve stemmed from two quarters. First, he did not like the idea of putting God on trial, as it were. 'Like this is the conduct of those who resolve to treat the Almighty with dispassionateness, a judicial temper, clearheadedness and candour.'[8] This disposition implies, when it does not actually insinuate, that the subject-matter of faith and theology is to be treated like the subject-matter of the natural scientist. This, surely, is an enormous mistake in method, which Aristotle highlighted in the *Nicomachean Ethics* when he considers the variations in the logical perfection of proof in various subject matters. 'A well educated man will expect exactness in every class of subject, according as the nature of the thing admits; for it is much the same mistake to put up with a mathematician using probabilities, and to require demonstration from an orator.'[9] Newman always feared the reduction of the divine Mystery to the proportions of a problem on which it would then be possible to descant.[10]

But there is also a second reason why this 'syllogistic method' is inadequate as an access to God. It assumes that human beings are perfectly rational, totally committed to the search for 'the truth that sets us free' (Jn 8:32), and unhindered by the power of passion and pride, and by attachment to prejudice. For Newman such dispositions are in the nature of an achievement, not a starting possession. 'Syllogistic method' is an approach which is 'theoretical and unreal'.[11] 'After all,' he writes, 'man is *not* a reasoning animal; he is a seeing, feeling, contemplating, acting animal. He is influenced by what is direct and precise.'[12]

What, then, is 'the Criterion of Truth'?
The truth is that 'our criterion of truth is not so much the manipulation of propositions, as the intellectual and moral character of the person maintaining them.'[13] The intellect is made for truth, its very homeland, but the rays of 'truth stream in upon us through the medium of our moral as well as our intellectual being; and that, in consequence, that perception of its first principles which is natural to us is enfeebled, obstructed, perverted, by allurements of sense and supremacy of self, and, on the other hand, quickened by aspirations after the supernatural.'[14] In that perspective it is easy to see why Newman did not follow 'modes of argument such as Paley's', where people 'act, not as suppliants but as judges' and 'sit at home, instead of stirring themselves to inquire.'[15]

The Way to the Truth: Right Reasoning
It is no surprise at all, then, that Newman should give a central importance to conscience in our access to moral, spiritual and divine truth. In doing so it is not his intention at all to denigrate the function and range of the human intellect. In fact, Newman is the great defender of the dignity of this level of human consciousness. The only formal treatise he ever wrote, *A Grammar of Assent*, set out

the modes of thought which are proper to our nature and insisted that we follow them in our intellectual exercises.[16] The principal thesis of that seminal work is that the restriction of mind to formal demonstration represents a gratuitous and unwarranted reduction of its range. The mind is greater than all its works, of which demonstration is only one, and science a product! In the power of the intellect to reach true judgement, which Newman colourfully calls 'the illative sense', the human person reaches reality, 'that which is'.

In an unfinished letter to the scientist William Froude, written in 1879, he claims,

> first that there is a mental faculty which reasons in a far higher way than that of merely measuring the force of conclusions by the force of premises; and next, that the mind has the power of determining ethical questions, which serve as major premises to syllogisms, without depending upon experience. And now I add a third, which is as important as any: the gradual process by which great conclusions are forced upon the mind, and the confidence of their correctness which the mind feels from the fact of that gradualness.[17]

This is as near a summary of the central insight in the *Grammar* as is possible and shows up this work as a masterpiece of epistemology, providing a succinct refutation of empirical narrowness in whatever guise.

And yet Newman gives the palm to conscience in our access to reality in its higher moral and spiritual echelons. We will now study in some detail his preference for this way of knowledge. Its importance resides in the fact that it enables us to reach God and, at the same time, to detect his presence in the centre of our being, 'closer to us than we are to ourselves' (St Augustine). This in turn will allow us to speak convincingly and critically of moral experience and of religious experience, yes even of moral experience as religious experience![18]

The Way to Truth: Conscience
On many and varied occasions Newman speaks of conscience.[19] We will expound the central content in his idea of conscience which 'is nearer to me than any other means of knowledge,'[20] and whose operations have the most momentous implications both for this and for the next life. For if human existence is uniquely an imperative to live by the truth and a call to advance towards one's original goal as given by God,[21] it must follow that the place and formation of conscience, 'the faculty for gaining moral truth' and spiritual reality,

play the decisive role in the drama of each person's existence, indeed of the whole human community.

What, then, is conscience? In the *Grammar* he answers thus, 'Conscience is a moral sense, and a sense of duty; a judgement of reason and a magisterial dictate.' These distinct aspects of conscience do not divide its act, as it were. 'Though I lost my sense of the obligation which I lie under to abstain from acts of dishonesty, I should not in consequence lose my sense that such actions were an outrage offered to my moral nature.'[22]

Since conscience is a moral judgement and a moral imperative or dictate, one and the same act has 'both a critical and judicial office.'[23] In its judicial sense, conscience is a faculty determining right and wrong. Here Newman takes issue with the view elaborated in the previous century by David Hume for whom conscience has a distinctly subjectivist connotation. For Hume conscience does not really know. It 'feels', and these feelings then become the guide to right behaviour. Conscience in this view 'operates without ratiocination, with the immediacy of feeling'.[24]

Newman repudiates this 'emotional' sense of conscience. Conscience is able to know what is right and what is wrong. It determines these two ultimately definitive qualities of every human action. It is therefore an act of our rational and intelligent nature. Grave notices how Newman already stresses this point in the *Oxford University Sermons* where conscience 'seems to detect moral truth wherever it is hid.'[25]

Knowing the Truth

Its mode of knowing is 'an implicit act of reasoning'. Here one is face to face with a quintessential Newman distinction between explicit and formal reasoning, on the one hand, and implicit and informal reasoning, on the other. In the realms of history, ethics and theology, implicit reasoning is the normal mode of reasoning, which the mind cannot 'count up and methodise in an argumentative form.'[26]

The process of reasoning by which conscience makes moral judgements is not available to experience. It shows up as a simple act, so that it is both unconscious and implicit.[27] Since this dimension of conscience involves an act of reasoning, it is quite inaccurate to substitute 'perception for reasoning in matters of religion', or 'logically immediate insight,'[28] or an intuitionist view of our moral knowledge. These are misleading directions in the investigation of the nature of conscience which always involves a practical judgement terminating the process of reasoning just described. This

'judgement of reason' bears upon a particular matter or course of
action that has been done or is about to be done. In order to elabo-
rate it further Newman compared and paralleled it to Aristotle's
teaching on *phronesis* or practical judgement.

Light from Aristotle

Edward Sillem and Gérard Verbeke rightly alert us to the preponderant
influence of the ethical works of the great Greek upon the developing insight of Newman. The ethical works, not the metaphysical.[29]
Newman admits his debt. 'As regards moral duty, the subject is
fully considered in the well known ethical treatises of Aristotle. He
calls the faculty which guides the mind in matters of conduct, by
the name of *phronesis*, or judgement.'[30] In a note added in the 1889
edition of the *Grammar* Newman specifies that the treatment of
phronesis in the *Nichomachean Ethics* highlights this faculty's ability
to determine truth in the concrete and contingent domain (*ta prak-
ta*), and not 'in its general relation to truth and the affirmation of
truth.'[31] For Newman, Aristotle's doctrine of *phronesis* is 'undoubtedly true' and particularly helpful in the understanding of the judicial side of the act of conscience.

Comparing like unto like, then, Newman describes the nature of
conscience as a moral sense. His words speak eloquently:

> This (*phronesis*) is the directing, controlling, and determining
> principle in such matters, personal and social. What it is to be
> virtuous, how we are to gain the just idea and standard of
> virtue, how we are to approximate in practice to our own
> standard, what is right and wrong in a particular case, for the
> answers in fullness and accuracy to these and similar ques-
> tions, the philosopher refers us to no code of laws, to no
> moral treatise, because no science of life, applicable to the
> case of an individual, has been or can be written.[32]

Still, it would be premature to conclude that 'Newman borrowed
his teaching on the illative sense from Aristotle'. It is more accurate,
continues Verbeke to see in the illative sense Newman's own particular employment of Aristotle, and this results in 'some striking like-
nesses between both teachings, especially in the relative value of
formal arguing and the close connection between concrete knowledge and the moral character of the subject.'[33]

Conscience and the Science of Ethics

It is from this dimension of conscience that the science of ethics
flows. Here the supreme enterprise of determining the moral good

is undertaken. The fact that every person has by definition a conscience is a first principle of this science which is central to human beings, human society and human history, since society is the person written large, and history is society written long, as Plato observes. Newman saw full well that this science of morality was an enduring imperative for the whole human family, but one continually imperilled also. Writing in 1875 he frankly comments, 'Words such as these are idle verbiage to the great world of philosophy now ... Literature and science have been embodied in great institutions in order to put it (conscience) down ... We are told that conscience is but a twist in primitive and untutored man.'[34] It is but little wonder that Pope John Paul II finds it necessary to write an encyclical on the very subject of the knowability of the moral good which opens up 'the path of the moral life' and where 'the way of salvation is open to all'. In a very scriptural key the Pope discusses the judgement of conscience, asserting that it 'is a *practical judgement*, a judgement which makes known what man must do or not do, or which assesses an act already performed by him'.[35]

Conscience Reads Out the Content of the Natural Law
As an act of cognition, conscience reaches after the knowledge of the good intended by the creator for his creatures. In the Christian tradition this good is imprinted on the heart of the creature and is called the Natural Law. Numerous texts of holy scripture either describe or refer to it. The text from Romans 2:14-15 stands out vividly. 'Pagans who never heard of the Law but are led by reason to do what the Law commands, may not actually "possess" the Law, but they can be said to "be" the Law. They can point to the substance of the Law engraved on their hearts – they can call a witness, that is, their own conscience – they have accusation and defence, that is, their own inner mental dialogue.'

In A *Letter to the Duke of Norfolk* Newman quotes both St Augustine and St Thomas on the nature of this law, and summarises them as follows:

> God has the attributes of justice, truth, wisdom, sanctity, benevolence and mercy, as eternal characteristics of his nature, the very law of his Being, identical with himself; and next, when he became Creator, he implanted this Law, which is himself, in the intelligence of all his rational creatures. The Divine Law, then, is the rule of ethical truth, the standard of right and wrong, a sovereign, irreversible, absolute authority in the presence of men and angels.[36]

Now conscience reads this Law in the individual mind and for the particular contingent course of action to be entered upon or which has already been performed. In that sense conscience exercises a mediational role since it detects the good of the natural law that is to be chosen and done 'here and now'. Newman quotes Cardinal Gasset, 'This (that is the divine) law is the rule of our conduct by means of our conscience; as the Fourth Lateran council says, *"quidquid fit contra conscientiam, aedificat ad gehennam"*.'[37] On this cognitive side of conscience, Newman uses the classical description of 'the voice of God'. Conscience is nothing less than 'the voice of God in the nature and heart of man as distinct from the voice of revelation.[38] But more about the voice of revelation later. In the meantime we must deal with the other dimension of conscience as a 'magisterial dictate', unlike any other in all creation.

Conscience as a Magisterial Dictate

To speak of conscience as a voice is to highlight its cognitive side, the fact that it is a judgement of reason in which the human being knows the good. But this voice is not only informative, it is more particularly imperious and commanding, 'a term which we should never think of applying to the sense of the beautiful; and moreover a voice, or the echo of a voice, imperative and constraining, like no other dictate in the whole of our experience'.[39] In its indivisible act, therefore, conscience tells us of the good and commands us to do it. The result is that we know ourselves to be addressed by a voice requiring obedience, 'a stern monitor'.[40] Furthermore, for Newman this latter sense is 'its primary and most authoritative aspect; it is the ordinary sense of the word'.[41]

The Experience of This Echo: What Does it Mean?

The sensitive, dutiful person grows and advances in his sense of God in proportion as he listens to the echo of that voice of conscience. Newman provides a fascinating analysis of this appearance of God in conscience. It involves three stages or moments. First, there is the 'emotional' phase where the specific 'phenomena of conscience'[42] register their presence. These phenomena are more generally classified under the headings of a 'good' and a 'bad conscience'.

On doing wrong one is possessed by a plethora of emotions including distress and apprehension, compunction and regret, confusion, self-reproach, poignant shame, haunting remorse, chill dismay at the prospect of the future, and the like. On obeying conscience one senses the very opposite sequence of emotions such as self-approval, inward peace, lightness of heart and so forth. Here Newman provides a kind of phenomenology, even pathology, of the emotions associated with our acceptance or rejection, as the case may be, of the sovereign commands of conscience.

But now, secondly, all this raises a central quest. Since 'we are not affective towards a stone, nor do we feel shame before a horse or a dog', the cause of these emotions cannot belong to this world. Instead 'these feelings in us are such as require for their exciting cause an intelligent being'. The gamut of emotions of a good or bad conscience powerfully argues the existence of a Person 'to whom we are responsible, before whom we are ashamed, whose claims upon us we fear'.[43] In this way 'its very existence carries on our minds to a being exterior to ourselves ... Its very existence throws us out of ourselves to go and seek for him in the height and the depth, whose voice it is'.[44]

Thirdly and finally, this reflection on 'the exciting cause' of these emotions brings home to us not only the existence of a Personal Being, but, more precisely, the exact attributes of the Supreme Being. This third phase in the ascent of conscience to the 'ethical character' of the Creator is of huge significance for Newman, since he is concerned to show how we actually gain an 'imaginative' or 'real apprehension' of his Being, and how we give a real assent to the proposition that 'there is one God, such and such in nature and attributes'.[45] In this context, he asks the famous question, 'Can I believe as if I saw?'[46]

'Can I Believe as if I Saw?'

Now clearly the answer to this question has to be negative. God is not an object among others, and still less an object within the world surrounding us. 'Si comprehenderis, non est Deus' (St Augustine). But this does not deter Newman from the effort to show that we can arrive at a real apprehension of God's attributes. The way thereto is the way of conscience on its imperative side. The function performed by the mind with regard to the external world has its precise parallel in the function performed by conscience with regard to the Supreme Being. 'From the perceptive power which identifies the intuitions of conscience with the reverberations or echoes (so to say) of an external admonition, we proceed on to the notion of a Supreme Ruler and Judge, and then again we image him and his attributes in those recurring intuitions, out of which, as mental phenomena, our recognition of his existence was originally gained.'[47] So vivid is this perception of the attributes of God, his truth, holiness, justice, that conscience may be declared 'the connecting principle between the creature and his creator'.

What stands out here is the place given to conscience in our knowledge of God. Or should we say the importance given to obedience to conscience. Since only a delicate instrument can receive distant transmissions, only a delicate and obedient conscience is capable of apprehending the attributes of God in 'the phenomena of conscience'. Thus fidelity to conscience is the royal road to God and the great internal teacher of religion, without which no external teacher will be of lasting value. It is on this premise that Newman drinks to conscience first and to the Pope afterwards.[48] Conscience enjoys an existential, not an ontological, primacy over Pope and council. A practised and sustained fidelity to the sovereignty of conscience sharpens, as it were, the one instrument we possess to hear and take to heart the voice of God, whether in nature or in revelation. 'If then, the light inside you is darkness, what darkness that will be!' (Mt 6:23).

A Theocentric Religion

Newman's religion, then, has both a theocentric character and an anthropocentric character since 'conscience is the connecting principle between the creature and the Creator'. As the dictates of conscience are accepted and obeyed, as the one acting in and through these same dictates is apprehended and noticed, so his character as holy and just and good is apprehended. 'For Newman the encounter with God in conscience is a profoundly religious experience, indeed, it is for him *the* foundational religious experience.'[49]

Now it would be altogether mistaken to think that because Newman places such an accent on the divine pole in the experience of conscience that he must inevitably neglect the human pole. More mistaken still would be any idea that such a focus must lead inevitably to alienation from the human. The truth is that for Newman conscience is not only an address from God, as being his voice, but also that this same address and voice constitute a call, and this call reaches down to the very roots of our being. The objectivity of the voice as coming from outside reaches our subjectivity and invites us *personally*.

> The authoritative dictate touches us at the most intimate and sacred centre of our being, and it actualises this centre. In being morally bound we are aware of 'quickening' as per-

sons in a unique way, of coming to life as persons ... In neglecting our obligation in favour of our selfish wants and desires we are aware in conscience of being wounded in the very centre of our being, and of having corrupted the well-springs of all our deepest happiness.[50]

Religious and Human

The operation of conscience is human and religious at one and the same time. The imperatives of conscience manifest God at the same time as they call forth the freedom, responsibility and goodness of our human being. Conscience is, in other words, the awareness of existing from and under this divine Ground.[51] 'It is a messenger from him who, both in nature and in grace, speaks to us behind a veil.'[52]

Conscience therefore has a content, the glorious content of the Infinite Being who elicits a deep fascination with himself and so quickens in us an unsuspected depth of personhood and humanity. Conscience, though a stern monitor, brings home to us our true greatness in the truth that 'he alone is sufficient for the heart, who made it'.[53] This truth that conscience has a content, this bi-polar content of God and of the self as called by the voice of God, has central significance in the thinking of the cardinal. For here is the arena in which authentic human flourishing occurs. Only here can human beings advance towards the fullness of their original destiny, since we begin with nothing achieved, as it were.[54]

The Conspiracy against the Duties of Conscience

When in 1875, five years after the conclusion of the First Vatican Council, Newman came to write his reply to Gladstone's expostulation against the decree of papal infallibility proclaimed by the council, he first saw a huge shift against this classical understanding of conscience, which had been shared by pagan and Christian, by Catholics and Protestants. His words are evocative.

> All through my day there has been a resolute warfare, I had almost said conspiracy against the rights of conscience ... Literature and science have been embodied in great institutions in order to pull it down. Noble buildings have been reared as fortresses against that spiritual, invisible influence which is too subtle for science and too profound for literature ... We are told that conscience is but a twist in primitive and untutored man; that its dictate is an imagination ...[55]

Now this diagnosis of his times with his prognosis of the future will be sufficient to qualify him for the praise lavished on him by Jean Guitton for being 'the good prophet of what we are now experiencing'.[56] Freud is still a long way down the road! And the other philosophers of will and of power!

In 'the popular mind' also the emptying out of 'the old, true, Catholic meaning of the word' advances vigorously on all sides. People speak about the 'rights of conscience' in order to be emancipated from conscience altogether! The language is changed to mean 'the right of thinking, speaking, writing, and acting, according to their judgement or their honour, without any thought of God at all'. In the nineteenth century conscience 'has been superseded by a counterfeit, which the eighteen centuries prior to it never heard of, and could not have mistaken for it, if they had. It is the right of self-will.' Here is a masterly analysis of how language persists though with its meaning being totally subverted. A new rhetoric of rights has emerged. This rhetoric abolishes the idea that conscience has duties: 'In this age, with a large portion of the public, it is a very right and freedom of conscience to dispense with conscience, to ignore a Lawgiver and Judge, to be independent of unseen obligations.'[57] Newman draws the inevitable conclusion that his words outlining the nature of conscience 'are idle empty verbiage to the great world of philosophy now'.[58]

The final outcome of this view of conscience is its dissolution or its replacement by some counterfeit. But in the measure in which this happens two dangers threaten. The first consists in the destruction of 'the light inside you', coupled with the affirmation that there is only opinion but not truth, and that even if moral and spiritual truths exist, they are beyond the scope of our knowledge. This affirmation of moral agnosticism – we cannot know right and wrong and so are free to do as we please or as is fashionable or as society proposes – amounts to a veritable deformation of the mind. And the deformation of reason is the abolition of humankind since, although reason functions in the fields of science, both natural and human, its further and higher employment in the fields of history and ethics, natural theology and spirituality, is rendered obsolete or at least suspect. Here Newman's thought comes close to that of Eric Voegelin, who claims, 'We do not live in a "post-Christian", or "post-philosophical", or "neo-pagan" age, or in an age of a "new myth", or of "utopianism", but plainly in a period of massive deculturation through the deformation of reason.'[59] It is well within the mark to claim that Newman anticipated this diagnosis.

The second danger is a consequence of the first. To abolish conscience by explaining it away is to open the way to the law of might, of will, and of self-will. Might is now right. Since there is no God, nor final truth and good to which we are beholden, we are free to do as we please. We do not need the good, we only need the will and the desire. 'The destruction of the conscience is the real precondition for totalitarian obedience and totalitarian domination ... Only the absoluteness of conscience is the complete antithesis to tyranny; only the recognition of its inviolable ability protects human beings from each other and from themselves; only its rule guarantees freedom.'[60]

The prophetic voice of Alexander Solzhenitsyn, who lived much of his life under a régime based on the denial of human transcendence towards God and of the authentic rights of conscience, shows how once it is proclaimed that above man there is no other, then the very weaknesses and defects of men are proclaimed as imperatives.[61] Might is right! Desire is the way to flourish! An action to be chosen and done requires neither moral truth as its essential presupposition nor moral goodness as its indispensable quality. It only requires will and desire! The appalling corollary of this is the loss of the divine in the human being. In the words of a contemporary philosopher, 'We are witnessing the erosion, perhaps the final erosion, of the idea of man as something splendid or divine, and its replacement with a view of man, no less than nature, as simply more raw material for manipulation and homogenisation.'[62]

If Conscience, why also Revelation?
For Newman, 'conscience is a stern monitor', for after its cognitive dimension it commands the performance of the good and the avoidance of the bad. However, one's consistency in fidelity to this voice, 'unlike any other in the whole of creation', normally leaves much to be desired. The result is that 'the more a person tries to obey his conscience, the more he gets alarmed at himself, for obeying it so imperfectly'. His moral experience of the call and quickening of his central humanity, on the one hand, and his imperfect response, on the other, is the basic source of this inquietude. Like St Paul, he realises he is divided and broken. 'I fail to carry out the things I want to do, and I find myself doing the very things I hate' (Rom 7:15). This brings the painful awareness that 'the voice of conscience has nothing gentle, nothing of mercy in its tone. It is severe and even stern. It does not speak of forgiveness, but of punishment. It suggests to him a future judgement; it does not tell him how he can avoid it'.[63]

The Sternness of Conscience makes us look out for Revelation

The experience of the theonomous side of conscience, then, throws us between our real perception of the goodness and holiness of God, on the one hand, and the perception of our moral and religious misery, on the other. This being-thrown-between the good God and the miserable self creates, engenders and inspires the desire that God might speak a word of pardon to us.[64] Here is how Newman expresses the dilemma: 'Those who know nothing of the wounds of the soul, are not led to deal with the question, or to consider its circumstances; but when our attention is roused, then the more steadily we dwell upon it, the more probable does it seem that a revelation has been or will be given to us.'[65] Seen in this way, a revelation would be the greatest possible boon that could be vouchsafed to you.[66]

Conscience: The First, but Feeblest, Teacher

But it is not only our inability to obey consistently the imperative side of conscience that engenders the anticipation of a revelation from the God imaginatively or 'really apprehended' by this aspect of conscience. The other judgemental or informative side of conscience is also defective in the concrete, practical order. How else explain the vast variety of positions on central moral questions such as the permanence of marriage, the value of the person in all situations and the like? The fact is that 'this sense is at once the highest of all teachers, yet the least luminous'.[67]

What is the meaning of this tragic state of affairs? And it is particularly tragic since, as we have seen, conscience is central to the science of religion, being the source of ethics on its judgemental side and of the experiential knowledge of God on its imperative side. While all scientists have their certainty in themselves, whether they follow deductive or inductive methods, the science of religion has a necessary instrument of unsurpassable worth which is still a vulnerable and fallible calculus. Here is how Newman puts it:

> The sense of right and wrong, which is the first element in religion, is so delicate, so fitful, so easily puzzled, obscured, perverted, so subtle in its argumentative methods, so impressible by education, so biassed by pride and passion, so unsteady in its course, that, in the struggle for existence amid the various exercises and triumphs of the human intellect, ... the church, the Pope, the hierarchy, are, in the divine purpose, the supply of an urgent demand.[68]

In this perspective it is true to say that Newman never conceives of conscience as being simply opposed to authority.[69] *Au contraire!* Newman's conception of conscience requires authority for its counter-point.[70]

Conscience: 'The Aboriginal Vicar of Christ'

By the time he wrote *Norfolk* his theology of the church was fully evolved. Only two years later he was to write the famous preface to the third edition of the *Via Media*. It is enough to cite the key paragraph in *Norfolk*. 'Conscience is the aboriginal vicar of Christ, a prophet in its informations, a monarch in its peremptoriness, a priest in its blessings and anathemas, and, even though the eternal priesthood throughout the church could cease to be, in it the sacerdotal principle would remain and would have a sway.'[71] One sees at once the three dimensions or offices of 'the first element in religion'. However, what is perhaps most significant is his calling conscience 'the aboriginal vicar of Christ'. This appellation sets up what may be called 'the christological context of conscience' which, as a component of human nature, belongs to creation, but belongs to Christ in virtue of the incarnation and resurrection. He who speaks in nature and creation by way of conscience is the same person who will speak in revelation, 'the initial and essential idea of Christianity'.[72]

The Authority of Revelation and the Authority of Conscience: a Clash or a Dovetail?

As Christ is Prophet, Priest and King (and this is the unfolding teaching of both the Old and New Testaments), and as Christ is the fullness and mediator of all revelation, it follows that Christianity has to be a prophecy, a priesthood and a polity. And just as Christ expresses the visibility of the divine in the world, so too these 'layers of Christianity' will also enjoy a certain visibility or objectivity.

What, then, is Christianity? Newman defines it Christologically in these striking terms which are at once the key to his understanding of the church: 'Christianity, then, is at once a philosophy, a political power, and a religious rite: as a religion, it is holy; as a philosophy, it is apostolic; as a political power, it is imperial, that is, One and Catholic. As a religion, its special centre of action is pastor and flock; as a philosophy, the schools; as a rule, the papacy and its curia.'[73] Basing itself on the revelation of Christ, the church has an objective authority, a worship given by God, and divinely guaranteed teachers and prophets who speak with authority because they speak in Christ's name.

What is truly striking, however, is the fact that revelation provides the divine prototypes, as it were, for the figures manifested in conscience. There is, as a result, a perfect isomorphism between revelation and conscience. This relationship provides the true setting for understanding conscience and its phenomena. Revelation may not usurp its place. In fact, 'did the Pope speak against conscience in the true sense of the word, he would commit a suicidal act ... On the law of conscience and its sacredness are founded both his authority in theory and his power in fact'.[74] In that sense, we must drink to conscience first and then to the Pope!

As conscience, however, is not infallible and is particularly swayed and affected by innumerable forms of human conditioning, it cries out for completion, correction and reinforcement. The internal authority of conscience is presupposed by, and yet fulfilled in, the external authority of revelation in Pope, council and hierarchy. 'The supremacy of conscience is the essence of natural religion, the supremacy of apostle, or Pope, or church, or bishop, is the essence of revealed.'[75] And so it is well within the mark to say that 'Newman's acceptance of authority relates to his sense of our personal limitations when we are confronted by the structure of Christian revelation.'[76] Instead of complaining that one has to accept the church's teaching on morality, mature Christians are thankful that the first intimations of truth and its splendour are completed, purified and guaranteed by the infallible voice of revelation. 'The guide of life, implanted in our nature, discriminating right and wrong, and investing right with authority and sway, is our conscience, which revelation does but enlighten, strengthen and refine. Coming from one and the same Author, these internal and external monitors of course recognise and bear witness to each other.'[77] It is for this reason that Erich Przywara describes Newman as the 'great synthesiser of interiority and church'.[78]

CHAPTER 8

The Gospel of Joy

In his article, 'Newman's Gospel of Gloom',[1] Arthur Burton Calkins charaterises Newman's Anglican preaching as a 'gospel of gloom'. Contradicting the view held by Charles Stephen Dessain, hailed as the *éminence grise* of Newman scholars[2] who lauded Newman's preaching as 'complete and balanced' and permeated by 'the joyful optimism which pervades the teaching of St Ambrose, St Athanasius and the Greek Fathers',[3] Calkins sets out to substantiate his claim 'that Newman's was not the joyful optimism of the Greek fathers or, even more basically, the joyful optimism of the gospel'. He concludes his exposition by saying that 'what he (Newman) preached was neither joyful nor optimistic because it was not the Good News. It was terrible, subtle and refined, but it was devoid of that spontaneous joy which Paul VI considered an authenticating hallmark of the gospel of Jesus Christ.'[4]

The article of Calkins claims 'to distill the research of several years'.[5] It has the further merit of using as criteria of the Christian gospel two apostolic constitutions of great authority and richness, *Gaudete in Domino* and *Evangelii Nuntiandi*.[6] In the light of these criteria Calkins assesses Newman's gospel as he delivered it during his Anglican years. It is precisely such research and method that make Calkins' conclusion so serious. His contention simply demands a response and I shall indeed be happy if what I write will go, even a little way, towards providing a response and perhaps a refutation. Most of all, however, this chapter has the positive purpose of sketching Newman's gospel of joy.

The Case Against Newman
Our author begins with an analysis of a text from the first volume of Newman's *Parochial and Plain Sermons*. The particular sermon is called 'Scripture, a Record of Human Sorrow'.[7] 'The bible is full of descriptions of human misery ... human tales and poems are full of pleasant sights and prospects; they make things better than they are and portray a sort of imaginary perfection; but scripture (I repeat)

seems to abstain even from what might be said in praise of human life as it is.'[8] His analysis of this text argues in favour of the view that Newman's view of the bible was both 'negative and impoverished, not to say misdirected'.[9] Then he proceeds to show that Newman's *'praeparatio evangelica'* centred in the human experience of misery, moral, personal and social: 'Let us set it down, then, as a first principle in religion, that all of us must come to Christ, in some sense or other, through things naturally unpleasant to us.'[10] This seems an amazingingly morose starting point for the preaching of the Good News. Consistent with this morbid approach, Newman proclaims a proportionately morose and so distorted Christian kerygma.

To prove the point Calkins analyses in detail a homily on the mystery of Easter:

> At Christmas we joy with the natural unmixed joy of children, but at Easter our joy is highly wrought and refined in its character. It is not the spontaneous and unartificial outbreak which the news of the redemption might occasion, but it is thoughtful … On such a day, then, from the very intensity of joy which Christians ought to feel, and the trial they have gone through, they will often be disposed to say little. Rather like sick people convalescent, when the crisis is past, the illness over, but strength not yet come, they will go forth to the light of day and the freshness of the air, and silently sit down with great delight under the shadow of that tree, whose fruit is sweet to their taste. They are disposed rather to muse and to be at peace, than to use many words; for their joy has been so much the child of sorrow, is of so transmuted and complex a nature, so bound up with painful memories and sad associations, that though it is a joy only the greater from the contrast, it is not, cannot be as if it had never been sorrow … Christ indeed, though he suffered and died yet he rose again vigorously on the third day, having loosed the pains of death; but he cannot accomplish in our contemplation of him, what he accomplished really; for he was the Holy One; and we are sinners. We have the languor and oppression of our old selves upon us, though we be new.[11]

Calkins is satisfied that this text and others[12] illustrate the degree to which Newman 'manages to dilute the strength of the Good News of Jesus' resurrection', denying in the process the doctrine of baptismal regeneration.[13]

An Apparent Contradiction

The foregoing presents both the contention and case of Calkins. Amazingly, however, a paradox presents itself at once, at least in reply to his thesis, if not in actual contradiction of it! For the same Newman writes, 'Gloom is no Christian temper; that repentance is not real, which has not love in it; that self-chastisement is not acceptable, which is not sweetened by faith and cheerfulness; we must live in sunshine even when in sorrow; we must live in God's presence, we must not shut ourselves up in our own hearts, even when we are reckoning up our past sins.'[14] In an earlier sermon in the same volume Newman seems to highlight joy and peace as the very portion of the Christian in the world: 'The Christian has a deep, silent, hidden peace, which the world sees not ... He can (as it were) joy in himself, for it is the grace of God within him, it is the presence of the Eternal Comforter in which he joys ... More thankfulness, more holiness, more of heaven he needs indeed, but the thought that he can have more is not a thought of trouble but of joy.'[15] Now these texts are as striking in one direction as the texts quoted above are in the opposite direction.

As if to reinforce this contrary thrust of his teaching Newman characterises the mystery of the incarnation *and* the mystery of Easter[16] as fountainheads of joy for the sincere Christian, wellsprings of peace that will not run dry: ' ... that dreadful yet most joyful event, the passion and death of Our Lord', and again, 'The lesson of joy which the incarnation gives is as impressive as the lesson of humility.' He emphasises the truth that all that happens to the Christian works together towards his upbuilding and firm establishment in the peace of God, 'All God's providences, all God's dealings with us, all his judgements, mercies, warnings, deliverances, tend to peace and repose as their ultimate issue ... after our soul's anxious travail; after the birth of the spirit; after trial and temptation; after sorrow and pain; after daily dyings to the world; after daily risings unto holiness; at length comes that "rest which remaineth unto the people of God".'[17] Newman seems in these passages and in many others to be of the mind and conviction that 'a religious life is true happiness',[18] and that this is so true that Christians ought to 'rejoice even while they are in trouble'.[19] In the striking homily, 'The Cross of Christ the Measure of the World', he urges his hearers to remember that 'it must not be supposed, because the doctrine of the cross makes us sad, that therefore the gospel is a sad religion. The psalmist says, "They that sow in tears shall reap in joy"; and Our Lord says "They that mourn shall be comforted". Let no one go away with the impression that the gospel makes us take a gloomy view of the world and of life.'[20]

Towards a Higher Viewpoint

We are face to face, then, with an extraordinary state of affairs. Calkins is 'convinced that what he presents is genuinely representative of what Newman preached and believed during his Anglican career'.[21] On the other hand, a mere perusal of the eight volumes of the *Parochial Sermons*[22] throws up a phalanx of texts the direction of which runs counter to the direction described by Calkins. If Calkins portrays Newman's gospel as a 'gospel of Gloom', it seems just as easy to describe it as a 'Gospel of Joy' prohibiting gloom and inculcating unequivocally genuine Christian joy! Is there any way out of this dialectic of position and counterposition? I believe we must move upwards towards what Bernard Lonergan calls 'the higher viewpoint',[23] where seemingly clashing positions can be harmonised, and the antithetical quality of earlier viewpoints seen as stages on the road to fuller understanding. The remainder of this chapter has this precise aim.

The Religion of Newman's Time

Newman wrote these sermons in the first half of the last century in an England which he saw moving towards infidelity[24] and the gospel of liberalism, what he chose to call 'the religion of civilisation'. The subsequent history of that nation has vindicated Newman's prophetical insight. 'I know,' he writes in 1873, 'that all times are perilous, and that in every time serious and anxious minds, alive to the honour of God and the needs of man, are apt to consider no times so perilous as their own. At all times the enemy of souls assaults with fury the church which is their true Mother, and at least threatens and frightens when he fails in doing mischief. And all times have their special trials which others have not. And so far I will admit that there were certain specific dangers to Christians at certain times which do not exist in this time. Doubtless, but still admitting this, still I think that the trials which lie before us are such as would appal and make dizzy even such courageous hearts as St Athanasius, St Gregory I or St Gregory VII ... Christianity has never yet had the experience of a world simply irreligious.'[25] But much earlier, in fact in the very first volume of the *Parochial Sermons*, in a homily significantly named 'The Religion of the Day', he describes 'the shallowness of the religion' he saw around him as 'a general plague in the land'.[26]

The Religion of the World

His words are penetrating:

> What is the world's religion now? It has taken the brighter
> side of the gospel – its tidings of comfort, its precepts of love;
> all darker, deeper views of man's condition and prospects
> being comparatively forgotten. This is the religion *natural* to a
> civilised age, and well has Satan dressed and completed it
> into an idol of the truth … Thus elegance is gradually made
> the test and standard of virtue, which is no longer thought to
> possess an intrinsic claim on our hearts, or to exist, *further*
> *than* it leads to the quiet and comfort of others … Human society
> has a new framework, and fosters and develops a new char-
> acter of mind; and this new character is made by the enemy
> of our souls, to resemble the Christian's obedience as near as
> it may, its resemblance all the time being but accidental.[27]

Within the British Empire, especially at its centre, this lukewarm-
ness was growing, supported by the assumptions of the day, and
inculcated by the cultural ethos prevailing among the well-off and
the educated. It was this attitude, spreading over the land like
autumn after summer, which in the ultimate analysis stimulated
the Oxford Movement.[28]

'The Religion of Civilisation'

This 'religion of civilisation' tended to elicit two distinct responses,
both of which Newman adjudicated to be seriously defective,
deforming the Christian gospel. The one response erred on the side
of enthusiasm, focusing the attention on oneself, the other exaggerated the sobriety and ordinariness of the gospel, considering that
the gift of the Holy Spirit was almost peculiar to the apostles' day.[29]
Newman set out to steer a way between these extremes.

It was this ethos, and the diagnosis he made of it, that led
Newman along the homiletic pathway peculiar to the *Parochial
Sermons*. As an antidote to the religion of the day he proposed a personal obedience to Christ and to his word, 'Obedience, not a frame
of mind, is the test'.[30] He wrote in only his second sermon, 'I want a
man on the one hand to confess his immortality with his lips, and
on the other, to live as if he tried to understand his own words, and
then he is in the way of salvation.'[31]

Newman's Purpose

What, then, did Newman aim at in the Anglican sermons? His personal diaries tell us the answer: 'My sermons are on subjects con-

nected with sanctification. My reason for dwelling on the latter subject was my conviction *that we required the Law*, not the gospel in this
age – we want rousing – we want the claims of duty and the details
of obedience set before us strongly.'[32] The emphasis on the law in
contradistinction to the gospel seems to identify Newman rather as
a neo-Judaiser rather than a bearer of the Christian gospel (see Mk
1:15, Mt 3:2, Lk 3:8, Rom 1:1-2)! It is obvious, however, that he is
deliberately using the technique of contrast to make his point in the
strongest possible terms, namely, that Christ demands obedience as
the first elementary step from his disciple. 'It is obedience which
brings a man into the right path; it is obedience keeps him there and
strengthens him in it. Under all circumstances, whatever be the
cause of his distress, – obey.'[33] It is this diagnosis of the dangers
threatening the faith in England from without and within, that
accounts for the pronounced ethical and moralistic quality of the
earlier sermons.

Does this mean, then, that Newman did not preach the gospel
delivered once and for all to the saints (Jude 3)? Certainly not! I will
soon demonstrate that he preached the great Christian gospel privileges profoundly and comprehensively in the Anglican homilies.
But first let me state and expound what I judge to be Newman's
stance in those sermons which Gladstone predicted in 1879 would
be read one hundred years later.[34] I find this stance delicately articulated in a homily in volume seven, 'Religion Pleasant to the
Religious'.[35]

Religion is Pleasant to the Religious
The homily begins with a strong statement of the 'excellence and
desirableness of God's gifts', 'a subject again and again set before us
in holy scripture' (and let it be added, a subject equally loved by the
fathers both Greek and Latin).[36] Quoting the words of Psalm 24:8,
'O taste and see how gracious the Lord is: blessed is the man that
trusteth in him', he comments:

> You see by these words what love Almighty God has
> towards us, and what claims he has upon our love. He is the
> Most High, the All-Holy. He inhabiteth eternity: we are but
> worms compared with him. He would not be less happy
> though he had never created us; he would not be less happy
> though we were all blotted out again from creation. But he is
> the God of love; he brought us all into existence, because he
> found satisfaction in surrounding himself with happy crea-
> tures.[37]

For almost four pages he cites texts from both the Old and New Testaments in order to bring out powerfully the scriptural doctrine on the intrinsic joy of the Christian life. He comments thus on his teachings:[38]

> You see all images of what is pleasant and sweet in nature are brought together to describe the pleasantness and sweetness of the gifts which God gives us in grace. As wine enlivens, and bread strengthens, and oil is rich, and honey is sweet, and flowers are fragrant, and dew is refreshing, and foliage is beautiful; so, and much more, are God's gifts in the gospel enlivening, and strengthening, and rich, and sweet, and fragrant, and refreshing, and excellent. And as it is natural to feel satisfaction and comfort in these gifts of the visible world, so it is but natural and necessary to be delighted and transported with the gifts of the world invisible; and as the visible gifts are objects of desire and search, so much more it is, I do not merely say a duty, but a privilege and blessedness to 'taste and see how gracious the Lord is'.[39]

This is what the Christian religion is for Newman – the presence of Persons, the Divine Persons of the Blessed Trinity drawing us into their blessed company through the Paschal Mystery of the Son incarnate and the outpouring of the Holy Spirit in the church and the sacraments. And this what it *ought* to be for each Christian. But is it? Newman answers in tones betraying an unmistakable regret.

> I wish it were possible, my brethren, to lead men to greater holiness and more faithful obedience by setting before them the high and abundant joys which they have who serve God … but this is, I know, just what most persons will not believe. They think that it is very right and proper to be religious; they think that it would be better for themselves in the world to come if they were religious now. They do not at all deny either the duty or the expedience of leading a new and holy life; but they cannot understand how it can be pleasant: they cannot believe or admit that it is more pleasant than a life of liberty, laxity, and enjoyment. They, as it were, say, 'Keep within bounds, speak within probability, and we will believe you; but do not shock our reason. We will admit that we *ought* to be religious, and that, when we come to die, we shall be very glad to have led religious lives: but to tell us that it is a *pleasant* thing to be religious, this is too much: it is not true; we feel that it is not true; religion is something unpleasant,

gloomy, sad, and troublesome ... ' Alas! I cannot deny that
this *is* true in the case of most men. Most men do not like the
service of God, though it be perfect freedom; they like to follow their own ways, and they are only religious so far as their
conscience obliges them.[40]

The Attraction of the Gospel

I excuse the length of this excerpt on the grounds that it brings
together in one place what might be called the 'ideal' and the 'real'
orders. It expounds the delights of the gospel, and then the delights
that fascinate and attract even religious people. 'This is the point. I
do not say that it (religion) is pleasant to most men; but I say that it
is in itself the most pleasant thing in the world. Nothing is so pleasant as God's service to those *to whom* it is pleasant ... O that I could
get you to believe this!'[41] It would have been hard for Newman, in
spite of his incomparable ability to express his thought, to have
been more explicit in his articulation of the gospel and its struggle
for the heart of the Christian. 'Such is our miserable state: we are
blind to the highest and truest glories, and dead to the most lively
and wonderful of all pleasures – and no one can describe them to
us. None other than God the Holy Spirit can help us in this matter,
by enlightening and changing our hearts.'[42]

The Gospel is for Everyone

It would be wrong, however, to conclude from this that Christianity
and its joy are beyond most Christians or, worse still, that it cannot
be lived. Newman underlines the fact that it *is* lived and *is* experienced as delightful by those who obey the word of God. 'I hope
there are some of those who hear me', he writes in the same homily,
'who take a pleasure in coming to church, in saying their prayers, in
thinking of God, in singing psalms, in blessing him for the mercies
of the gospel, and in celebrating Christ's death and resurrection ...
These persons have 'tasted' and tried. I trust they find the taste so
heavenly, that *they* will not need any proof that religion is a pleasant thing; nay, more pleasant than anything else, worth the following above all other things, and unpleasant only to those who are not
religious.'[43]

A Willingness to be Changed

It is now time to fulfil our promise to describe briefly Newman's
preaching of the outstanding privileges of the gospel and of the
'narrow door' that leads to them. The 'narrow door'[44] of the gospel

consists in repentance and obedience to Christ and to his word in the gospel and the church. 'What then is it that we who profess religion lack? I repeat it, this: a willingness to be changed, a willingness to suffer Almighty God to change us. We do not like to let go our old selves... But when a man comes to God to be saved, then, I say, the essence of true conversion is a *surrender* of himself, an unreserved, unconditional surrender.'[45] Following closely upon this indispensable first step in Christian living – here Newman is clearly in line with the synoptic gospels[46] – is the need for a 'detailed obedience'.[47]

The Management of our Hearts

Underlying and strengthening Newman's therapy of obedience was his doctrinal conviction of 'the depths and the deceitfulness of the human heart, which we do not really know'. Like St Augustine before him,[48] he tells us that 'the management of our hearts is quite above us',[49] and so he reinforces the need for us to 'watch and pray' for the strength to obey God's will as he reveals it to us. Such obedience is what Newman calls true faith: 'It (faith) may be described to be the temper under which men obey; the humble and earnest desire to please Christ which causes and attends on actual services. He who does one little deed of obedience, whether he denies himself some comfort to relieve the sick and needy, or curbs his temper, or forgives an enemy, or asks forgiveness for an offence committed by him, or resists the clamour or ridicule of the world – such a one evinces more true faith than could be shown by the most fluent religious conversation, the most intimate knowledge of scripture doctrine.'[50] A sizeable proportion of all the sermons in the first volume have obedience as their theme.[51] With an uncanny knowledge of the human heart, with a real grasp of the society of his day, and with a wisdom drawn from his own spiritual odyssey,[52] Newman spelled out the elementary claims of Christian duty. He roused Christians from the slumbers which made them drift with the current, and challenged them to live lives worthy of their real vocation.

The Power of the Word of God

Newman lamented how his contemporaries commonly read scripture, which should always be 'a living word to the benefit of our souls'. 'Alas, those who hear the Word of Life continually, know it, admire it, do all but obey it.'[53] They failed to realise the authority of the Divine Word and its basic claim on their obedience. Newman recalled the New Testament teaching on the authority of the word,

'If anyone loves me he will keep my word', 'My mother and my brother and those who hear the word of God and keep it', 'It is not those who say to me, "Lord, Lord" who will enter the kingdom of heaven, but the person who does the will of my Father in heaven', 'We must not be hearers of the word only, but doers', 'Man's days are like grass and his glory like the flower of the field. The grass withers and the flower fades, but the word of the Lord remains for ever', 'Blessed are they that do his commandments'.[54]

These sermons are biblical through and through.[55] Not only does a distinct scripture text stand over each one, but frequently their author begins with a gospel event or parable and then proceeds to draw out its doctrinal and practical meaning for living. The manner in which he elaborates and expands on the text seems both faithful to its literal sense and helpful to the situations and needs of his listeners. What strikes their reader today is the power of the word of God which suffuses with authority and light and love their every page.[56] Newman enables the reader to encounter the inspired word through the medium of his own text which seems to become transparent to the word in scripture. In this way one easily forgets Newman as one reads and in his place finds the living God addressing his living word to the heart and conscience. 'See, I set before you today a blessing and a curse, a blessing if you obey the commandments of Jahweh your God.'[57]

Obedience Leads to Transparency

It seems impossible that anyone could become so transparent to the word of God if he had not first become its obedient hearer and dutiful executor in his own daily life. Newman comes through as an outstanding prophet of God's word: like the biblical prophets, the living word lives and burns in him, and so lights fires in the hearts of those who hear and read him.[58] In his sermon 'The Self-Wise Inquirer', he unfolds St Paul's teaching on false wisdom which consists in an 'unfounded confidence in our own reasoning powers which not only leads to pride, but to "*foolishness*" also, and destructive error, because it will oppose itself to scripture.'[59] In such opposition to scripture Newman located the basic evil of his own and indeed all ages.

Insight into the Human Condition

One of the outstanding fruits of Newman's use of scripture was the insight it provided into the problems and conditions of the human family. He shows how the sustained biblical view of the world and human suffering both confirms and interprets human experience for those willing to learn.[60] In the same Good Friday homily, 'The Cross of Christ, the Measure of the World', the Redeemer's holy cross is the true yardstick with which to assess the manifold events that make up life in the world. He encourages all Christians to see in the cross the most learned book ever written, to learn to read this book with ease, and so to grow in the wisdom of God.[61] Perhaps here we are close to Newman's own wisdom of the cross and his love and union with the Crucified, 'the power and wisdom of God' (1 Cor 1:25).

The Trinitarian Indwelling

Numerous studies bear witness to the treasures of Newman's teaching on the divine indwelling of the Three Divine Persons in the heart of the justified Christian,[62] a matter which concerned us particularly in the opening chapter. It is true that Newman spoke, particularly in the early volumes of the *Sermons*,[63] more on the law than on the gospel,[64] to use his own words. But even in those early volumes mention of the indwelling of the Holy Spirit and of Our Lord is frequent and revealing. 'We are assured of some real though mystical fellowship with the Father, Son, and Holy Spirit, in order to this: so that both by a real presence in the soul, and by the fruits of grace, God is one with every believer, as in a consecrated temple.'[65] Without the power of such grace it would in fact be impossible for the Christian to will and to do the will of God, what is pleasing to his heavenly Master (see Phil 2:12-13).

This is Newman's clear theological teaching even in the case of his most ethical sermons. For example, in his very first Sermon he concludes with these comforting words: 'While we thus labour to mould our hearts after the pattern of the holiness of our Heavenly Father, it is our comfort to know ... that we are not left to ourselves, but that the Holy Ghost is graciously present with us, and enables us to triumph over, and to change our own minds. It is a comfort and encouragement, while it is an anxious and awful thing, to know that God works in and through us.'[66]

This magnificent teaching is rooted in the New Testament, particularly in Paul and John. It is expounded and drawn out into clear shape with the help of the Greek fathers for whom Newman had a unique affection.[67] In his sermon 'The Indwelling Spirit', he provides a superlative statement of the theme, 'the merciful office of God the Holy Ghost towards us Christians'. The Holy Ghost dwelling within the Christian applies 'to us individually the precious cleansing of Christ's blood in all its manifold benefits'. He fixes the eyes of our mind on our Father and on our Saviour with true love and a loyal heart. In a striking manner Newman shows how the Holy Spirit, far from replacing Christ, actually places him in the heart.[68] 'Let us not for a moment suppose that God the Holy Ghost comes in such sense that God the Son remains away. No, he has not come so that Christ does not come, but rather he comes that Christ may come in his coming. Through the Holy Ghost we have communion with the Father and Son.'[69]

So great a truth, however, must be received with reverence and love, for it is there not for our unbecoming curiosity but rather for our humble obedience, to be lived with reverence. Newman concludes the sermon on 'The Gift of the Spirit':

> For ourselves, in proportion as we realise the higher view of the subject, which we may humbly trust is the true one, let us be careful to act up to it. Let us adore the Sacred Presence within us with all fear and 'rejoice with trembling'. Let us offer up our best gifts to him who, instead of abhorring, has taken up his abode in these sinful hearts of ours ... In this then consists our whole duty, first in contemplating Almighty God, as in heaven, so in our hearts and souls; and next, while we contemplate him, in acting towards him and for him in the works of every day.[70]

Once again active obedience is the only authentic response to such ineffable truths of revelation. In this way Newman strives to aid his listeners to base their Christian living on the firm rock of New Testament doctrine, in particular on the reality of the Indwelling Trinity.

Self-Denial: The Law of the Cross

In terms reminiscent of St Augustine, Newman warns people, 'Dare not to think that you have got to the bottom of your hearts; you do not know what evil lies there. How long and earnestly must you pray, how many years must you pass in careful obedience before you have any right to lay aside sorrow.'[71] In this manner Newman encourages his hearers to work out their salvation in fear and trembling, especially as it was still fashionable in the England of his day to be religious, at least externally. Christianity, however, remains the 'narrow way' and the truth of Our Lord 'is against the current of human feeling and opinion'.

In order to avoid self-deception Newman recommends the discipline of self-denial as this is set forth in the scriptures. 'Let your very rising from your bed be a self-denial; let your meals be self-denials. Determine to yield to others in things indifferent, to go out of your way in small matters to inconvenience yourself, rather than you should not meet with your daily discipline. This was the Psalmist's method, who was, as it were "punished all day long, and chastened every morning" (Ps 63:14). It was St Paul's method who "kept under" or "bruised" his body and brought it into subjection ... Try yourself daily in little deeds, to prove that your faith is more than a deceit.'[72] Newman teaches a self-denial that must be daily, performed in little things, and especially in weak points. 'Never think yourself safe because you do your duty in ninety-nine points; it is the hundredth which is to be the ground of your self-denial, which must evidence, or rather instance your faith.'[73] With all the power of a St Paul, all the practical sense of a pastor of souls, Newman encourages his listeners to become sincere athletes of the Spirit in the following of Christ. Every day they ought to look for the cross in order to be close to their Lord.

Realisation
John Henry Newman had a horror of 'unreal words', by which he meant all forms of insincerity in religion. Convinced that 'it is not easy to learn that new language which Christ has brought us',[74] he set out to help his listeners to 'realise' or grasp the realities of the 'unseen world' which Christian faith put before them but which many people often failed to apprehend in any meaningful or personally involving manner. 'Christ has interpreted all things for us in a new way; he has brought us a religion which sheds new light on all that happens. Try to learn this language. Do not get it by rote, or speak it as a thing of course. Try to understand what you say. Time is short, eternity is long. God is great, man is weak; he stands between heaven and hell; Christ is his Saviour; Christ has suffered for him. The Holy Ghost sanctifies him; repentance purifies him, faith justifies, works save.'[75]

In this and in many parallel passages it is easy to detect Newman's abiding pastoral concern to focus the heart of the believer on the realities of revelation. Each Christian needs to bring home vividly to himself the great objects of faith, 'to realise the unseen world'.

> We are born into a world of sense, that is, of real things which lie around us ... But all this does not interfere with the existence of that other world which I speak of, acting upon us, yet not

impressing us with the consciousness that it does so ... It
appears, then, that the things which are seen are but a part,
and but a secondary part of the beings about us. Once, and
only once, for thirty-three years has he condescended to
become one of the beings that are seen, when, in the Person
of his only-begotten Son, he was, by an unspeakable mercy,
born of the Virgin Mary into this sensible world.[76]

In this way Newman tries to help his hearers to realise the reality of
the incarnation. The realisation of the mystery of the crucifixion he
attempts to bring home to his listeners in the same manner.

It is the death of the Eternal Word of God, made flesh, which
is our lesson how to think and how to speak of this world ...
Go to the political world ... to the world of intellect and science ... look at the misery, look at poverty and destitution,
look at oppression and captivity; go where food is scanty and
lodging unhealthy ... Would you know how to rate all these?
Gaze upon the cross.[77]

In this way he tries to put flesh and blood on the elementary
Christian belief that 'Christ was bearing our faults in his own body
on the cross' (1 Pt 2:24).

I am not at all surprised, then, that Newman should have made
such an impact on those who heard him and read him. I have no
difficulty in accepting the verdict of Newman's eminent contemporary, Dean Church: 'The most practical of sermons, the most real in
their way of dealing with life and conduct, they are also intensely
dogmatic.' And again, 'They made men think of the things the
preacher spoke of, and not of the sermon or the preacher.'[78] The
things he spoke of were the great privileges of the gospel, and I
have tried to show that Newman employed his outstanding talents
to communicate them as good news to his Anglican congregations.

CHAPTER 9

A Builder of Unity

On 16th October 1845, barely one week after John Henry Newman's reception into the church he called 'the one fold of the redeemer', one of his closest colleagues and dearest friends, E. B. Pusey, wrote that Newman's conversion to Catholicism was 'perhaps the greatest event which has happened since the communion of the churches has been interrupted'. Pusey provided at once a reason for his judgement: 'If anything could open their (Roman Catholic) eyes to what is good in us, or soften in us any wrong prejudices against them, it would be the presence of such a one, nurtured and grown to such ripeness in our church and now removed to theirs'.[1] Newman is a bridge between Rome and Canterbury! With the hindsight of a century and a half, Pusey's prediction can be seen as a prophecy generously fulfilled: Cardinal Newman has indeed been a bond of understanding and a stimulus to dialogue between the Catholic and Anglican churches. On the day of his requiem the *Cork Examiner* wrote, 'Cardinal Newman goes to his grave with the singular honour of being by all creeds and classes acknowledged as the just man made perfect.'[2]

When Pope John Paul II went to Coventry in 1982 he praised the ecumenical contribution of Newman in these terms: 'I cannot come to the Midlands without remembering that great man of God, that pilgrim for truth, Cardinal John Henry Newman ... His teaching has great importance today in our search for Christian unity too, not only in this country but throughout the world.'[3] Newman seems to be an instrument chosen by that kindly providence whose leading he trusted throughout his life, an instrument employed by God to heighten among Christians of different churches the spirit of the gospel and, especially, the conviction that what makes us credible in the world and most pleasing to our one Lord and Saviour is mutual love of which unity is the fruit (see Jn 13:34-5; 15:12; 17:21f). Convinced always that 'the division of the churches is the corruption of hearts', he prayed and wrote, worked and suffered for the restoration of unity between Rome and the Anglican communion.[4]

Newman's journey of faith acquires, according to Archbishop Runcie, 'a universal meaning', particularly in its ecumenical dimension. 'If for Anglicans the move he made in 1845 sets a question mark against the permanence of their position, perhaps for Roman Catholics his concern to maintain the unity between his earlier and later life demands readiness to look more closely at where he came from.'[5] Anticipating the conviction of a Second Vatican Council that the lack of unity between Christians 'inflicts damage on the most holy cause of proclaiming the good news to every creature', he could write, 'The absence of visible unity between ... different communions is so great a triumph, and so great an advantage to the enemies of the cross.'[6]

The Evangelicals set him on his Way

It needs to be remembered that the instruments, under God, of the first teenage conversion of Newman were the Evangelical principal of Newman's school, Walter Mayers, and the Calvinist, Thomas Scott. With the benefit of hindsight Newman described Scott as the man 'to whom, humanly speaking, I almost owe my soul'.[7] The nominal Anglican first discovered revealed religion from these Evangelicals. He was never to forget the gift thus given him. In fact, he was destined to repay it through his own work for revealed religion. This work was increasingly well received in the other denominations during his lifetime. In the 1870s a Methodist minister who had never actually met Newman wrote to express his thanks: 'Almost four years ago I came by the first three volumes of the *Parochial and Plain Sermons* ... these sermons are all that I have read of your writings ... my life has been changed, my spirit has been fashioned, the mind that was in Christ Jesus has been communicated to me.' And he continues, 'There is one precious and profound doctrine which you teach us, which is that the best part of the Christian life remains hidden ... you may be able to understand how rich, and, I hope, how lastingly rich you have made me in that inward light.'[8] This reciprocal influence between Newman and the Evangelicals has an important significance for ecumenism.

In what follows, I should like to treat the following themes as being central to Newman's ecumenical calling and mission. First, there is Newman's witness as a man of communion and life-long commitment to the gospel spirit of unity. Then there is the specifically theological level of ecumenism where we can outline his particular methodology in four interlocking steps. And finally, there are the specific guidelines for the practice of ecumenism today which emerge from his witness, theology and practice of ecumenism during his life.

A Man Who Gathered

C. S. Dessain has ably demonstrated that the restoration of unity between the churches was an abiding and central concern of Newman's whole life. 'If the return to unity was a dream he dreamed as an old man, it was also a vision he had seen as a young one.'[9] From the time of his conversion he prayed that the holy church would enfold all in its embrace. One of these prayers, dated the 17th November 1817, runs as follows: 'Enlighten all by the Holy Spirit: turning all Jews, Musselmans (sic!) and Pagans to thee; converting all atheists and infidels, whether so in principle or practice; recovering all heretics from the error of their ways, and restoring all schismatics to thy holy church; that there may be one fold and one shepherd'.[10] The ideal of the unity of all in Christ and by means of the one holy church was a sustained object of his prayer.

In 1824-25 he drew up a further list of intentions. On Sunday there was to be intercession for the 'universal Church of Christ – Church of England – other Christian churches – for nominal Christians – for heretics, schismatics, papists, etc. – for Jews, Mohammedans – for heathens'.[11] It was soon clear to him, however, that the very idea of the church had so largely disappeared from the minds of his contemporaries that he needed to restore it and to provide a theology for it. During the Oxford Movement this became a principal objective in order to bring out the revealed truth about the church. To resist the Erastian tendencies by which the government claimed ascendancy over the church and in which the ruling party in the Anglican Church and the establishment acquiesced, Newman and his fellow tractarians highlighted 'the great truth that Our Lord had instituted, and still acknowledges and protects, a visible church'.[12] For a time he accepted the 'Branch Theory' of the Church forwarded by the two William Palmers, the one of Magdalen, the other of Worcester. The former tried to persuade the Greek and Russian churches to accept it, the latter expounded his ecclesiology in his, *Treatise on the Church of Christ.*[13]

As a Catholic Newman did not and could not accept this view, seeing it as 'paradoxical when regarded as a fact', and 'heterodox when regarded as a doctrine'. Still, the motives leading Anglicans to accept it betokened 'a goodwill towards Catholics, a Christian spirit, and a religious earnestness, which Catholics ought to be the last to treat with slight or unkindness'.[14] What stands out in partic-

ular relief during his Anglican days is his desire for union with
Rome coupled with an equal realisation that this is, when practically
and theologically considered, simply beyond the limits of possibility.
'Till she ceases to be what she (Rome) practically is, a union is
impossible between her and England; but if she does reform (and
who shall presume to say that so large a part of Christendom never
can?) it will be our church's duty at once to join in communion with
the Continental churches, whatever politicians at home may say to it'.[15]

Setbacks

After 1839 when the first shadows concerning the validity of his
Anglican position had emerged, his first feeling 'was to pray for
unity'. He made a collection of prayers for this purpose, drawn
from the Anglican Prayer Book, but later adopted formulae for the
same object from two Tractarians, Arthur Acland and Robert
Williams. These prayers were called *Prayers for Unity*, and were to
be recited on Thursdays. Pusey also warmly welcomed the idea.

Living in Communion

With his genius for friendship – 'I lived in my friends' – and his
visionary leadership in the Oxford Movement, it was little wonder
that a party gathered around Newman. After the *Tract 90* shock,
when he saw the general rejection of his claim that the principal
Anglican doctrines were simply compatible with the Roman (diver-
sity and difference coming in only with the medieval and
Tridentine decrees), he abandoned his tenure of St Mary the Virgin
in Oxford and withdrew to Littlemore. Here he lived with close colleagues a life of deep communion, convinced that the church was a
communion requiring a life of communion from its members.[16] It is
legitimate to see in his choice of the Oratorian way upon becoming
a Catholic the logical continuation of this commitment to a collective spirituality aspiring towards 'a collective holiness'.[17] His
model he found in the churches and communities of the great
fathers, always his guides and mentors. And from this lived basis,
this daily experience of communion in faith, prayer and charity,
Newman aspired towards the building of that communion between
the churches, which was shattered in the West at the Reformation,
so that 'now all this beauty (of unity) ... is miserably defaced'.[18]
Thus Newman was no ivory tower ecumenist, no dreamer living in
Utopia, but a man whose ideal was that of unity and whose life was
a relentless practical enterprise to turn ideal into reality.

Newman's Ecumenical Method

Upon entry into the Catholic Church, Newman did not forget his friends nor their Communions. In 1841 he wrote in his private notebook that

> ... Catholics in England, from their very blindness cannot see that they are blind. To aim at improving the condition, the status, of the Catholic body, by a careful survey of the argumentative basis of their position relatively to the philosophy and the character of the day, by giving them juster views, by enlarging and refining their minds, in one word, by education, is (in their view) more than a superfluity or a hobby, it is an insult. It implies that they are deficient in material points.[19]

The Catholics had the full truth, but that did not mean that they either knew it or lived it. That something was true was no reason that it be said, but that it be done and lived. He set himself about 'the edification of Catholics'. But he led by example. He threw himself into the Catholic system with all the ardour of a neophyte, like a Hopkins who burns all his poems upon becoming a Catholic or a Merton who destroys his novels and poems when he is baptised and enters the Cistercians!

Of course, for two decades following upon his turning to Rome, he was largely estranged from his many friends of Oxford days. Pusey continued to write, but Keble and Church faded off the scene in the early years. The Catholics, his new brothers and sisters, found it hard to employ him, and even when they did, many of his projects for the raising of standards in the Catholic community were there either misrepresented and stymied through the fears and jealousies of lesser people. 'From the time of the *Apologia*, however, he was an ecumenical figure, loved and trusted and consulted by innumerable Christians, Anglicans, and others, and by those in doubt and unbelief'.[20] Thus a most theological ecumenism emerged which can be described under four headings which are also the elements constituting it as an ecumenical methodology. The four stages involved in this ecumenical methodology are as follows:

1. The acknowledgement of all that is true and valuable among our fellow Christians who are separated from us.
2. An exact and realistic measuring of the differences that keep us apart.
3. The effort to remedy all that is amiss and a hindrance to unity in our own church.

4. Following on this, the most important of all, a balanced exposition of the total Christian truth in all its aspects.

I. ACKNOWLEDGING ALL THAT IS TRUE

In the 1850s the cry 'No Popery' went up all over England. The
Pope himself was burned in effigy. Newman wrote to J.M. Capes
who was attacking the Church of England, 'Can we *at the moment*
wish the destruction of the Establishment? ... Are not numbers kept
in a sort of grace of congruity state, which may be the beginning of
better things, and who at *this moment* would anyhow not adopt
Catholicism, but go the other way, were the Establishment
destroyed?'[21] Thus the Church of England was a value to a large
number of sincere Christians.

In his own person he was grateful for all he had received from
this church while ripening within her. 'The church of England has
been an instrument of Providence in conferring great benefits on
me; ... had I been born an English Presbyterian, perhaps I should
not have known our Lord's divinity; had I not come to Oxford, perhaps I should never have heard of the visible Church, or of tradition, or other Catholic doctrines'.[22] He had a special affection for
Oxford: 'Catholics did not make us Catholics; Oxford made us
Catholics'. Besides, 'the Establishment has ever been a breakwater
against Unitarianism, fanaticism, and infidelity'.[23]

The Unity of Baptismal Grace

And of course there was the sacrament of baptism. 'Of the great
mass of religious persons in the Anglican communion, we may say
that they are living on baptismal grace.'[24] In the same spirit he
wrote of the teaching of the Evangelicals as 'a great blessing for
England; it had brought home to the hearts of thousands the cardinal and vital truths of revelation, and to himself among others'.[25]

II. THE DIFFERENCES SEPARATING: A REALISTIC APPRAISAL

On the other hand, however, Newman was quite unwilling to allow
that the Church of England was part of the Catholic Church, not
even in any kind of revamped 'Branch Theory' which he subscribed
to for some years during the Oxford Movement. In the *Apologia* he
writes, 'Unwilling as I am to give offence to religious Anglicans, I
am bound to confess that I felt a great change in my view of the
Church of England, ... an extreme astonishment that I had ever
imagined it to be a portion of the Catholic Church ... I am not
speaking of the Anglican Church with any disdain, though ... I

seem contemptuous. ... It may be a great creation, though it be not divine, and this is how I judge of it.'[26]

The 'Ecumenical Revolution' has occurred in the meantime, and the Vatican Council *Decree on Ecumenism* recognises the Anglican Church as a church. Newman's formula was that the Anglican Church was 'to a certain point a witness and a teacher of religious truth', but not 'an oracle of revealed truth'.[27] Accordingly, Newman's ecumenical attitude was, in the judgement of Ian Ker, 'typically mixed: uncompromising but pragmatic, critical but open, hopeful yet realistic'.[28] Avery Dulles speaks of 'the tension between the convert and the ecumenist, the apologist for Catholicism and the friendly observer of other Christian communions'.[29] The hope for the future lay in the Church of England becoming more Catholic, and the Catholic Church more Christian in the sense of increase in gospel and collective holiness.[30]

Corporate Unity: A Possibility?
Perhaps Newman's attitude to the real differences separating Canterbury and Rome emerges best in his relations with an enthusiastic ecumenist, Ambrose Lisle Phillips. In 1857 Phillips with others founded the *Association for the Promotion of the Unity of Christendom*, his great aspiration being that of corporate unity of the two churches. A lengthy correspondence with Newman ensued. Newman viewed the idea as theoretical and quite impossible of realisation, 'Can the Thames flow into the Wash?' As there have always been three great parties in the Anglican communion – the Evangelical, the Liberal and the Erastian – the Anglican Church would first have to raise the perceptions and tones of these parties to the level of being truly Catholic. As this was for Newman extremely unlikely, he felt the prospects of the Anglican Church becoming a Uniate Church of Rome was something in the category of the miraculous.

It would be quite inaccurate, however, to feel that Newman saw absolutely no hope for something of the kind in the future. Thus in the Catholic edition of the *Via Media*, II, in 1878, he writes, 'It is observable that at the commencement of the Oxford Movement in 1833, the insuperable obstacle, felt by High Anglicans, to communion with Rome, was the doctrine of the Tridentine Council. By 1865 they seemed to have got over it, and the Vatican decrees are the obstacle now. Will they be such in another forty years?'[31] Such change would not occur suddenly. In the meantime Catholics were to 'pray for the conversion of individuals, and for a great many of them'.[32] Underlying Newman's conviction of the proper manner of making converts was his insight, born out of the history of his own great journey, that Catholic faith is a gift and that conversion cannot be programmed and planned, like a pastoral project, but must be the result of grace, and the insight of faith and the drawing of charity.

III. REMEDYING ALL THAT IS A HINDRANCE TO UNITY IN OUR OWN CHURCH

A motto of Newman was that 'life is for action'. If the Anglican Church in the 1830s needed, as he then saw, 'a second reformation', in the sense that the principles of the fathers needed to infiltrate it to make it Catholic, the Catholic Church needed its own renewal. True, the faith was there in its pristine purity, but the practical deficiencies were also evident. Newman saw them, saw them with all the keenness of a convert and of one steeped in the early normative portion of the Church's life. 'The church must be prepared for converts, as well as converts prepared for the church.'[33] A number of items were on his agenda at once.

First, there was the issue of the laity who were in need of education and formation. Their position in the church was sadly underestimated, as indeed was that of the bishop. 'To me, conversions were not the first thing, but the edification of Catholics.'[34] Newman was so preoccupied with this that his stance was interpreted as a coolness towards the idea of conversion.

Raising the Catholic Temper
But there was only limited value in talking about the laity without first educating them. This idea runs through so much of his work as a Catholic: the experience in Dublin with the incipient Catholic university, the ill-fated project of the Oxford college, the foundation of the Oratory school in Birmingham and others. Education was his scene. 'What I want is a laity not arrogant, not rash in speech nor disputatious but who know their religion, who enter into it, who know just where they stand, who know what they hold, and what they do not, who know their creed so well that they can give an account of it, know so much of history that they can defend it ... what are the bases of Catholicism... In all times the laity have been the measure of the Catholic spirit.'[35]

In his long essay, *On Consulting the Faithful in Matters of Doctrine*, he outlined a theology of the laity, which situates them in the apostolic church and gives them a commission in both the church and the world. Their consensus throughout the church is the voice of the infallible church, without prejudice to the Pope and the bishops. Consequently, the teaching church is more happy when she is surrounded by enthusiastic partisans who appreciate their faith 'than when she cuts off the faithful from the study of her divine doctrines and the sympathy of her divine contemplations, and requires of them a *fides implicita* in her word, which in the educated classes would terminate in indifference, and in the poorer in superstition.' Famous indeed are the comments of Monsignor Talbot on this Newman enterprise: 'What is the province of the laity? To hunt, to shoot, to entertain. These matters they understand, but to meddle with ecclesiastical matters they have no right at all.'[36]

A second item on his agenda was that of 'the intellectual defence of revealed religion against the rising tide of unbelief'. This concern eventually produced the innovative and seminal work, *An Essay on a Grammar of Assent*. By it he wished to cultivate 'a philosophy of religion among Catholics', convinced that this would also be a necessary first step in the conversion of England.[37]

IV. A BALANCED EXPOSITION OF THE TOTAL TRUTH

Newman laid it down that it is almost the definition of a heresy to say that 'it fastens on some one statement as if the whole truth, to the denial of all others, and as the basis of a new faith'.[38] When a heresy actually occurs, the church, yes, will repudiate it, but in doing so the popular exposition of the injured area of truth may often suffer an exaggeration. For example, the teaching on justification at the time of the Reformation was counteracted by the Council of Trent and further corrected by the Counter Reformation, but at the expense of the full scriptural and patristic view of the subject. More of this shortly. In this way Newman anticipates the desire of Pope John XXIII and the council to make the church and her teaching shine out before the world with original harmony.

It may be useful to take just two instances of Newman's exposition of the faith in illustration of his marvellous ability to touch into life forgotten or underemphasised areas of faith. The first is the area of grace. He deals with the subject in a special way in the 1837 volume, *Lectures on Justification*. Recently hailed as 'soaring above the unsatisfying aridities of textbook theology' and discovering 'in the wealth of Catholic tradition the spirit that might have given the original Protestants complete satisfaction, fulfilling their aspirations and removing all risk of their falling into heresy or schism,'[39] the lectures on justification wanted to overcome the deadlock between the Lutheran and popular Roman view of justification by having recourse to the New Testament and patristic teaching on the divine indwelling of the Blessed Trinity. '*This* is to be justified, and to receive the divine presence within us, and to be made a temple of the Holy Ghost.' Thus what is given to us is not only faith, not only renewal, 'but through God's mercy, the very presence of Christ'.[40]

In that way Newman got beyond the popular Protestant and Catholic notions and their tragic dialectic, and reconciled them both in the revelation of the Divine Indwelling, as this is taught particularly in St John and St Paul. Of course, Newman was almost reticent to talk about a subject so sacred and, as an antidote to the danger of irreverence towards so momentous a gift, demanded reverence and obedience to the divine gift and the practice of prayer of which the indwelling is source and stimulant. 'O my God, can I sin, when thou art so intimately with me? Can I forget who is with me, who is in me? Can I expel a divine inhabitant?'[41]

A second instance might be his theology of 'the mother of Jesus'. C.S. Dessain perceptively remarks that 'the only book which Newman wrote *ex professo* on Mary had an ecumenical purpose, his *Letter to Pusey*',[42] a work written in reply to Pusey's perplexity at Pius IX's definition of the Immaculate Conception as a divinely revealed truth. He outlined the principle on which he would base his reply: 'The fathers made me a Catholic ... as regards our teaching concerning the Blessed Virgin, with the fathers I am content'.[43] He produces a mariology that is biblical, balanced, patristic, and derived from the central areas of revelation such as the incarnation and grace, the resurrection and intercessory prayer.

In Fr Dessain's judgement, 'Newman's greatest contribution to ecumenical work' is 'his balanced exposition of the total Christian truth'.[44] He applies this antidote to the not infrequent caricatures of certain aspects of the faith. Still, the first need for all is to improve the temper of faith in ourselves. When that happens, the level of faith of those around us will also improve.[45] This led at once to the importance of prayer in action, or, in the language of the *Decree on Ecumenism*, spiritual and practical ecumenism. 'Everyone who desires unity, who prays for it, who endeavours to further it, who witnesses for it, who behaves Christianly towards the members of churches alienated from us, who is at amity with them, (saving his duty to his own communion and to the truth itself), who tries to edify them, while he edifies himself and his own people, may surely be considered, as far as he himself is considered, as breaking down the middle wall of division, and renewing the ancient bonds of unity and concord by the power of charity.'[46]

Ecumenical Guidelines and Principles

In 1864 while writing the *Apologia* Newman realised, better than ever before, that his own toilsome, profound itinerary which led eventually into the fullness of faith followed a route which could not be mapped by logic nor explained in the neat operations of syllogisms. That journey, in fact, was much more like the dismantling of horizons as further and higher ones came into view. It was a growing, developmental movement of mind and heart, a verification of the truth that 'growth is the only evidence of life'. This led Newman on 'to examine more attentively what (he) doubted not was in his thoughts long before, viz. the concatenation of argument by which the mind ascends from its first to its final religious idea'.[47] He then added the startling conclusion, 'I came to the conclusion that there was no medium, in true philosophy, between Atheism and Catholicity.'[48] The religious scenario was one where halfway houses would not survive, but also a scenario obliging Catholics to look with new and kinder eyes on believers in the Anglican and other communions.

An Ascending and Descending Scale of Thought

Sixteen years later he explained what he meant. He pointed out that there is a certain *'organon investigandi* given us for gaining religious truth'. This *'organon investigandi'* consists in 'a certain ethical character, one and the same, a system of first principles, a mode of viewing the question and arguing, which is formally and morally, naturally and divinely the *organon investigandi* given to us for gaining religious truth'. Newman had appropriated the method during his own lonely and painful odyssey. Its employment, he is sure, 'would lead the mind by an infallible succession from the rejection of atheism to theism, and from theism to Christianity, and from Christianity to Evangelical religion, and from these to Catholicity'. Of course, he well realises from experience that many people are not serious and in earnest: they 'are not consistent, logical or thorough; they obey no law in the course of their religious views'. The result is that they 'are set down at this or that point in the ascending or descending scale of thought, according as their knowledge of facts, prejudices, explanation, domestic ties, social position and opportunities for inquiry determine'.[49]

It is time to list and explain briefly the ecumenical guidelines emerging from Newman's journey of faith and practice of ecumenism, particularly those most relevant to the dialogue of the churches today.

First Guideline: Conversion of Life
In Christian life conversion is an indispensable foundation. Jesus in fact began the preaching of the Good News with a call for a change of heart. This conversion consists in that most personal journey of each and all Christians into the very mystery of God. The imperative of conversion is ongoing reform and remedy of life. It is expressed in the attitude of looking out from ourselves to God, in waiting on him and in obedience to his will and word in our lives. 'To live is to change and to be perfect is to have changed often'. By conversion we become 'Advent persons' like Abraham, John the Baptist and especially Mary, the great 'Advent person' of the scriptures, who did not sit at home, but went out from herself on the beckoning of God and thus facilitated the entry of God into her own life and into the hearts of humankind.

A Permanent Dialogue
Conversion sets up a permanent dialogue between each Christian and Christ. It allows the Kingdom of God to come into our flesh, enter our society and influence our history. It asks each Catholic to intensify this dialogue between himself and God and between himself and others. It asks each Anglican to intensify this dialogue, as well as each Methodist, each Free Church member. And as the rays of the sun come closer to each other to the degree they come closer to the sun, so Christians come closer to each other to the degree they love and obey the one Lord. 'While Christians do not seek after inward unity and peace in their own breasts, the church itself will never be at unity and peace in the world around them.'[50]

Source of Desire for Unity
Conversion, then, prevents ecumenism degenerating into a vague religiosity, a sentimental feeling, an effete desire, a dialogue of the deaf, for it roots ecumenism in Christ the Lord of all the churches and of each church. It is impossible to turn and come near to Christ without hearing in the process 'the deepest desire in his heart', 'Father, may they all be one' (Jn 17:21). Conversion then becomes the source and inspiration of the desire to work and pray for the unity of all who are true Christians because converted to the one Lord. Here we see Newman's own life-long praying for the unity of believers in its own proper context.

His Own Witness
Newman personified this guideline admirably. In his own life he always lived at once what he learned and understood. 'I have not

betrayed the light'. The whole duty of a Christian – in any church – consists in looking off towards Christ and in obedience. He was convinced of the promise of Christ, 'Anybody who receives my commandments and keeps them ... I shall love him and show myself to him' (Jn 14:21). This was the very drama of his life, as it advanced towards the fullness of faith and faith-life which God's providence had intended.

Anticipating Vatican II

We notice here the originality of Newman who anticipates the teaching of Vatican II's *Decree on Ecumenism.* 'There can be no ecumenism worthy of the name without a change of heart. For it is from newness of attitudes (see Eph 4:23), from self-denial and unstinted love, that yearnings for unity take their rise and grow towards maturity ... Let all Christ's faithful remember that the more purely they strive to live according to the gospel, the more they are fostering and even practising Christian unity' (7). When Newman was still an Anglican he was busy with attempts and projects to improve his own communion. Upon entering 'the one fold of the Redeemer' his concern was 'the edification of Catholics'.[51]

Second Guideline: Recourse to Revelation

The church's life-flow is revelation. From divine revelation it is come, for the transmission of revelation it exists, and in the full appropriation and everlasting enjoyment of revelation in heaven the church will be both completed and fulfilled. Revelation, as Newman loved to stress, is 'the initial and essential idea of Christianity'.[52] His own religious journey began with revelation and only unfolded and developed as he recovered and personally appropriated the constitutive areas of revelation. This we saw in our opening two chapters. The very renewal of the church depends upon her faithful remembering of revelation and her active translation of revelation into life.

The Stream of Living Water for All

All the churches must look to this one revelation. It is their origin and only source of renewal, their foundation, strength and nourishment. Accordingly, they must avoid whatever deflects attention from this abiding supernatural source. They must absolutely repudiate the human tendency to trust in the world, or to look for its approval as the criterion of what is true or what is worthwhile in her mission. Here all churches must examine their consciences as to possible inordinate links with the political structures surrounding them or in which they happen to be found. The leader of the Oxford Movement wanted an end of Erastianism, the bold affirmation of the church's transcendent origin, and the practical promotion of her sovereignty. In the *Letter to the Duke of Norfolk* one finds a masterly statement of the church's dependence on revelation and independence of the secular realm. Many observers today speak of the cancer of 'civil religion' by which the gospel is made to compromise with the particular body politic surrounding the church. Such a liaison paralyses the church's essential prophetical task of proclamation, and, worst of all, takes the church's eyes off Jesus, our unique consoler and companion along the roads of history and the byways of the world (see Mt 28:20).

Third Guideline: The Normative Patristic Church

In the problem of the one church and the many churches, Newman had recourse to the church of the fathers, what he sometimes called 'the undivided church', though the term is misleading as even in the fourth and fifth centuries there were numerous heretical churches, such as the Arian, the Nestorian, the Monophysite and the Donatist. Still, it is true to say that Newman reached back to Christian origins, to the early church which he named as the true exponent of Christianity. From this early church he learned the three principles of a living Christianity in a living church: the dogmatic, the sacramental and the hierarchical.

Reverence towards Antiquity

The lesson for the churches in the twentieth century is crystal clear. They can look to the early church as to a model to be imitated. They must be neither afraid nor immersed in history. Much has happened in the meantime to alter the climate of contact between the churches. The result is that no church can simply appeal to the few centuries preceding the century of the Reformation in explanation of that great turmoil that, in the effort to renew the Catholic Church, tragically scattered the one flock of Christ resulting in schism and separation, and the rending of the seamless robe of Christ to the point where the World Council of Churches now numbers a membership of more than 270! Such multiplicity is a kind of condemnation. The first five centuries are simply normative. 'Where, what is this thing in this age which in the first age was the Catholic Church?'[53]

In the early centuries the once-for-all revelation recorded in sacred scripture was expounded in creed, celebrated in sacrament and expressed in the daily living of the church. The great

Ecumenical Councils confessed the faith often in the teeth of heresy, while the church's theologians explained, defended and elaborated it. Tradition thus has an importance which cannot simply be ignored. In fact, a characteristic of that doctrinal liberalism, which makes the tragic 'mistake of subjecting to human judgement those revealed doctrines which are in their nature beyond and independent of it',[54] and which held that 'one doctrine is as good as another',[55] was its 'irreverence towards antiquity ... (and) the growing indifference to the Catholic Creed'.[56] If Christianity is an historical religion, even though its influence is in the present, its historical course must be taken seriously, especially the early centuries which display and manifest its living organism, as well as its doctrine, sacramental life, and ancient but permanent structure.

Fourth Guideline: Conscience

C. S. Dessain has written that 'Newman's costly act of becoming a Catholic was an example of the fundamental ecumenical principle of the primacy before God of a conscience sincere in its convictions'.[57] Newman is the Catholic theologian of conscience which he describes and defines in a memorable passage in the *Letter to the Duke of Norfolk*, 'When Anglicans, Wesleyans, the various Presbyterian sects in Scotland, and other denominations among us, speak of conscience, they mean what we mean, the voice of God in the nature and heart of man, as distinct from the voice of revelation ... It is a message from him, who, both in nature and grace, speaks to us behind a veil, and teaches us and rules us by his representatives. Conscience is the aboriginal Vicar of Christ, a prophet in its informations, a monarch in its peremptoriness, a priest in its blessings and anathemas.'[58] The ecumenical movement is founded on this aboriginal Vicar of Christ. Through it God addresses us and we know ourselves to be in the presence of God, the creator of the world and the giver of revelation. Conscience is an instrument for detecting moral truth, and, as such, it is the key to ethics and vital to moral theology. But besides being a moral sense, it is also a sense of duty and this aspect of conscience makes it 'a connecting principle between the creature and his Creator',[59] and 'a dutiful obedience to what claims to be a divine voice, speaking within us'.[60]

The Finest Hold on Revealed Truths

Newman always saw obedience to conscience as the way to the truth. The more a person tries to obey his conscience and succeeds through grace, the more he advances in the personal appropriation and realisation of the faith.[61] 'The firmest hold of theological truths is gained by habits of personal religion'.[62] The truth is that Newman had 'always contended that obedience even to an erring conscience was the way to gain light'.[63]

In that way conscience becomes a source of religious truth, of the natural religious truth. But it also prepares us to be on the look-out as it were for the infallible teaching of revelation,[64] and when that revelation is encountered it enables us to believe with quick-ness, hope against all hope, and love with all our heart. As the late and respected Newman scholar, H. F. Davis pointed out, Newman focuses on an analysis of our moral experience as the key to the unique relationship between 'our own soul and the God who made it', and he does this in clear Augustinian terms. As all Christian churches emphasise conscience thus understood, here is a wonder-ful common ground for the faithful believer as for the learned theolo-gian: for the faithful who ought to obey the truth in order to follow the kindly light of God and Christ; for the theologian who would find in Newman's linking of conscience and revelation a most orig-inal and unifying theological method.[65]

Fifth Guideline: The Exhibition of Christian 'First Principles'
It is not an exaggeration to say that the methodological differences between the churches all have to do with clashing positions regard-ing the interpretation and transmission of divine revelation as God's ultimate word to the world. Now Newman saw with great clarity that interpretation always follows and depends upon 'first principles' which are so deep and profound as to be ordinarily well out of view even though they are powerfully active. In this way he anticipates the insights of the philosophers of hermeneutics of the twentieth century, such as H. G. Gadamar who writes, 'Properly speaking history does not belong to us but we belong to history.'[66]

First principles are 'the propositions with which we start in rea-soning on any given subject matter. They are in consequence very numerous, and vary in a great measure with the persons who rea-son, according to their judgement and power of assent.'[67] They are the key to the identity, history and destiny of each church and of all churches. Just as they 'constitute the difference between man and man',[68] so too do they constitute the differences between the Christian communities. They are the concrete starting points in all questions as addressed by a particular church.

First Principles in Theological Dialogue
In the work of ecumenical dialogue, particularly on the theological

level, the task is to enable one another to bring out, a difficult task, the respective first principles relevant to the subject matter under consideration. A good instance of such work is Newman's *Tract 90* whose main thesis was the contention that the Thirty-nine Articles do not oppose Catholic teaching. 'It aimed at showing that the Thirty-nine Articles, although admittedly their animus was un-Catholic and they were not intended to inculcate Catholic doctrine, did not in their literal sense contradict it, and could be accepted by those who believed the Catholic truths as expounded by the Tractarians.'[69] The *Essay on Development* is his classical employment of revealed first principles in his attempt to find an explanation for the apparent contradiction of doctrinal development and continuity in Rome. One of the criteria of true development of doctrine as opposed to its corruption, is 'continuity of principles'.[70]

The main point, then, in ecumenical dialogue, is not to oppose arguments founded on your own first principles to the arguments of the other church from its first principles. Rather ecumenism is an art that uncovers the first principles of the churches who are party to the dialogue. Once this is done the further step would be that of checking these first principles against the revelation, the creeds, the tradition, and the liturgy,[71] for all the churches claim that their first principles are revealed.

Principles More Basic than Doctrines!
The practicality of Newman's insight here is striking. Principles are related to doctrines as general law to its expression. Doctrines exhibit the life of a principle and are manifestations of it, while the principle being larger than a doctrine protects, justifies and enhances the doctrine. The first principle of the incarnation not only contained all the doctrines of Christology, but also many of the other first principles of revelation.

In the memorable Oxford Symposium of 1966, Professor Cunliffe-Jones wrote on the subject of the Free Church attitude to Newman, and concluded, 'In his life as a whole, he emerges not only as a great teacher of the Roman Catholic Church, but also as a great teacher of all twentieth-century Christians.'[72] His comment reinforces those of Pope John Paul II and Archbishop Runcie. The inevitable tension between the ardent convert and wise ecumenist only adds soul and spice to the ecumenical praxis he portrays for our times. His spirit and method are capable of promoting unity 'between estranged communions and alienated hearts'[73] in the present, and, in the future, who knows what further unity.

Conclusion

CHAPTER 10

The Meaning and the Message

The final chapter of a book should perhaps set out its principal conclusions and, in the case of a theological work such as the present, provide some indication as to the significance of these conclusions for the life of faith and the work of theology today. In any case this is going to be the goal of this chapter: we will state the principal insights of Newman and try to highlight their value for our very different times when, as Nicholas Lash rightly comments, 'we have need of him'.[1] Our conclusions ought to show how his thinking increasingly meets the needs of our times and provides a reliable orientation for all those seeking to live a life inspired by faith and rooted in love today. To this end we will look at each Part in turn.

A. THE DEEP ROOTS OF FAITH AND LIFE

The opening Part shows the deep roots of Newman's whole life. There is the fact of his emphasis on revelation as 'the initial and essential idea of Christianity',[2] the role of the fathers, and his grappling with the true way of appropriating revelation. His elaboration of a theology of revelation is of great interest, though not all accept the claim that this theology is significant.[3] The fathers expounded this revelation and even suggested to Newman the genuine road to its heart.

I. TOWARDS A THEOLOGY OF REVELATION

'The fundamental interest of Newman's life is his devotion to the cause of revealed religion ... This devotion gave his life its unity.'[4] This verdict of C. S. Dessain is no exaggeration. Rather, it justifies the subject of the first chapter. There we focused on Newman's theology of revelation. His sources were biblical and patristic. These two goldmines furnished him with the most authentic and most stimulating theology of revelation. We noted how, from the point of view of content, his theology of revelation linked the various layers of the Christian mystery. These included the trinitarian, christological,

174

pneumatological and anthropological layers of the revealed mystery. The many component mysteries fold outwards from the one scriptural mystery and fold back into the same primordial mystery.

The Many Mysteries in the One Original Mystery

Christ is the fullness of revelation since he brings the life of the Holy Trinity into history. We noted the fact that Newman highlighted the role of the Holy Spirit in finishing the work of the revealing Christ. 'The birth, the life, the death and resurrection of Christ, has been the text which he (the Holy Spirit) illuminated. He has made history to be doctrine.'[5] It is the Spirit who enables us to perceive Christ as the revelation of the Father and in that way to perceive the Father as well. He places the one Christ in the many believers, and draws the many believers into the dying, rising and glorified Christ.

> Christ was born of the Spirit, and we too are born of the Spirit. He was justified by the Spirit, and so are we. He was pronounced the well-beloved Son, when the Holy Ghost descended on him; and we too cry Abba, Father, through the Spirit sent into our hearts. He was led into the wilderness by the Spirit; and he did great works by the Spirit; he offered himself by the Eternal Spirit; he was raised from the dead by the Spirit; he was declared to be the Son of God by the Spirit of holiness on his resurrection: we too are led by the same Spirit into and through this world's temptations; we, too, do our works of obedience by the Spirit; we die from sin, we rise again unto righteousness through the Spirit; and we are declared to be God's sons – declared, pronounced, dealt with as righteous – through our resurrection unto holiness in the Spirit.[6]

Inspired by scripture and the fathers, and linking together the many strands of the mystery, his theology of revelation highlights revelation's cumulative, varied, complex and developmental nature. Like St Augustine, he can speak of 'revelation to the devout pagan',[7] what he calls 'the Dispensation of Paganism' so that 'there never was a time when God had not spoken to man, and told him to a certain extent his duty'. But 'what the church of God ever has had, and the rest of mankind never has had, are authoritative documents of truth and approved channels of communication with him'.[8] This revelation, however, is always vaster than what human beings are capable of realising in the present world. In the future world we will be enabled to see God face to face (1 Cor 13:12).

The Structure of Revelational Experience: Brightness and Darkness
This brings us to the matter of the structure of the revelational experience. This structure is a tension between mystery and light, darkness and brightness. 'Revelation is religious doctrine viewed on its
illuminated side; a mystery is the self-same doctrine viewed on the
side unilluminated.'[9] Revelation in that way increased the mysteriousness of our present existence. 'We gain spiritual light at the
expense of intellectual perplexity.'[10] Newman deftly relates mystery and doctrine. He shows how the divine mystery 'far from
being compassed by those very propositions (of doctrine), would
not be exhausted, nor fathomed by a thousand'.[11] The mysteriousness of revelation results from the depths of the divine abyss
encountering the limitations of the human spirit, which they blind
even as they illuminate.

Personal and Propositional
Finally, revelation is both personal and propositional. It is personal
in that it is a personal God who addresses human beings, sending
them his eternal Son and sanctifying Spirit. 'True Christianity is the
Presence of Persons – to know Christ and through him, the
Father'.[12] It is propositional and so doctrinal because the very idea
of revelation insinuates that *something* is spoken to humankind and
speaking is only verbiage if *nothing* is affirmed. Newman would
have rejoiced to see Vatican II describe revelation in personal categories as when it taught, 'In his goodness and wisdom, God chose
to reveal himself and to make known to us the hidden purpose of
his will (cf. Eph 1:9) by which through Christ, the Word made flesh,
man has access to the Father in the Holy Spirit and comes to share
in the divine nature (cf. Eph 2:18; 2 Pt 1:4).'[13] He would have been
equally pleased to see the council's emphasis on the truth communicated in and by divine revelation, as when it teaches, 'By (this)
revelation then the deepest truth about God and the salvation of
man is made clear to us in Christ.'[14] In fact, since revelation is
divine truth expressed in human language, and truth for its annun-
ciation presupposes formulation in propositions, revelation would
be as if not given if there were no propositions in revelation. That is
why dogma has to be one of the constitutive principles of
Christianity[15] if revelation is to be the initial and essential idea of
Christianity.

II. THE SECOND ROOT: THE FATHERS

If revelation is the first root of the faith for Newman, the fathers are the second. They are such as the first and gifted expositors of the divine revelation transmitted in scripture and tradition. Of course, the apostolic fathers, like Ignatius and Irenaeus, predate the final determination of the canon of scripture. In the fathers Newman saw the face of early Christianity, its principles and practices, its doctrines and sacraments, its constitution and polity, its witness and struggles. 'Persons influence us, voices melt us, looks subdue us, deeds inflame us,'[16] he once wrote. As soon as he learned to read the fathers correctly – and that was only after several years of misreading – the true and fair form of the early church rose up before him. They became for him a goldmine of the faith, second only in eminence to that of scripture. It is impossible to study Christianity effectively without immersing oneself in these mouthpieces of the early church, what he liked to call antiquity.

Neither Antiquarianism nor Adulation

Newman, however, carefully avoids all antiquarianism and adulation in his fondness for the fathers. They are never museum exhibits from an earlier age. He is able to have recourse to them when dealing with difficulties which were unknown to their age. In Newman's treatment of one such difficulty, namely, the question of grace and justification which we looked at in Chapter II, we saw how he transcended the *popular* Protestant and Catholic notions of justification by a patristic reading of the matter. In the long article, *On Consulting the Faithful in Matters of Doctrine*, he once again displayed a deep familiarity with them as he elaborated a theology of the lay faithful, as surprising for the last century as it was a commonplace for the fathers of the fourth century.[17] The same facility shows itself six years later as he grounds Pius IX's definition of Our Lady's immaculate conception in the teaching of Justin, Irenaeus and Tertullian on Mary as 'the Second Eve'.[18] The imaginative employment of the fathers stands out again in his reply to Gladstone's expostulation against the decrees of the First Vatican Council. There he shows from the fathers that bold independence of the church in the first centuries, an independence by which she defied her persecutors in the ante-Nicene period and ruled them afterwards.[19]

Steeped in the Truth of Revelation

The fathers, then, are the first expositors of the divine revelation.

But they are expositors only to be pioneers of new pathways of life and thought. Their most daring initiatives can and should inspire the thinking of the church in later ages. The source of their perennial fruitfulness, however, is to be found in one fact: they are steeped in the truth and life of revelation, 'the eternal life which was with the Father and has been made visible to us' (1 Jn 1:2). The fathers have a life, this life.[20] Their persons, their writings and their churchmanship breathe this life. This faith-life, hope-life and love-life is the secret of the attraction which they unceasingly exerted on Newman until, in the end, they made him a Catholic. The life of faith, hope and love is the final gift of divine revelation. It may be contrasted with a more vague faith and lesser level of life of some Christians. St Thomas Aquinas distinguishes the two levels in terms of 'unformed faith' (*fides informis*) and 'faith formed by charity' (*fides charitate formata*). Here surely is a clear parallel with Newman's distinction between real and notional apprehension of, and assent to, the realities communicated in revelation.

This brings us face-to-face with the now familiar phenomenon of the separation of theology and spirituality, and not merely their distinction. The former is seen as a science with its specific methods, criteria and goals, the latter as an important dimension of Christian living seeking its nourishment and finding its direction from sources other than the doctrines of faith. Hans Urs von Balthasar makes the point powerfully and in terms reminiscent of Newman.

> This impoverishment brought about by the divorce between the two spheres (of theology and spirituality) is all too plain; it has sapped the vital force of the church of today and the credibility of her preaching of eternal truth. (The result is) on the one hand, the bones without the flesh, 'traditional theology'; on the other, the flesh without bones, that very pious literature that serves up a compound of asceticism, mysticism, spirituality and rhetoric, a porridge that, in the end, becomes indigestible through lack of substance.[21]

Newman's wisdom lies largely in his detection of the true rapport of faith and life, while his influence as pastor, teacher and theologian is attributable to his ability to translate the message, style and ethos of the fathers into his own very different religious and cultural setting. This puts Newman, as Nicholas Lash saw, 'somewhere near the heart of the Second Vatican Council's achievement ... healing within Catholicism ... that dissociation of mind and heart, of argument and experience, of structure and feeling, which is our negative legacy from the Enlightenment's achievement'.[22] 'The fathers made me a Catholic' is indeed his grateful tribute to them, but it is hardly inordinate to suggest that they also owe him a debt of gratitude for the new currency which he minted for their practical and theological re-issue in the Anglican and Catholic churches of the nineteenth century and since!

III. THE THIRD ROOT: A WAY OF MAKING FAITH ONE'S OWN

The third root in Newman's treatment of divine revelation deals with its appropriation by individuals and the church. Here some of his most original thinking is to be found, as our third chapter claimed. What conclusions should be drawn from it? The following seem unavoidable.

While many currents of contemporary theology begin from the premise that we know the faith, and can begin to think out the faith from this very knowledge, Newman puts us at once on our guard. Is this faith a faith-life or a faith-belief? As we have just seen, there is a drastic difference of quality between the two. In God's providence this modern church father, this *Augustinus Redivivus*, as Erich Przywara described him, came to personal Christian faith by way of conversion. He did not arrive at this happy destination through yielding to proofs in a textbook, though such proofs and evidences are very important to him.[23] And he came to *Catholic* faith only after a series of conversions that traced out a mighty itinerary. This explains his fondness for the dictum of St Ambrose, 'It did not please God to save his people by means of logic,' and his aversion to what he called 'paper logic'.[24] All the way from *The Tamworth Reading Room Articles* of 1841 until the *Grammar of Assent* in 1870 he stresses both the necessity and the inadequacy of logic in the theological enterprise. [25]

Newman's own faith-life and, in particular, his journey pointed out a dramatic contrast between 'proof' and 'conversion' as rival and competing ways to the truth. He clearly opts for the latter in the fields of the human sciences and theology, without denying the former its appropriate place. Perhaps Bernard Lonergan, himself an admirer of much that is in the English cardinal,[26] is most precise of all his commentators when he describes Newman's way of the appropriation of faith as the breakthrough from classicism to concreteness, and from proof to conversion. We will let him speak for himself:

> Basically the issue is a transition from the abstraction of classicism to the concreteness of method. On the former view

what is basic is proof. On the latter view what is basic is conversion. Proof appeals to an abstraction named right reason.
Conversion transforms the individual to make him capable
of grasping not merely conclusions but principles as well.[27]

Now the significance of Newman's breakthrough here is far-reach-
ing. The central question for theology becomes, What is the true, the
'real' way, to appropriate 'the unsearchable riches of Christ' (Eph
3:8 RSV) in revelation? How are believers to 'realise the invisible'[28]
world which revelation opens up? More accurately, since Christ is
the fullness and the heart of Christianity, how should theology conceive its task of introducing Christians to Christ? Clearly this will
involve, as Bernard Lonergan remarks, 'far less talk about proofs,
and … far more about conversion'.[29]

That is the question. But the answer to the question preoccupied
Newman his whole life long, and issued eventually in the *Grammar
of Assent* where he stated the method of appropriation which he
believed to be the true one. 'I will add,' he wrote in a note for the
second edition of this great work, 'that a main reason for my writing this *Essay on Assent* … was, as far as I could, to describe the
organum investigandi which I thought the true one.'[30] As we saw in
Chapter III, Newman did not evaluate the *Grammar* as a *Novum
Organon* so much as an *organum investigandi*.

An Instrument of Investigation

The distinction is significant. Newman, who knew his Aristotle,[31]
particularly the ethical, rhetorical and logical works, realised that
the great Greek gave two distinct, if connected, meanings to the
term, *organon*. The primary sense is biological, focusing on the
heart, lungs and other organs of the body, each with its specific
function and each serving the good of the whole body. The secondary sense of the word consists in that of an instrument or means
for hunting. Now it is this secondary sense of the word that
Newman recalls and evokes when he describes the *Grammar of
Assent* as an *organon investigandi*. The *Grammar* outlines an instrument for the investigation of the Christian revelation. It is not a
Novum Organon, in the Baconian sense. This Newman recognises in
an exchange of letters with Robert William Dale upon the first
appearance of the work in 1870.[32] 'I shall be truly glad if I shall be
found to have made any suggestions which will aid the formation
of such a calculus,' that is, a *Novum Organon* for theology. Clearly,
he sees the *Grammar*, as a lesser, though connected, reality, namely,
an *organon investigandi*, an instrument or means for the unfolding of

the riches of revelation. The theologian employing this method, however, needs 'what Aristotle would call a *pepaideuménos* investigator, and a process of investigation *sui similis*'.[33]

These, then, are our conclusions on Newman's statement of the roots of the faith. It is now time to go to the shoots that spring from these roots.

B. THE THEOLOGICAL SHOOTS

The young Newman was brought up on scripture. His adolescent conversion deepened his regard for the written word. The scriptures and, later, the fathers were his spiritual and mental nourishment, but soon he began to make other discoveries. They are all shoots springing from his encounter with divine revelation in scripture and the fathers. A principal discovery was going to be that of tradition and the necessity of a credal Christianity in the context of an apostolic church.

I. TRADITION: A GRADUAL DISCOVERY

His first introduction to the theme of tradition came from Edward Hawkins (1789-1882) who in 1818 put Sumner's treatise on the subject into his hands, and then preached the famous sermon on the subject which Newman heard. Given Newman's rather Calvinist leanings in the years immediately succeeding his first conversion in 1816, there was little room on his theological horizon for the idea of tradition, and any room there was began to be filled by his progressive reading of the fathers.

The mode of his discovery of tradition was theological, that is, as insight flowing from either earlier beliefs or tasks undertaken. Thus his researching of the First Ecumenical Council for *The Arians of the Fourth Century* was the entry into church history as a systematic discipline. Rowan Williams has shown that the young Newman, while appreciating the work on pre-Nicene theology of the 'standard divines' like Bull, Waterland, Petavius and Baronius, considering them to be 'magnificent fellows but ... antiquarians or doctrinists, not ecclesiastical historians', is sensitive to the category of history.[34] Revelation is committed to a community which must move through history, indeed *make* history.

Still, Newman is at first reticent to admit the need of doctrinal formulation. He fears the irreverent exposition of the pearls of the gospel. He is suspicious that such exposition may detach these treasures from their native and proper location in the bosom of the church. The *Arians* project, however, alters that perspective substantially. 'His sense of the legitimacy and necessity of doctrinal definition seems to have developed actually *in* the process of endeavouring to write church history'.[35] This begins with the history of the Arian hurricane. It will be his persistent involvement with those great christological controversies of the fourth and fifth centuries, controversies providing the theological and cultural context for the golden age of the fathers, that will both occasion and cause his gradual discovery of the reality of tradition. He will discover it, in fact, as a component and carrier of revelation through the waves and storms of church history. And this is precisely the thesis of the great 1837 work, *The Prophetical Office of the Church*. Tradition will be *the* plank in the raft which the *Via Media* must sail between Protestant reduction to scripture only, and Roman exaggeration towards authority, even infallible authority.

Episcopal and Prophetical Tradition

The *Prophetical Office* expounds a fertile theology of tradition. Louis Bouyer sees in it 'a view of the Catholic tradition which is not only a most inclusive but also a most synthetic one'.[36] Newman's view distinguishes two kinds of tradition, episcopal and prophetical. The latter is powerful but subtle, 'pervading the church like an atmosphere'.[37] It both parallels and fills in the gaps in the episcopal form. It is drawn on, and witnessed to, by the fathers. It also flows in many channels and so enjoys multiple media, including the *consensus fidei* of the lay faithful. Here is the germ of the theology of the laity. The advancing insight of Newman buoys him up in his resistance to both the Reformers and the Romanists. The Anglican communion, after all, may have more than a mere 'paper theology'.

As he notices the varied and subtle contours of tradition, and, in particular, as he sees the fathers' respect for it and the early Ecumenical councils' use of it in their decrees determining the faith to be believed by all, he realises that tradition is a special carrier of the faith. It is there since the beginning as the apostolic tradition, and this authoritative tradition is the proper matrix, nourishment and critique of all subsequent traditions.

Scripture and Tradition: Witnesses to Revelation

Tradition exists alongside scripture, not in competition with it since both spring from the same fountainhead in revelation. Scripture is the more authoritative of the two, a view which he held throughout his life. Through his reading in the early 1840s of the history of the Monophysites and of the fifth century councils, the collaborative nature of scripture and tradition dawns upon him. He sees them as expressions of the fullness of revelation. Furthermore, as a Catholic, he saw only verbal differences between the Catholic and Anglican theology of scripture and tradition in the transmission of divine revelation.[38] Catholics, of course, believed in the church's divinely given authority and infallible competence to teach the faith, the proof of which was in scripture and tradition. To refresh our memories on the point, we only need to recall Newman's own demonstration of the dogma of the immaculate conception in the *Letter to Pusey*,[39] where he draws on early apostolic tradition in the mouths of second and third century fathers and doctors in order to ground the papal definition.

II. VINDICATED AT THE SECOND VATICAN COUNCIL

As we have so often stressed, Newman loved the early centuries of the church. This love made him study with care the councils of the early centuries and the controversies which they settled. It seems providential that a council of this century should vindicate many of his own concerns and insights. The Second Vatican Council has done this, particularly with regard to his theology of tradition. Now if one accepts with Nicholas Lash, following Bishop B. C. Butler, that Newman's *direct* influence on the recent council was 'exceedingly limited',[40] one may see in that council's espousal of a theology of tradition in the *Dogmatic Constitution on Divine Revelation*, which is so like that of Newman, a singular legitimation of his understanding of tradition. Here, in fact, is an instance of the convergent testimony of different witnesses.

The *Dogmatic Constitution on Divine Revelation* recovered the patristic notion of tradition in its relation to revelation, scripture and the teaching office. It defined scripture and tradition as functions of revelation[41] which consists in the word and event of Christ, who is 'the mediator and at the same time the fullness of all revelation' (2). It vindicated for the magisterium 'the task of authentically interpreting the word of God, whether written or handed on', but stressed that its 'teaching authority is not above the word of God but serves it' (10). Above all, the council's emphasis on the living quality of this tradition, and its consequent development in and through the concrete life of the church (8), seems to bring Newman's insight centre-stage.

III. DOCTRINE: THE NEED TO KNOW BEFORE WE CAN LOVE!

Always the most practical of thinkers, particularly since he was primarily a pastor, Newman realised slowly the indispensable place of doctrine in the exposition of faith. 'We must know concerning God, before we can feel love, fear, hope, or trust towards him. Devotion must have its objects; those objects, as being supernatural, when not represented to our senses by material symbols, must be set before the mind in propositions.'[42] Religion is intrinsically doctrinal and dogmatic, or it will not be at all.

The climate of Newman's day tended to water down this dimension of revelation. It reduced religion to feeling, and dogmas to opinions or beliefs that happened to be held by groups. Newman saw here the central mischief of his own age and of the age to come. He called it liberalism. In his novel, *Loss and Gain*, he portrays, ingeniously and with irony, a fictitious Truth Society whose patrons were Abelard, Benjamin Franklin and Julian the Apostate, and whose guiding principles were 'first, it is uncertain whether truth exists, and, second, it is certain that it cannot be found'.[43]

Truth Exists and is Attainable

In our sixth chapter we showed the philosophical genius of Newman as he studied the human mind. The *Grammar of Assent* is the resultant epistemology. Truth there is and attainable it is. The moment of the mind's judgement is the moment of truth's attainment, when the faculty of judgement, the illative sense, reaches the truth, that which *is*. In that way, the illative sense grounds philosophically the validity of a propositional and doctrinal Christianity. In the process he is able to refute the liberals and to relativise the relativisers of doctrinal Christianity.

A Surprising Parallel

The philosophical and theological greatness of Newman's achievement in this respect is only slowly gaining the recognition it deserves.[44] Neither the formal inference, nor the methods of the natural sciences have a monopoly on truth: there is also true judgement as the act of the illative sense. Not only that, but there is a basic similarity of type, what Bernard Lonergan calls an 'isomorphism', between the scientific method and the mind's journey to the truth in the fields of history, ethics, natural theology and faith.[45] In his attempt to write ecclesiastical history scientifically he discovered the fact of dogma, and its necessary place in Christianity; in the *Grammar* he worked out philosophically the foundation of dogma in the mind's relentless drive towards the truth of reality. Dogma is to faith what conscience is to religion.

So much, then, for the first two Parts of our exposition. There is still a third Part. It consists in the fruits of Christian living.

C. THE LIVING FRUITS:
A RELIGION FOR THE BUSY WORLD

Newman stressed the fact that 'Christianity is a religion for the world, for the busy and influential, as well as for the poor'.[46] He warned of the temptation 'to undervalue this life altogether, and to forget its real importance'. He reminded those who heard him in the 1830s not to succumb to any of the various ways 'the thought of the next world would lead men to neglect their duty in this'. Still, he entered into the difficulty which many sincere Christians would find in harmonising life in the Two Cities. The acute tension in the lives of such people consists in the effort 'steadily to contemplate the life to come, yet to act in this'.[47] Newman spent the greater part of his life communicating the truths of the Christian life to lay men and women. In that task he showed himself a master.

Master Teacher of the Christian Life
He was equipped to fulfil this mission with exceptional distinction. First of all, he had appropriated the life given in revelation, expounded by the fathers, witnessed to by tradition and suffered for by the great cloud of martyrs and saints through the ages. He had roots and so a life. Next, he had the benefits of a theological education and, especially, the insight into the faith which his theological discoveries brought to him. He enjoyed, in other words, the wisdom and so also the skill necessary to impart to others, whether friends, colleagues, students or parishioners, the truth and life of revelation. What is vital for the living of Christians in the world? In the third part of this work there is a presentation of some of the essentials, without any claim whatsoever to completeness. These essentials are provided by revelation and theology. They are, in fact, the fruits of this very revelation and theology.

I. THE 'ABORIGINAL VICAR OF CHRIST' AND THE FIRST FRUIT

As a moral imperative conscience places one before a personal source of moral authority: one feels oneself to be in the presence of a Person, and knows oneself to be addressed by that Person. Thus conscience is 'the connecting principle between the creature and his Creator'. It impresses upon the mind a 'real' or 'imaginative apprehension' of God and the unseen world. In that sense conscience is our foundational teacher of religion, being 'the aboriginal Vicar of Christ, a prophet in its informations, a monarch in its peremptoriness, a priest in its blessings and anathemas'.[48]

Conscience, then, is the sanctuary where God and the concrete life of the individual meet. They encounter at the sacred core of human consciousness, where man is present to God, to himself and to others. This is indeed the highest level of consciousness. Obedience to the voice of God in conscience is the way both to the deepest hold on the truth of religion and to the heights of self-identity. The arrival of revelation and its correlative, faith, do not render conscience obsolete. On the contrary, revelation is the divinely provided antidote to the vulnerability of conscience to bad influence, evil habit, wrong education and human sinfulness. With revelation the voice of conscience grows louder and more distinct, as it were.

The Voice of Conscience and the Voice of the Holy Spirit

It becomes the voice of the Holy Spirit speaking within our hearts (Gal 4:6; Rom 8:15) and coming to complete revelation. Our duty now becomes that of listening attentively for that voice and acting accordingly. The Holy Spirit is the Spirit of love and truth, with his sevenfold gift and twelve fruits. He is the one who enables us to discern the call of Christ the Good Shepherd and to translate that call into the ordinary and the everyday. He is the Spirit of unity between religion and morality, and so the source of harmony between life in the Two Cities. 'A true Christian,' he writes in 1830, 'may almost be defined as one who has a ruling of God's presence within him ... present not externally, not in nature merely, or in providence, but in his innermost heart, òr in his *conscience*.'[49] And if we fail and sin, he is that good Spirit that does not condemn, but convicts of sin while he beckons to repentance and gives the confidence needed to start again, trusting not in ourselves but in the power of God who is 'greater than our conscience and (he) knows everything' (1 Jn 3:20).

II. THE GIFT OF THE SPIRIT: THE SECOND FRUIT

The gift of the Holy Spirit, then, is the second fruit, as it were, of the Christian life, following upon that of conscience. His presence far increases rather than diminishes the responsibilities of each Christian. He focuses the attention of Christians on single-minded devotion to God, both in heaven and in their hearts, and on 'acting towards God and for him in the works of every day'.[50] His presence, however, is costly because demanding. C. S. Dessain appositely remarks that for Newman 'what matters in the church is the invisible part of it, God's grace in the soul and its union with him'.[51] Thus in 1873, when preaching at the opening of St Bernard's seminary in Birmingham, he chose as his subject the apostasy from faith and morality which he saw approaching. His sermon proposes a clear remedy:

> We must gain the habit of feeling that we are in God's pres-
> ence, that he sees what we are doing; and a liking that he
> does so, a love of knowing it, a delight in the reflection, 'Thou
> God seest me' ... Thus an elevation of mind will be created,
> which is the true weapon we must use against the infidelity
> of the world.[52]

The indwelling of the Holy Trinity is, Newman repeats, the most sublime and, at the same time, the most characteristic gift of the New Testament, but it is a gift for daily living. It is an eminently practical gift, albeit a mysterious and demanding one. His attitude as a teacher of Christian lifestyle may be caught in a saying attributed to him, 'If you have a religion like Christianity, think of it and have it worthily.'[53] Vatican II's stress on the universal call to holiness for all the baptised would have delighted him.[54]

III. THE THIRD FRUIT: THE SOURCE OF JOY

The third fruit of revelation and theology for the Christian life is what we have called the 'gospel of joy' in chapter VIII. The spirit of the world tends to dilute the message of revelation and to infiltrate its own atmosphere into the minds and hearts of Christians. To the extent that it succeeds, Christians will live a compromised Christianity, a kind of 'pagan Christianity'. A lot of the Christianity of Newman's day belonged unfortunately to that category. Its practitioners could not realise that they were temples of the Holy Spirit, and so 'raised in the scale of being'.[55] They did not appreciate and could not see what this entails.

The result was a religion which for many became a burden rather than a blessing, a hindrance to the pursuit of their personal pleasures. The Christianity they portrayed was not attractive. It consisted in *not* doing rather than in doing, in avoiding major wrongdoing rather than in living for God and his Kingdom. These Christians might respect their religion, be convinced of its necessity for salvation, and even show a certain perseverance, but would find the idea that the religion of Christ brings joy and freedom simply incredible, indeed impossible.

And yet the revelation of Christ is the joy of women and men. 'The thought of God, and nothing short of it, is the happiness of men ... He alone is sufficient for the heart who made it.'[56] It is not easy for us to realise this, since the management of our hearts is not in our control. Our hearts require the promptings of the Holy Spirit, the coaxing of indwelling grace, the corrections of a lifetime, the assistance of the church, the nourishment of the Eucharist, the healing of penance so that we develop what is in effect a new and second nature – the love of religion. Now such a love is not static but dynamic. It is, in fact, a holy journey, which presupposes the increasing willingness to change and to be changed.[57]

The only authentic joy in life is to be found in this communion with God the Holy Trinity and with God's will. The art of Christian living consists in living from 'the life that is hidden with Christ in God' (Col 3:3). 'The Christian can bear himself; he can (as it were) joy in himself, for it is the grace of God within him, it is the presence of the Eternal Comforter in which he joys ... More thankfulness, more holiness, more of heaven he needs, indeed, but the thought that he can have more is not a thought of trouble but of joy.'[58] The joy of the Christian, then, is not superficial nor unreal. It is rather the promised gift of the Saviour (Jn 15:11; 16:20-4) and the effect of his cross. It is the fruit of the Holy Spirit, and the proof that 'our hope is not in vain' (Rom 5:5).

IV. THE FOURTH FRUIT: THE LIFE OF COMMUNION

The fourth and final fruit of revelation and theology for the Christian life is that of the life of communion. From the scriptures and the fathers Newman learned the doctrine of the unity of the baptised and the corresponding imperative of communion among believers as the law of all laws, the norm of all norms.

> This, then, is the special glory of the Christian Church, that its members do not depend merely on what is visible, they are not stones of a building, piled one on another, and bound together from without, but they are one and all the births and manifestations of one and the same unseen spiritual principle or power, 'living stones', internally connected, as branches from a tree, not as the parts of a heap.[59]

Christians must live by the truth of *who* they are, members of each other and all members together of the one Christ. 'He loves the unseen company of believers who loves those who are seen. The test of our being joined to Christ is love; the test of love towards Christ in his church, is loving those whom we actually see'.[60]

A Man of Ecumenism

Newman's life was that of a man who cherished communion and built unity with and among people. This is surely the fundamental meaning of his enormous correspondence sustained to the end of his long life. In that sense he was a *'homo ecclesiasticus'*, a man of the church. Raised to maturity in the Anglican Church, he was transplanted midway through life into the Catholic Church. Still, the fervent convert remained the committed, albeit realistic, seeker for the unity of Christians. Since unity is *the* sign of Christianity, and mutual love the convincing evidence that those calling themselves Christians actually belong to Christ, Newman worked for the ecumenical cause both within the Catholic Church and beyond.

As we have seen in the previous chapter on Newman as a builder of unity, he worked out a thorough ecumenical method for Catholics consisting of four specific steps. He also listed five guidelines for the wider ecumenism between all the churches. This makes him a theologian of ecumenism and, since he anticipated the modern ecumenical movement as such, a pioneer of ecumenism. But it was as a practitioner and teacher of ecumenism that he shone out most. His ecumenism consisted in the living out of the gospel. 'We are to begin with loving our friends about us, and gradually enlarge the circle of our affections, till it reaches all Christians, and then all men ... The real love of man *must* depend on practice.'[61] Christians who live in that fashion are truly alive. That matters, indeed only that matters finally, because 'you God made alive' (Eph 2:1) and only *this* life gives life.

A Marian Paradigm

When composing in 1843 the sermon, *The Theory of Developments in Religious Doctrine*, one of his most original pieces and the conclusion of the *Oxford University Sermons*, Newman makes a significant, if brief, reference to the place of the Blessed Virgin in revelation and theology. He points to the infancy narrative of St Luke. He saw that Mary welcomed the gift of God's eternal Son, pondered the meaning of what had been given to her, and then lived by this light in her daily life. She gave a singular testimony to the interdependence of revelation, theology and Christian praxis.

Revelation had come to the Blessed Virgin in a unique, indeed incomparable, fashion, since God offered her his eternal Son, the fullness and completion of the revelation growing in the Old Covenant. She conceived him by the overshadowing of the Holy Spirit. In God's design Mary stands at the junction of the Old and

New Covenants, where man is united to God in the word made flesh. There the synagogue becomes the church. There the new People of God begins to be formed as 'a people made one with the unity of the Father, the Son and the Holy Spirit'.[62] Mary is therefore the supreme witness, and custodian of the revelation of the Father through his Son, Jesus Christ in the Holy Spirit.[63]

The Mother of Jesus, however, was not content merely to receive by faith and to conceive by love the Son of God: she also 'treasured', 'pondered' and 'stored' (Lk 2:19, 51) the reality of the Son. The three verbs used by St Luke, with their different nuances, highlight Mary's thought-life, her theologising.[64] Using the logical device called a sorites, which contrasts a later with an early affirmation in such a way that the earlier seems to be denied but only in order to place more emphasis on the later, Newman comments:

> Thus St Mary is our pattern of faith, both in the reception and in the study of divine truth. She does not think it enough to accept, she dwells upon it; not enough to possess, she uses it; not enough to assent, she develops it; not enough to submit the Reason, she reasons upon it; not indeed reasoning first, and believing afterwards, with Zacharias, yet first believing without reasoning, next from love and reverence, reasoning after believing. And thus she symbolises to us, not only the faith of the unlearned, but of the doctors of the church also, who have to investigate, and weigh, and define, as well as to profess the gospel; to draw the line between truth and heresy; to anticipate or remedy the various aberrations of wrong reason; to combat pride and recklessness with their own arms; and thus to triumph over the sophist and the innovator.[65]

Mary, in a word, *does* theology. From the revelation made to her there flows the reflection and thinking which underline the place of theology and the need for theologians. This activity in the Seat of Wisdom is a witness to the vitality of revelation. It highlights revelation's inherent power to make its recipients think, ponder and speculate. Revelation thus leads to thinking, and inspires theology, both the informal variety of all believers and the formal variety of the minority of believers who enjoy the opportunity of studying the texts of the faith and the great tradition under the guidance of experts.

From revelation, then, to theology. There is still a third moment. It consists in Mary's living out the revelation she had received by faith and thought out by her treasuring, pondering and storing. Newman identifies this moment in her concrete action on the occasion of the miracle at Cana (Jn 2:5). 'And accordingly, at the marriage-feast in Cana, her faith anticipated his first miracle, and she said to the servants, "Whatsoever he saith unto you, do it".'[66] Mary welcomes revelation, does theology, but now lives *from* this revelation and *by* this theology. As the Mother of 'the root of Jesse', the Seat of Wisdom and the Help of Christians, the Blessed Virgin is the personal focus of revelation, theology and the Christian life. In her these components of Christian existence converge to create a marvellous icon. The glory and grace of being such an icon, however, 'are not for her own sake, but for her Maker's,'[67] for her divine Son and for our encouragement. He it is who is the life of revelation, the truth of theology, and the way for every man and woman coming into this world (see Jn 14:6; 1:9). Mary's glory is but the reflected glory of this life, this truth and this way. She enables us to see that 'in him was the life' (Jn 1:4) offered 'for the life of the world' (Jn 6:51). In the final analysis, only this life gives life.

NOTES

PRELUDE

1. Coulson, John and Allchin, A. M., (eds.), *The Rediscovery of Newman*, London 1967.
2. Ker, Ian, *John Henry Newman*, Oxford-New York, 1990; Gilley, Sheridan, *Newman and his Age*, London 1990.
3. *Catechism of the Catholic Church*, Dublin 1994, paragraphs 157 (quoting the *Apologia*), 1723 (quoting the *Discourses to Mixed Congregations*), 1778 (quoting the *Letter to the Duke of Norfolk*), and 2144 (quoting *Parochial and Plain Sermons*, V).
4. *The Rediscovery of Newman*, 216f.
5. Pope Paul VI, *l'Osservatore Romano*, 28 October 1963: AAS, 1963, 1025.
6. Liddon, H. P., *Life of Edward Bouverié Pusey*, London 1894, II, 461.
7. Chadwick, Owen, *Newman*, Past Masters Series, Oxford-New York 1983, 5.
8. *CS*, 123.
9. *Apo.*, 108.
10. *Diff.*, II, 24.
11. *Diff.*, I, 370
12. *VM*, I, Preface, xlvii.
13. *Apo.*, 150; see *Dev.*, 359-60.
14. *Diff.*, II, 248.
15. *SSD*, 133.
16. *US*, 313.
17. O'Loughlin, T., 'Newman on *Doing* Theology', *New Blackfriars*, 76 (1995), 97.

CHAPTER 1

1. Bouyer, Louis, *Newman's Vision of Faith*, San Francisco 1986, 18; see 47.
2. *US*, 197; PS, II, 27: 'when love waxed cold'.
3. Bouyer, op. cit., 15.
4. *SD*, 117.
5. *LD*, XXIX, 91.
6. *Diff.*, II, 86-7.
7. *Ess.*, I, 23.
8. Dawson, C., 'Newman and the Modern World', *The Tablet*, London, Aug. 5 1972, 733-4.

9. Ward, II, 415-6.

10. St Augustine, *De catechizandis rudibus*, IV, 8: PL 40:316; quoted in Vatican II, *Dei Verbum*, 1.

11. *Apo.*, 49.

12. Dessain, C. S., *Life*, 44. Perhaps Paul Misner is a little premature in concluding that Newman 'needed a more adequate notion of revelation than was then available', in 'Newman's concept of revelation and the development of doctrine', *Heythrop Journal*, 1 (1970), 32-47 at 47.

13. *PS*, I, 210.

14. ibid.

15. *PS*, II, 35.

16. Quoted in Guitton, Jean, *The Church and the Laity*, New York 1964, 6.

17. Bouyer, op. cit., 14.

18. *PS*, I, 211.

19. ibid., II, 155.

20. ibid., VI, 57.

21. ibid., 58.

22. ibid.

23. First Preface for Christmas.

24. *PS*, IV, 202-3.

25. ibid., II, 168.

26. ibid., IV, 208.

27. ibid., II, 153.

28. ibid., VI, 74.

29. Dean Church, *The Oxford Movement*, 191-2.

30. von Balthasar, Hans Urs , *Man in History*, London 1972, 271.

31. See *PS*, VI, 83-4.

32. ibid., VI, 84-6.

33. *Jfc.*, 203-7.

34. *PS*, II, 229-30.

35. ibid., V, 138-40.

36. ibid., II, 222-3.

37. *Jfc.*, 201.

38. *PS*, II, 217.

39. ibid., V, 138; 'the Spirit revealing it' (the gospel), *PS*, II, 227.

40. *Apo.*, 93.

41. *PS*, V, 337.

42. ibid., I, 203, 204, 203, 208.

43. ibid., 208.

44. ibid., 211.

45. Dessain, C. S., *Life*, 30; see *US*, 172.

46. *PS*, I, 211.

47. ibid., 209.

48. See *PS*, IV, Sermon 19; III, Sermon 12; II, Sermon 8.

49. *Ess*, II, 242.

50. *PS*, I, 211-2, 212-3.

51. *Ess*, II,242.

52. ibid., I, 41-2.

53. *D.A.*, 388.

54. See Ker, *Healing the Wound of Humanity: The Spirituality of John Henry Newman*, London 1993, 43-50.

55. *Apo.*, 27.

56. *Ari.*, 37.

57. *Jfc.*, 316.

58. *US*, 336.

59. ibid., 332.

60. *PS*, III, 250.

61. *US*, Sermon 2.

62. *US* 28; see Mix, 174.

63. *PS*, VI, 69-82.

64. *US*, 27.

65. Soloviev, V., *God, Man and the Church*, London 1938, quoted in von Balthasar, H. U., *The Glory of the Lord*, III, Edinburgh 1986, 287.

66. *US*, 172.

67. *DA*, 296.

68. *PS*, V, 29-45; VI, 94-104.

69. ibid., I, 24.,

70. Kasper, W., *ITQ*, 2 (1989), 97.

71. See *GS* 24.

72. *DV*, 2.

73. Dessain, C. S., *Life*, 22.

74. See von Balthasar, H. U., 'God is his own Exegete', *Comm*, 4 (1986), 280-7.

75. *PS*, VI, 58-9.

76. von Balthasar, H. U., *The Glory of the Lord*, I, Edinburgh 1982, 125-6.

77. Solzhenitsyn, A., *A Documentary Record*, (ed.) L. Labedz, Penguin 1970, 151.

78. Bertoldi, F. 'Henri de Lubac on Dei Verbum', *Comm*, 1 (1990), 91.

79. de Lubac, H., *La Rivelazione Divina*, Milano 1985, 33.

80. See O'Collins, G., SJ, *Fundamental Theology*, London 1981, chapter 3; Rahner, K., *Theological Investigations*, XVIII, London 1984, passim.

81. *PS*, II, 154; *Call*, 222.

CHAPTER 2

1. de Lubac, Henri, *Catholicism*, London 1950, 150.

2. Gilley, Sheridan, *Newman and his Age*, London 1990, 91.

3. *LD*, II, 150.

4. *Diff.*, I, 370.

5. ibid., p.388.

6. *Diff.*, II, 24.

7. Quoted in Guitton, J., *The Modernity of St Augustine*, London 1959, 65.

8. *Ess..*, I, 23.

9. *Diff.*, I, 370-1.

10. *Apo.*, 7.

11. Dessain, C. S., *John Henry Newman*, London 1960, 10.

12. *Apo.*, 26.

13. Quoted in Ker's definitive biography, 56.

14. Tristram, H., *John Henry Newman: Autobiographical Writings*, London and New York 1956, 82-3.

15. *LD*, II, 30.

16. ibid., 369.

17. Mitchell, Basil, 'Newman as a Philosopher' in Ker and Hill (eds.), *Newman after A Hundred Years*, Oxford 1990, 223.

18. *Moz.*, I, 184.

19. *Apo.*, 25.

20. *Diff.*, I, 371.

21. *LD*, V, 133.

22. Ker, 120; see LD, V, 133.

23. *Diff.*, I, 371-2.

24. Apo., 26.

25. Dessain, C. S., *Life*, 11.

26. *Ess.*, I, 228; see his Tract, *On the Text of the Epistles of St Ignatius*, begun with notes in 1828 and completed in 1870, in TTE, 93-135.

27. *Ess.*, I, 233.

28. ibid., 236.

29. ibid., 238.

30. ibid., 228.

31. *Diff.*, II, 24.

32. Ker, I., *Reader*, 21.

33. St Ambrose, *De Fide ad Gratianum*, I.V.42: PL 16:537, and CSEL 18:78, edited by Faller, Otto, SJ; it is the epigram of the *Grammar of Assent* and is quoted in *Arians*, 29, n.9; *Ess.*, II, 42; *LD*, XXIII, 275.

34. *Jfc.*, 2; see Flynn, J., *John Henry Newman on Grace and Mind*, unpublished doctoral dissertation, St Patrick's College, Maynooth, 1992, 171-83.

35. *Jfc.*, 217; see St Augustine, *Sermo* 143: PL 38:784-7; St Leo, *Sermo* 74, 4: *PL* 54: 360-7.

36. *Jfc.*, 144.

37. ibid., 175.

38. ibid., 214; see St Augustine, *Sermo* 143, PL 38: 784-7.

39. See St Athanasius, in *Ath.*, II, 380.

40. *Jfc.*, 206-7.

41. ibid., 50-1; see St Augustine, *Sermo* 169, 8:PL 38:921; also *De spiritu et littera*, 15: PL 44:209; H. Chadwick makes no reference to the contribution of the fathers to Newman's treatment of justification in his splendid essay on *Justification*, 'The *Lectures on Justification*', in Ker and Hill (eds.), *Newman After A Hundred Years*, Oxford 1990, 287-308.

42. Ker, I., *Reader*, 29; see *Salvation and Grace*, Irish Inter-Church Meeting, Dublin 1993, passim.

43. *Jfc.*, 31, n.1.

44. ibid., 265.

45. ibid., 121.

46. *Dev.*, New York 1956, 90-1.

47. See Finan T., 'St Augustine on the *'mira profunditas'* of Scripture: Texts and Contexts', in Finan, Thomas and Twomey, Vincent (eds.), *Scriptural Interpretation in the Fathers*, Dublin 1995, 163-99.

48. *Diff.*, I, 400.

49. *Apo.*, 43.

50. ibid., 27.

51. *Ess.*, II, 193.

52. *VM*, I, 60.

53. *PS*, VII, 149.

54. Dragas, G., 'John Henry Newman: A Starting-Point for rediscovering the Catholicity of the Fathers Today', *The Greek Orthodox Theological Review*, 3 (1980), 279.

55. *TT*, 170-1; *VM*, I, 51.

56. *Diff.*, I, 373; Apo., 182.

57. *Apo.*, 116.

58. St Augustine, *Contra epistulam Parmeniani*, III, IV, 24: PL 43:101; see two translations in the *LD*, 'The whole church has no chance of being wrong' (XXV, 220), and 'The Christian commonwealth judges without misgiving, (XXIV, 354); Artz, 'Newmans Vier Maximen' in *Catholica*, 2(1979), 134-52.

59. *Apo.*, 117.

60. Dulles, A., 'Newman, Conversion, and Ecumenism', *TS*, 4(1990), 438

61. *Diff.*, I, 373.

62. *Diff.*, II, 24.

63. See Kannengiesser, C., 'Listening to the Fathers', *Comm*, 3(1989), 415.

64. See Dragas, G., 'Conscience and Tradition: Newman and Athanasius in the Greek-Orthodox Church', *Newman Studien*, II, 73-84.

65. See relevant entries in *Artz, Lexikon*.

66. See *Diff.*, I, 400.

CHAPTER 3

1. Simpson, Richard, *The Rambler*, December 1858.

2. Pope Paul VI, Address to Newman Symposium, Rome, 1975, in *l'Osservatore Romano*, April 17, 1975.

3. *GA*, 487-8.

4. Novak, M., 'Newman on Nicea', *TS*, 21 (1960), 449-50.

5. *Moz.*, II, 129-30.

6. See *Mix*, 342-76.

7. *Apo.*, 80.

8. Dessain, C. S., *Life*, London, 1966, 22; see Hans Urs von Balthasar, *Herrlichkeit*, I, Einsiedeln, 1961, 158.

9. *PS*, I, 210.

10. ibid., 80; see *GA*, 425.

11. OS, 57, 53; see Artz, J., 'Newman Heute', *Theologische Quartalschrift*, 2 (1977), 119-39.

12. *Dev.*, 304, 186.

13. *Ath.*, II, 51; see HS, I, 209-10.

14. *Dev.*, 186, HS, I, 402-3.

15. *US*, 317.

16. *VM*, I, XL.

17. *Ess.*, I, 23.

18. ibid., 69-70.

19. ibid., 30-101.

20. *Campaign*, 394-5; see *Apo.*, Note A, 285-97.

21. *GA*, 387.

22. See fascinating statement on 'Catholic Fullness' in *Ess.*, II, 231-3.

23. Pope Paul VI, *l'Osservatore Romano*, October 28, 1963.

24. *Dev.*, 444-5; see, *LD*, XI, 109-110.

25. Dessain, C. S., 'Newman's First Conversion', *Newman Studien*, III Folge, Nürnberg, 1957, 37-53.

26. *GA*, Note II, 495-501.

27. *Apo.*, 169: emphasis my own.

28. See my book, *Newman and his Theological Method*, Leiden, 1977, 88-9; *DA*, 294.

29. Lonergan, B., *Method in Theology*, London, 1972, 338.

30. *GA*, 288.

31. *LD*, XI, 190-10; see *US*, 198-9.

32. *DA*, 295.

33. *Idea*, 121.

34. *DA*, 294. Newman quotes a large portion of this article in the *GA*, 88-92.

35. Ker, I., *Newman and the Fullness of Christianity*, Edinburgh 1993.

36. *GA*, New York 1955, 21; N. Lash calls it 'a seminal work in the philosophy of religion' in his introduction to the 1979 edition of the work, Notre Dame and London, 12.

37. ibid., 499; see 316.

38. See Fey, W., *Faith and Doubt*, 1976.

39. Bacchus, F., 'How to Read the Grammar of Assent', *The Month*, 1926; see also Ker, 'Newman and Truth', *ITQ*, 1(1977), 67-8.

40. *GA*, 263f; see Rombold, Günther, *Das Wesen der Person nach John Henry Newman*, *Newman Studien*, IV Folge, Nürnberg, 1960, 19.

41. Novak, M., 'Newman on Nicea', *TS*, 21 (1960), 444-53.

42. A keyword and concern in all his writing.

43. Crowe, M., 'Intuition', *New Catholic Encyclopaedia*, VII, 700; see Worgul, G. S., 'The Ghost of Newman in the Lonergan Corpus', *The Modern Schoolman*, 5 (1977), 319.

44. *GA*, 271.

45. ibid., 384-5, 409; see Sillem, E., *The Philosophical Notebook*, I, London, 1969, 67-148.

46. See *PS*, V. 127; IV, 82-3.

47. *Dev.*, 99-121.

48. See my book, *Newman and his Theological Method*, chapter 4, 'Theology and its Methodical Foundations', 84-111.

49. *GA*, 288.

50. ibid., 288, 343-83, 320-3.

51. *LD*, XXIV, 375.

52. Gal 4:4; Heb 1:3.

53. See *GA*, 318; note the vital role played by conscience in the work of appropriation, ibid., 101-21, 500-1.

54. ibid., 133.

55. ibid., Note II, 495-501; *DA*, 367; note the striking parallel with von Balthasar, *Herrlichkeit*, I, 160; see E. D'Arcy, 'The new catechism and Cardinal Newman', *Comm*, 3 (1993), 485-502.

56. Govaert, L., *Kardinal Newmans Mariologie und sein persönlicher Werdegang*, Salzburg, 1975.

57. *Apo.*, 196.

58. *US*, 317; see Artz, J., 'Newman Heute', *Theologische Quartalschrift*, 2 (1977), 128.

59. *Apo.*, 95; *Ward*, II, 275.

60. *LD*, XXIV, 212-3.

61. ibid., 213.

62. *GA*, 410-1.

63. ibid., 414-8.

64. *Apo.*, 198.

65. *GA*, 495-501.

CHAPTER 4

1. *Weidner*, 58; *GA*, 191; see Biemer, G., *Newman on Tradition*, London 1966, passim.

2. *US*, 313; see O' Loughlin, Thomas, 'Newman on DOING theology', *New Blackfriars*, 76(1995), 92-8.

3. See Bouyer, L., *Newman's Vision of Faith*, San Francisco 1986.

4. *Ess.*, I, 125-6.

5. For a treatment of the issue see Brown, Raymond E., Fitzmyer, Joseph A., Murphy, Roland E., *The New Jerome Biblical Commentary*, London 1990, 770-1; the idea of the 'Depositum Fidei' occurs three times in *The Catechism of the Catholic Church*, nn. 84, 97, 175.

6. *Apo.*, 4.

7. ibid., 5.

8. ibid., 9.

9. See Ker, 162; see Nockles, P., 'The Oxford Movement: The Historical Background', in G. Rowell, (ed.), *Tradition Remembered. The Oxford Movement Conference Papers*, London 1986, 24-50, especially 34-5.

10. *Apo.*, 26.

11. *Ath.*, I, vi.

12. *Apo.*, 26.

13. See, for example, Kelly, J. N. D., *Early Christian Creeds*, London 1968, 223-51 with extensive bibliography; Twomey, V., *Apostolikos Thronos*, Münster 1982, passim; Williams, R., *Arius. Heresy and Tradition*, London 1987.

14. *LD*, XXX, 105, 240.

15. *US*, 82.

16. Acts 9:2; 18:25,26; 19:9,23; 22:4; 24:14,22.

17. St Jerome, in *Dialogus contra Luciferos*, 19: *PL* 23:191: cited in Ari, 350.

18. *Ari*, 445-6; see Stern, J., 'Le Magistére et les Théologiens', in *Seminarium*, XXIX (1989), 384.

19. *US*, 96.
20. *Cons.*, 64, 73.
21. ibid., 65, 72-3.
22. See Note V (1873) to the Third Edition of the *Arians*, 445-68.
23. *Tract One*, Published by the Rocket Press, 1985, 17.
24. ibid., 18; *Apo.*, 50, 'As to the Episcopal system, I founded it upon the Epistles of St Ignatius, which inculcated it in various ways.'
25. *Apo.*, 43.
26. ibid., 56f.
27. ibid., 49.
28. *Ath.*, II, 193.
29. *PS*, III, 290-1.
30. *Apo.*, 51.
31. *Ess..*, I, 102-37, 'Apostolical Tradition'.
32. ibid., 117.
33. ibid., 117, 118, 121.
34. *Ath.*, II, 231.
35. ibid., 125.
36. *Weidner*, XXXIV.
37. ibid., 79; see VM, I, 158.
38. *DV*, 10.
39. *Apo.*, 55f.
40. ibid., 55.
41. ibid., 54.
42. ibid., 53.
43. *VM*, II, 28.
44. *Apo.*, 166.
45. Gilley, 157.
46. Lease, G., *Witness to the Faith*, Shannon 1969, 57.
47. Gilley, 156; see VM, I, 77; *Apo.*, 63f.
48. *LD*, VI, 13.
49. ibid., 250-1.
50. *VM*, I, 49, 51, 71.
51. ibid., 38.
52. ibid., 249.
53. Ker, I., *The Achievement of John Henry Newman*, Notre Dame and London 1990, 105.
54. *VM*, I, 250.
55. ibid., 251.
56. *Weidner*, 270.
57. *Apo.*, 114f.
58. For a detailed account of the incident in Newman's life, see Lease, 62f.

59. Ward, M., *Young Mr Newman*, 462; see also *Correspondence with John Keble*, 16-25.

60. *Apo.*, 115-6.

61. *Ath.*, II, 51.

62. St Athanasius, *de Decr.*, 27.

63. *Orations*, II, 34.

64. *Ath.*, II, 312.

65. St Irenaeus, *Adv. Haer.*, III, 3, 4.

66. *Ath.*, II, 313.

67. *Weidner*, 321.

68. ibid.

69. See *Dev.*, ch. VII, 4, 2.

70. See *VM*, I, Lecture X, 'On the Essentials of the Gospel', 239-65.

71. *Diff.*, II, 11.

72. ibid., 12.

73. *Ath.*, II, vi.

74. ibid., 51.

75. *Cons.*, 63.

76. ibid., 55: it 'is a branch of evidence which it is natural or necessary for the church to regard and consult, before she proceeds to any definition, from its intrinsic cogency'.

77. ibid., 73; see Dragas, G., 'Conscience and Tradition. Newman and Athanasius in the Greek-Orthodox Church', *Newman Studien*, II, 73-84.

78. *GA*, passim.

79. *Cons.*, 72.

80. *Ineffabilis Deus*, DS 2800-4.

81. *DA*, 137.

82. *Diff.*, II, 140.

83. ibid., 138-9.

84. ibid., 139.

85. ibid., 31; see *Dev* (1845), 384.

86. See copious texts, ibid., 33-44.

87. ibid., 140-1.

88. ibid., 140.

89. ibid., 46.

90. See Lease, G., op. cit., ch. 5, 43-52.

CHAPTER 5

1. See the fine commentary on these words in St John of the Cross, *The Ascent of Mount Carmel*, Bk 2, ch. 22: 'The apostle gives us to understand that God has become as if dumb, with nothing more to

say, because what he spoke before in fragments to the prophets he has said all at once, by giving us the all who is his Son'.

2. Nicholas of Cusa, *Opera*, Basle 1565, 411-2: text in Henri de Lubac, *Catholicism*, London 1950, 283-4; Compare St Augustine, *Sermo* 288, 4-5.

3. See von Balthasar, *Love Alone the way of Revelation*, London 1975.

4. See Exodus 34:6 and the prophetical elaboration of this theme in Hosea 2:16-22.

5. Lash, N., *Change in Focus*, London 1973, 59.

6. Butler, B. C., *The Theology of Vatican II*, London 1967, 28.

7. Lash, *Change in Focus*, 3.

8. The Second Vatican Council, *Dei Verbum, The dogmatic constitution on divine Revelation*, Dublin 1975, ed. A. Flannery, 2: hereafter *DV*.

9. *DV*, 2, Abbot edition, Dublin and London 1966.

10. *DV*, 2; see von Balthasar, *Herrlichkeit: Eine theologische Ästhetik*, III, 2/2, Einsiedeln 1969; 'Zur Gestalt der Theologie', 93-104.

11. *DV*, 1, 10.

12. Congar, Y., *Tradition and Traditions*, London 1966, 3; see also 18, 22.

13. See Schillebeeckx, E., *Revelation and Theology*, London 1967, 215f.

14. Newman, J. H., *Select Treatises of St Athanasius*, Vol. II, London 1842, 51, 250; see footnote 36.

15. Schillebeeckx, E., *Revelation and Theology*, 216.

16. Congar, *Tradition and Traditions*, 24-5.

17. Newman, J. H., *On Consulting the Faithful in Matters of Doctrine*, in Guitton, J., *The Church and the Laity*, New York, 1964, 73; Newman's thinking throws considerable light on the contemporary problems posed by the moral attitude of those who oppose the official teaching of the church in certain moral areas.

18. Lash, *Change in Focus*, 40.

19. See Congar, *Tradition and Traditions*, 15.

20. Barth, K., *Vatican II: La Révélation Divine II*, Paris 1968, 522.

21. *DV*, 8.

22. *DV*, 10.

23. Kasper, W., 'The Relationship between Gospel and Dogma: An Historical Approach', in *Concilium* 1, 3 (1967), 77.

24. See Rom 3:3; 2 Thess 3:3; Hb 10:23; 11:11.

25. *DV*, 2, 4.

26. Ignatius of Antioch, *Epistle to the Ephesians* 4 as quoted in J. H. Newman, *Catholic Sermons*, London 1957, 120; see *Early Christian Writings*, London 1968, 76.

27. Vatican II, *Dogmatic Constitution on the Church, Lumen Gentium*, 4.

28. Vatican I, *Dei Filius*, DS 3016, 3020.

29. Voegelin, E., *Order and History*, vols I-IV, Louisiana State University Press 1956-1974.

30. Voegelin, E., 'Immortality: Experience and Symbol', in *Harvard Theological Review*, July 1967, 235.

31. ibid., 235.

32. ibid., 237.

33. von Balthasar, Hans Urs, *Prayer*, London 1961, 86.

34. Newman, J. H., *Oxford University Sermons*, Westminister, Md, 1966, 91-2, 95.

35. Newman, *On Consulting*, 103-4; compare with B. Lonergan, 'Theology in its New Context', *A Second Collection*, London 1974, 55-68.

36. See Pope Paul VI's description of Newman's journey into the Catholic Church ' ... the most toilsome, but also the greatest, the most meaningful, the most conclusive, that human thought ever travelled during the last century, indeed one might say during the modern era', *l'Osservatore Romano*, 28th October 1963, AAS, 1963, 1025; see Dragas, G., 'Conscience and Tradition, Newman and Athanasius in the Greek-Orthodox Church', in *Newman Studien*, Vol II, 73-84, Nürnberg 1980: 'He (Newman) sees Tradition as the fundamental intuition behind St Athanasius' arguments, which is connected with the inner 'subjectivity' of the church (the *Nous Christou* and the *Ecclesiasticon Phronema*), which finds its expression in the Church's witness through catechetical and liturgical practice and indeed historical action ... Particularly important is Newman's appropriation of Athanasian theological methodology', 77, 78.

37. Newman, *Moz.*, II, London 1891, 129-30.

38. Lockhart, W., *Cardinal Newman*, London 1891, 25-6.

39. Voegelin, E., *Immortality*, 240.

40. *DV* 8: the text speaks of 'tradition which ... develops'.

41. *Decree on Priestly Formation*, 16.

42. See *Pastoral Constitution on the Church in the Modern World*, 48; von Balthasar, 'Tradition', in *Elucidations*, London 1975, 73-82.

43. *DV*, 7.

CHAPTER 6

1. See *PS*, II, Sermon, 'The Incarnation', 26-40.

2. Montalembert, *Life of Fr Lacordaire*, 19.

3. *Apo.*, 285.

4. ibid., 286.

5. *Moz.*, I, 237.

6. Campaign, 394-5; see striking comments in *Apo.*, 191-2; 203; 297. In the field of education, however, 'liberalism' was Newman's preference.

7. *Apo.*, 48.

8. Walsh, D., 'The Challenge of Newman's Vision of the University', unpublished address to international Newman symposium, Dublin 1982, 11.

9. *Apo.*, 288. The 'sacrificium intellectus' 'was understood from Athanasius to Kant ... (as) the obligation not to operate with the human intellect in regions inaccessible to it', Voegelin, *The Philosophy of Order*, Stuttgart 1981, 451.

10. *Dev.*, 357-8.

11. *Apo.*, 49.

12. ibid., 4; Dessain, C. S., 'Newman's First Conversion', *Newman Studien*, III, Nürnberg 1956, 37-53.

13. See comment of Church, R. W., *Occasional Papers*, II, 457.

14. *Ess.*, I, 23.

15. See *PS*, II, 153-4.

16. Eph 3:8; Rom 16:25-7; Vatican II, *Dei Verbum*, 6.

17. Dessain, C.S., *Life*, 22.

18. *PS*, I, 24.

19. See *PS*, I, 54-6; 233; 335; VII, 203; von Balthasar, *Man in History*, London 1972, 271.

20. Vargish, Thomas, *Newman: The Contemplation of Mind*, London 1973, VIII, 25-71.

21. *Apo.*, 294.

22. ibid., 289.

23. *Idea*, 393.

24. ibid., 389.

25. ibid., 387.

26. ibid.

27. ibid.

28. ibid., 390.

29. See Lonergan's perceptive comments on Newman's analysis in *Collection*, I, London 1967, 114-120; and in *A Second Collection*, London 1974, 141f.

30. *Idea*, 397.

31. *Apo.*, 288.

32. ibid., 288-9.

33. See Dessain, *Life*, 36.

34. *Apo.*, 203, 214, 294.

35. ibid., 58.

36. Chesterton, G. K., *St Thomas Aquinas*, London 1933, 106.

37. Solzhenitsyn, A., *A Documentary Record*, L. Labedz, (ed.), Penguin 1970, 151.

38. *GA*, 46; *Dev*, 59-60.
39. *Campaign*, 395.
40. *Apo.*, 295.
41. See *DA*, ch. IV, 'The Tamworth Reading Room', 254-305.
42. ibid., 261.
43. Dessain, *Life*, 68f.
44. *DA*, 262, 264, 266, 268, 270, 273-4; see Ker, *Healing the Wound of Humanity. The Spirituality of John Henry Newman*, London 1993, passim.
45. *DA*, 254-305.
46. ibid., 201; see Vargish, op. cit., 127.
47. *DA*, 264.
48. ibid, 266.
49. See *Sermon* 'Unreal Words', PS, V, 29-45.
50. *DA*, 292.
51. *Campaign*, 398.
52. ibid.
53. ibid., 399.
54. *Apo.*, 295.
55. *VV*, 144.
56. *Apo.*, 14.
57. Dessain, *Life*, 12.
58. *Ward*, I, 444.
59. *PS*, II, 222.
60. *US*, 174.
61. *GA*, 488.
62. See Lash, N., *Change in Focus*, London 1973, 83-96.
63. *Apo.*, 197f.
64. Lash, *Newman on Development*, London 1979, 2.
65. *US*, 317.
66. Lash, *Change in Focus*, 59.
67. *Apo.*, 197.
68. *Diff.*, I, 368.
69. *LD*, XIII, 78; see *LD*, XI, 110; *LD*, XIII, 295; *Ward*, I, 237-8; *Dev*, conclusion.
70. *Apo.*, 198.
71. See *Ess.*, I, 30-101.
72. *Apo.*, 196-7.
73. Sillem, E., *The Philosophical Notebook*, I, 67-149.
74. *Idea*, 387f.
75. *GA*, 350; Sillem, ibid., 60-6.
76. *GA*, 164.
77. ibid., see ch. IX, 'The Illative Sense', 343-83.

78. Crowe, F., 'Intuition', *New Catholic Encyclopaedia*, VII, 700.

79. *GA*, 288.

80. ibid., 1870 edition, 346.

81. ibid., 259-69; see Lonergan, *Collection* I, 1, 2, 5, 6.

82. Voegelin, E., 'The Gospel and Culture', *Jesus and Man's Hope*, II, Proceedings of the Pittsburgh Festival on the Gospels, Pittsburg 1971, 65.

83. *PS*, III, 115.

84. *Moz.* II, 129-30.

85. *CS*, 121, 123.

86. *SE*, 104.

87. *Apo.*, 198.

88. *GA*, 499.

89. ibid.

90. See *Prepos.*, 279-91.

91. *DA*, 294.

92. *GA*, 94.

93. Lonergan, *Method in Theology*, London 1972, 338.

94. *GA*, 302; see 162f.

95. *US*, 198.

96. Quoted in Guitton, J., *The Church and the Laity*, New York 1964, 6.

97. *GA*, 499.

98. *LD*, XXV, 56.

99. ibid., 56-7.

100. Simpson, R., *The Rambler*, December 1859.

CHAPTER 7

1. See Artz, *Lexikon*, 'Gewisssen', 396-400.

2. See Grave, S. A., *Conscience in Newman's Thought*, Oxford 1989; *Newman Studien*, IX, 1974 and XI, 1980; J. Finnis, 'Conscience in the *Letter to the Duke of Norfolk*', in Ker and Hill, (eds.), *Newman After a Hundred Years*, Oxford 1990, 401-18.

3. *Apo.*, 241.

4. ibid.

5. *GA*, 424.

6. ibid., 425.

7. See my *Newman and his Theological Method. A Guide for the Theologian Today*, Brill 1977, 114-6.

8. *GA*, 426.

9. ibid., 414.

10. Gabriel Marcel centres his philosophy on this central distinction between mystery and problem.

11. *GA*, 164.

12. *DA*, 294.

13. *GA*, 302.

14. ibid., 311.

15. ibid., 425; he refers to Sermon V of *OS*, 'Dispositions for Faith', 60-74.

16. See *GA*, ch. IV, *Notional and Real Assent*, 36-97.

17. *Ward*, II, 589.

18. See Pope John Paul II, *Crossing the Threshold of Hope*, 34.

19. For references, see Artz, *Lexikon*, 396-400.

20. *GA*, 390.

21. ibid., 348-9.

22. ibid., 105, 106.

23. ibid., 106.

24. Grave, S.A., op. cit., 34.

25. *US*, 66.

26. ibid., 274; see 217-8 where Newman gives the analogy of the general assessing rapidly the battlefield; and Grave, op. cit., 45.

27. ibid., Sermon XIII, 'Implicit and Explicit Reason', 251-77; see comments of Grave, 45.

28. Grave, 46.

29. See Sillem, E., *The Philosophical Notebook*, I, Louvain 1970; and Verbeke, G., 'The Aristotelian Roots of the Illative Sense', in Bastable, James D., (ed.), *Newman and Gladstone*, Dublin 1978, 177-96.

30. *GA*, 353-4; see SE, 97-8.

31. *GA*, 353, referring to the *Nicomachean Ethics*, vi, 3;4.

32. ibid., 354..

33. Verbeke, G., op. cit., 191.

34. *Diff.*, II, 246-7.

35. Pope John Paul II, *Veritatis Splendor*, London 1993, sections 3; 59; see 57-60.

36. *Diff.*, II, 246-7; see J. Finnis' important correction of points of detail, 'Newman on Conscience', in *Newman after a Hundred Years*, 416-7. Finnis corrects Newman's contention that 'conscience cannot come into direct collision with the church's or Pope's infallibility' (*Diff.*, II, 256) by showing that '(1) Conscience is "engaged on" and makes "judgement upon" propositions more general than that this particular option is not to be made now by me. (2)And the general propositions which are the proper object of the church's infallibility include negative universals which, by absolutely excluding all actions of a specific type, exclude this particular option which could be made by me now' (412-3).

37. *Diff*, II, 247.
38. ibid.
39. *GA*, 107.
40. *Diff*, II, 250.
41. *GA*, 106.
42. ibid., 110.
43. ibid., 110, 109.
44. *OS*, 65.
45. *GA*, 101, 102.
46. ibid., 102.
47. ibid., 104.
48. *Diff*., II, 261; see Pope John Paul II, *Crossing the Threshold of Hope*, London 1994, 191.
49. Crosby, J., 'What is anthropocentric and what is theocentric in Christian existence?: The Challenge of John Henry Newman', *Comm*, 2 (1989), 253; see also his 'The encounter of God and man in Moral Obligation', *The New Scholasticism*, 3 (1986), 317-55.
50. ibid., 253.
51. See my *Newman and his Theological Method*, Leiden 1977, 91-5.
52. *Diff*., II, 248.
53. *PS*, V, 316.
54. *GA*, 348-9.
55. *Diff*., II, 249.
56. Guitton, J., *Newman and the Laity*, New York 1964, 8.
57. *Diff*, II, 250.
58. ibid., 249.
59. Voegelin, E., 'The Gospel and Culture', in *Jesus and Man's Hope*, II, Pittsburgh 1971, 65.
60. Ratzinger, J., 'Conscience in its Age', in *Church Ecumenism and Politics*, Slough 1988, 165 where he illustrates his position with chilling quotations from Hermann Rauschning's conversations with Adolf Hitler.
61. Solzhenitsyn, Alexander, *Alexander Solzhenitsyn Speaks to the West*, London 1978, 95-100.
62. Walsh, David, *After Ideology*, 14; see also Lewis, C. S., *The Abolition of Man*, London 1978; Frankl, V., *Man's Search for Meaning*, London 1989[3].
63. *OS*, 67.
64. *US*, 67.
65. See H. Fries' fascinating comparison of Newman and Rahner in *Newman Studien*, XI, 211-5.
66. *GA*, 425.

67. *Mix*, 276.

68. *Diff.*, II, 253-4; see 259.

69. Kent, J., 'Conscience and Authority: Newman and Tyrrell', *Newman Studien*, IX, 151-168.

70. See Holmes, J. D., 'Personal Influence and Religious Conviction: Newman and Controversy' in *Newman Studien*, X, 26-46.

71. *Diff.*, II, 248-9.

72. Preface Third Edition *VM*, I, XLVII.

73. ibid., XL.

74. *Diff.*, II, 252.

75. *Dev.*, 86.

76. Coulson, J., op. cit., 171.

77. *HS*, III, 79.

78. Przywara, E., 'Newman: möglicher Heiliger und Kirchenlehrer der neuen Zeit?', *Newman Studien*, III, Nürnberg 1957, 3: quoted by Merrigan, Terence, 'Newman's Catholic Synthesis', in *ITQ*, 1 (1994), 43.

CHAPTER 8

1. *ITQ*, 3 (1982), 184-94.

2. Strange, R., *Newman and the Gospel of Christ*, London 1981, vii.

3. Dessain, C. S., 'The Biblical Basis of Newman's Ecumenical Theology' in Coulson, John and Allchin, A. M., (eds.), *The Rediscovery of Newman: An Oxford Symposium*, (London 1967), 102; *John Henry Newman*, London 1966, 61.

4. Calkins, *ibid.*, 192; he is referring here to Pope Paul VI's Apostolic Exhortation for the Holy Year of 1975, *Gaudete in Domino*.

5. ibid., 184.

6. Pope Paul VI, *Evangelii Nuntiandi*, 1975.

7. *PS*, I, 325-35.

8. ibid., I, 326-7.

9. Calkins, ibid., 185.

10. *PS*, VII, 105-6.

11. *PS*, IV, 334-7.

12. See *PS*, V, 137, 204.

13. Calkins, ibid., 191.

14. *PS*, V, 271.

15. ibid., 69-70.

16. *PS*, VI, 70; VIII, 235 – here Newman proceeds to quote Phil 2:5-7 and 1 Pet 1:8-9: 'It (Christmas Day) is a day of joy; it is good to be joyful – it is wrong to be otherwise.' This last sentence seems to paraphrase the Christmas homily of Pope St Leo the Great, *Breviary*, Vol I, 185-6.

17. *PS*, VI, 369-70.

18. *PS*, VII, 184.

19. *PS*, VIII, 139; see Sermon 'Peace and Joy amid Chastisement' in *PS*, IV, 117-132; also VI, 96f.

20. *PS* VII, 90; see ibid., 96, 101, ll5; 70.

21. Calkins, ibid., 184.

22. In Ker's judgement, 'there is no doubt that they constitute one of the great classics of Christian spirituality', 90.

23. Lonergan, B. J., *Insight*, London-New York 1957, 13-18; *Method in Theology*, London 1972, chapter 'Dialectic', 235-66.

24. See *Idea*, London 1917; 381-404; *CS*, 117-134; SE, 104.

25. *CS*, 120-3.

26. *PS*, I, 322.

27. ibid., 311-2; see ibid., 27.

28. See *Apo.*, 36-91.

29. *PS*, III, 267-9.

30. Dessain, C. S., *Life*, 22.

31. *PS*, I, 24.

32. *LD*, V, 21-2; see the strong words in *PS*, I, 54-6; ibid., 233; 335; VII, 203; and the striking comment of von Balthasar, *Man in History*, London 1972, 271.

33. *PS*, I, 230; see ibid., 227; 'Men would willingly persuade themselves, if they could, that strict obedience is not necessary under the gospel, and that something else will be taken, for Christ's sake, in the stead of it', *PS*, VIII, 203. Compare with the thought of St Irenaeus, *Against the Heresies*, Bk 4:17.

34. Grant Duff, M. E., *Notes from a Diary*, 1837-1881, London 1898, II, 140; quoted in C. S. Dessain, *Life*, 44.

35. The fact that we are dealing with only one homily reduces the risk of selective citation!

36. Thus Augustine speaks of a 'Victrix Delectatio' and Maximus the Confessor (PG 90, 901A) makes the same point.

37. *PS*, VII, 192.

38. He quotes the following texts Ezek 33:11, Is 5:4, Ps 16:6, Ps 19:10, Ps 28:7, Ps 65:4.

39. *PS*, VII, 194.

40. *PS*, VII, 195-6; emphases throughout are Newman's.

41. ibid., 197, emphasis is Newman's; see ibid., 184f; 181-2; *PS*, VI, 209f, 239f.

42. *PS*, VII, 199; see Thomas Norris, *Newman and his Theological Method*, Leiden 1977, ch. IV, 84-111.

43. ibid., 200-1.

44. Lk 13:24.

45. *PS*, V, 241.

46. Mk 1:15, Mt 3:2; Lk 3:8.

47. See *PS*, I, 230, 54-5, 227, 172.

48. St Augustine, *Confessions*, VIII, 5, 8, 11, 12; IX, 1; PS, I, 172, 173.

49. *PS*, I, 173.

50. ibid., 172.

51. In particular 3, 5, 10-13, 18.

52. See the incisive words of Pope Paul VI in this regard, *l'Osservatore Romano*, 28th October 1963.

53. *PS*, I, 28, 29.

54. Jn 14:23; Lk 8:21; Mt 7:21; Jas 1:22; 1 Pet 1:24-5; Rev 21:23.

55. For example, I, Sermon 25; II, Sermons 1, 2, 3, 5.

56. See apposite comments of Archbishop Michael Ramsey, *The Rediscovery*, 7-8.

57. Deut 11:26-7.

58. See Dessain, C. S., *Life*, 63-5.

59. *PS*, I, 218; ibid., 327.

60. ibid., 336-49.

61. *PS*, VI, 83-93; ibid., 74f.

62. See *Jfc.*, passim.

63. Especially in volumes I-III.

64. See note 32 above.

65. *PS*, II, 35; see also 60, 'We are consecrated to be temples of the Holy Spirit, an unutterable privilege'.

66. *PS*, I, 13-14.

67. See HK, II; *Diff.*, II, *Letter to Pusey*, 24.

68. *PS*, II, 218, 224, 224-9.

69. *PS*, VI, 126.

70. *PS*, III, 269.

71. *PS*, I, 323; see also 333; 'Our Saviour gives us a pattern which we are bound to follow … to fast the more in private and to be the more austere in our secret hearts'.

72. ibid., 70-71.

73. ibid., 68.

74. *PS*, V, 44.

75. ibid., 44-5.

76. *PS*, IV, 201-3.

77. *PS*, VI, 84-6.

78. Church, R. W., *Occasional Papers* II, 457; *The Oxford Movement*, 130.

CHAPTER 9

1. Liddon, H. P., *Life of Edward Bouverié Pusey*, London 1984, II, 461.

2. 'The Cork Examiner', quoted in Blehl, V. F., SJ, *A Newman Prayer Book*, Birmingham 1990, iii.

3. Pope John Paul II, *The Pope Teaches*, 1982/5, London 1982, 72.

4. See Dessain, 'Cardinal Newman and Ecumenism', *The Clergy Review*, 1965, 119-37; 189-206.

5. Archbishop Robert Runcie, *Centenary Sermon at The University Church of St Mary the Virgin*, Oxford, 1890-1990, 6 in the unpublished text.

6. *LD*, XXIV, 22.

7. *Apo.*, 5.

8. Bouyer, L., *Newman. His Life and Spirituality*, London 1958, 386.

9. Dessain, op. cit., 121.

10. ibid.

11. ibid.

12. Preface to William Palmer, *Notes of a Visit to the Russian Church*, London 1882.

13. Dessain, op. cit., 122-3.

14. *Ess.*, I, 217.

15. ibid., II, 72.

16. See Tolhurst, J., *The Church – A Communion*, Leominster 1988, passim.

17. *US*, 82.

18. *PS*, III, 191.

19. *AW*, 258-9.

20. Dessain, op. cit., 128.

21. *LD*, XIV, 165; see also 173, 207.

22. *Apo.*, 341.

23. *Ward*, II, 57.

24. *LD*, XI, 185.

25. *AW*, 79.

26. *Apo.*, 339-40.

27. ibid., 340.

28. Ker, 569.

29. Dulles, A., 'Newman, Conversion and Ecumenism', *TS*, 51 (1990), 717.

30. *LD*, XXI, 299.

31. *VM*, II, 207.

32. *Addresses and Replies*, 271.

33. *AW*, 258.

34. ibid.

35. *Prepos.*, 388-91.

36. *Cons.*, 106; Dessain, *Life*, 117.

37. Dessain, *Spiritual Themes*, Dublin 1977, 25; see LD, XXV, 250.

38. *US*, 337.

39. Bouyer, L., op. cit., 171; see his comments in the preface he composed for Sheridan, Thomas L., *Newman on Justification*, New York 1967, 12; see also the eminent Anglican theologian, Henry Chadwick, 'The Lectures on Justification' in *Newman after a Hundred Years*, 287-308, especially his conclusion, 'Like much else in Newman, the book is among the major muniments of the modern ecumenical movement', 308.

40. *Jfc.*, 144, 152.

41. *MD*, 555.

42. Dessain, pamphlet 'Cardinal Newman's Teaching about the Blessed Virgin Mary', Birmingham, 1.

43. *Diff.*, II, 24.

44. Dessain, 'Cardinal Newman and Ecumenism', 205.

45. A recurring theme in the *PS*.

46. *Ess.*, II, 374.

47. *Apo.*, 198.

48. ibid.

49. *GA*, 499.

50. *PS*, III, 238; SD, 132.

51. *AW*, 258.

52. Preface to Third Edition of *VM*, XLVII.

53. *Diff.*, I, 368.

54. *Apo.*, 288.

55. *Dev.*, 357.

56. *US*, 174.

57. Dessain, 'Cardinal Newman and Ecumenism', 127.

58. *Diff.*, II, 247-8.

59. *GA*, 117.

60. *Diff.*, II, 255.

61. *US*, 67.

62. *GA*, 117.

63. Quoted in Ker, 284.

64. *US*, 66.

65. *Red.*, XVIII.

66. Quoted in Walgrave, J., *Unfolding Revelation*, London 1972, 30.

67. *GA*, 60.

68. *Prepos.*, 284.

69. Dessain, *Life*, 74.

70. See *Dev.*, II, vii.

71. *Prepos.*, 370-1; 297; 292.

72. *Red.*, 215.

73. Selection from the *Parochial and Plain Sermons*, Copeland, W. J. , (ed.), London 1878, vi.

CHAPTER 10

1. Lash, N., 'Tides and Twilight. Newman since Vatican II', in Ker and Hill (eds.), *Newman After a Hundred Years*, Oxford 1990, 464.

2. VM, I, XLVII; I. Ker, *Newman on being a Christian*, London 1990, has a chapter on revelation, 17-38.

3. See Misner, P., 'Newman's Concept of Revelation and the Development of Doctrine', *Heythrop Journal*, 1 (1970), 32-47.

4. Dessain, *Life*, xii.

5. *PS*, II, 227.

6. ibid., V, 139.

7. St Augustine, PL 44: 161, 315 and 974; PL 43:609-10.

8. *Ari.*, 80-2.

9. *Ess.*, I, 41.

10. *PS.*, I, 208.

11. *US*, 332.

12. Dessain, *Life*, 22.

13. *Dei Verbum*, 2.

14. ibid.

15. See *Dev.*, VII, 1.

16. *DA*, 293.

17. *Cons.*, 53-106.

18. *Diff.*, II, 31-44; 63-7.

19. ibid., 195-205; see HS, I, 339-74.

20. See Connelly, D., *The Letters of St Patrick*, Maynooth 1993, 185-94; *Jfc*, 31, n.1.

21. *Word and Redemption*, 2, New York 1965, 65.

22. *Newman After a Hundred Years*, 459.

23. See *GA*, Note II where he stresses the importance of evidences in his principal theological works.

24. *Apo.*, 198.

25. See *DA*, 254-305; *GA*, 89-94.

26. Crowe, F. E., SJ, *Lonergan. Outstanding Christian Thinkers*, London 1992, passim, especially 16f.

27. Lonergan, B. J., SJ, *Method in Theology*, London 1972, 338.

28. *PS*, III, 250.

29. Lonergan, B. J., SJ, *Second Collection*, London 1974, 237.

30. *GA*, Note II, 499.

31. See Sillem, E., *The Philosophical Notebook*, I and II, Louvain 1969-

70, passim; Verbeke, G., 'Aristotelian Roots of Newman's Illative Sense', in Bastable, James D., (ed.), *Newman and Gladstone*, Dublin 1978, 177-96; Artz, J., *Lexikon*, 'Aristoteles', 60-4; Newman shares with St Thomas Aquinas an esteem for Aristotle as 'the philosopher' (*Ath.*, II, 16; *LD*, XVI, 123).

32. *LD*, XXV, 56-7.

33. *GA*, Note II, 498.

34. Williams, R., 'Newman's Arians and the Question of Method in Doctrinal History', *Newman After A Hundred Years*, London 1990, 264.

35. ibid., 263.

36. Bouyer, L., 'The Permanent Relevance of Newman', *Newman Today*, Vol. I, San Francisco 1989, 168.

37. *VM*, I, 251.

38. *Diff.*, II, 12.

39. ibid., 31-9.

40. Ker and Hill (eds.), *Newman After A Hundred Years*, London 1990, 450, quoting Butler, B. C., 'Newman at the Second Vatican Council' in *The Rediscovery of Newman: an Oxford Symposium*, 244-5.

41. *Dei Verbum*, 8-10.

42. *GA*, 120-1.

43. See O'Connell, Marvin R., 'Newman and Liberalism', in *Newman Today*, Vol. I, San Francisco 1989, 79-93, the quote being from *LG*, 405.

44. See Lonergan, B. J., SJ, 'The Form of the Inference', in *Collection*, London 1978, 1-15, especially 1, 2, 5, 6: Crowe, F. E., SJ, *Lonergan*, London 1992, passim; Artz, J., 'Newman as a Philosopher', *International Philsophical Quarterly*, XVI (1976), 263-88.

45. See my *Newman and his Theological Method*, Leiden 1977, 208-10.

46. *HS*, II, 94.

47. *PS*, VIII, 154-5.

48. *Diff.*, II, 248-9.

49. *PS*, V, 225-6.

50. ibid., III, 269.

51. Dessain, *The Mind of Cardinal Newman*, vi.

52. *CS*, 133.

53. Dessain, *The Mind of Cardinal Newman*, vii.

54. *LG*, Ch. V.

55. *PS*, III, 266; see *PS*, II, 217, 220, 222.

56. ibid., V, 316.

57. See *PS*, V, 241.

58. ibid., 69-70.

59. ibid., IV, 170.

60. ibid., 184.

61. ibid., II, 54-5.

62. *Lumen Gentium*, 4, quoting St Cyprian, *De oratione Domini*, 23 in PL 4: 553; St Augustine, *Sermo* 71:20, 33 in *PL* 38:463f; and St John of Damascus, *Adversus iconoclastas* 12, *PG* 96:1358D.

63. See Mix, 349, ' ... to her is committed the custody of the Incarnation'.

64. The three verbs Luke uses – *suntéreo, sunballo* and diatéreo – point to the depth of Mary's thinking ('in her heart'), as well as to its quality of permanence.

65. *US*, 313; see O'Loughlin, T., 'Newman on *doing* Theology', New Blackfriars, 76 (1995), shows how 'the structure of paragraph 3 (of the Sermon) is a connected series of hypothetical propositions which form a single sorites', 93-4. Newman was an able logician who also did not hesitate to point out the limits of logic.

66. *US*, 313.

67. *Mix*, 349: see the two sermons concluding this volume, 'The Glories of Mary for the Sake of Her Son' and 'On the Fitness of the Glories of Mary', 342-59; 360-76.